George Hanger

George Hanger (1751-1824) by Thomas Beach *c.* **1785**
Reproduced by gracious permission of HM The Queen

George Hanger

The Life and Times of an Eccentric Nobleman

Ian Saberton

Grosvenor House
Publishing Limited

This book is published by
Grosvenor House Publishing Ltd
Link House
140 The Broadway, Tolworth, Surrey, KT6 7HT.

www.grosvenorhousepublishing.co.uk
info@grosvenorhousepublishing.co.uk

A CIP record for this book
is available from the British Library

ISBN 978-1-78623-163-5

To my wife and sons, Marcia, Bruce and Jonathan

CONTENTS

ACKNOWLEDGEMENTS

The author is grateful to the staff of the University of Sheffield Library, and the London Library, for courteously dealing with his various requests for assistance.

He is particularly indebted to Stephen J Dickens for meticulously checking the text and pertinently commenting on it.

Last but not least, his thanks go to Bruce Saberton for his technical advice.

INTRODUCTION

Adventurer, army officer, eccentric, humorist, practical joker and rake, George Hanger served as equerry to the Prince of Wales in the late eighteenth century and, as a member of the Prince's fast set, actively participated for over a decade in the dissolute life to which the coterie was accustomed. In doing so he added appreciably to his already notorious reputation. Eventually, says his obituary, "as the Prince advanced in life, the eccentric manners of the Colonel became somewhat too free and coarse for the royal taste" and he was dismissed.[1]

Together, his upbringing, entry into London high society and rake's progress through it; his service during the American Revolutionary War, association with the Prince, and friendship with Charles James Fox, the *de facto* leader of the Whig Party; his descent into debt and the King's Bench Prison, his entering trade as a "black-diamond" (coal) merchant, and inheriting the Barony of Coleraine but refusing to assume the title — all, *inter alia*, add to a life as colourful as it is fascinating. Mercilessly caricatured, as illustrated in this work, "he was," according to his obituary, "so marked a character that he might be considered as one of the prominent features of his time."

Yet today, outside the groves of academe, he is unknown.

---

[1] *The Gentleman's Magazine*, May 1824, 457-8.

CHAPTER 1

THE FORMATIVE YEARS

"The lives of malefactors in general are prefaced with a strong outline of their birth, parentage and education, with other peculiar circumstances belonging to them. As for instance, *A.B.* was born in the parish of —————, in the county of —————, of reputable and genteel parents, but falling early in life into bad company both of wicked men and lewd women, he contracted habits which ultimately led to the gallows." So begins George Hanger's picaresque account of his life, adventures and opinions, which, while extremely free with the last, is remarkably short with the rest.

George was born on 13 October 1751 at Driffield Hall, a country seat of his father Gabriel in the hamlet of Driffield near Cirencester. The youngest of three surviving sons, he has little to say about his birth: "I was born ... in the best bed in the state room, according to ancient custom. Whether I came headforemost or not into the world or whether I was born with teeth in my gums or with hair on my head it will not be expected that I should determine, having no other record to go by than a treacherous memory, but I am inclined to believe, if I may judge from the length of my nose, that at my birth the midwife committed some indignity to my person." Otherwise all he has left is the following quatrain:

Three pretty boys did Gabriel get,
The youngest George by name, Sir,
A funny dog, not favoured much
By fortune or by fame, Sir.

Gabriel was a son of Sir George Hanger Bt, a turkey merchant, and had gone out to Bengal with £500 in 1714, making his fortune as a merchant with the East India Company. When he returned to England in 1725, he had accumulated £25,000[2] and soon after became the sole legatee of his four brothers and two sisters, all of whom died without issue. An exceedingly wealthy man, he went on to become a Whig MP for Maidstone and then for Bridgewater in the Parliaments of 1753-61 and 1763-68. He was, according to George, "one of those respectable, independent, old English characters in the House of Commons called country gentlemen, who formerly had a considerable influence with the Ministers and to whose judgements and opinions every Minister paid the greatest respect ... I am confident he never received a bribe [*and*] I believe from my heart he was as honest a man as ever stepped in leathern shoe."

If we were to believe George, his father never solicited a place, but there exists a letter of his addressed to the Prime Minister, the Duke of Newcastle, in which he did solicit an honour:

My Lord Duke

The morning my Lord Gage did me the honour to introduce me to your Grace I found you so busy that I thought it then improper to mention what I had to say, which was this. As I make no doubt but His Majesty will against his coronation create some Irish peers as well as English, what I have to desire of your Grace is to ask the favour of His Majesty to make me a Peer of Ireland, to give me the tytle of Lord Colerane of that kingdom, that title [*of the first creation*] being extinct by the death of the last Lord Colerane, whose Lady was my first cozen and left me the greatest part of their estate. No one can be more zealously attached to His Majesty and his most illustrious family than I am, and I have a fortune equal to that of almost any title of nobility whatever. I have been in Parliament near ten years, and propose being in it again, and

_____
[2] Approximately £5,000,000 in today's money.

2

never did ask your Grace or anybody for anything yet. Therefore I hope I shall be indulged in this, to have your Grace's interest and recommendation to His Majesty to do me this honour. It makes no increase of the nobility of Ireland; it will be only reviving a title that died with the last Lord. Therefore I hope your Grace will oblige me in this request, and I shall at all times acknowledge the obligation with a great deal of gratitude.

I am
Your Grace's most obedient and very humble servant

GABRIEL HANGER

Pall Mall
December 12th 1760

The application was successful and on 26 February 1762 Gabriel was created Baron Coleraine of Coleraine in the County of Londonderry. He died in 1773, aged 76.

George's mother Elizabeth was the daughter of Richard Bond of Cobrey Court, Herefordshire, and married Gabriel in 1736. "In my mother," confides George, "I have experienced a most affectionate, kind and tender parent." Aged 65, she died in 1780.

George began his formal education at Reading School, an academy for boys founded in 1125 and still in existence. In his day the school was located in the former Hospitium of St John, the main building of which remains, but the refectory, which housed the schoolroom, was demolished in 1785 and is now the site of Reading Town Hall.

A very idle boy, George could never be induced to look into a book until it was forced under the shadow of his nose in the schoolroom. As a result he used to be beaten with such cruelty that on the representation of his brothers he was removed from the school. On the master who inflicted the punishment George remarked, "This tyrant did but seldom use the rod. His favourite instrument was a long rattan cane, big enough to correct a culprit in Bridewell. But this was not all. The savage used to refine on his punishment and to gratify his infernal feelings by varying the modes of it. The shrieks of the boys who were writhing beneath his blows were music to his soul." If the master ever found out that two of the big boys had been fighting, he would cause them to strip to their shirts in the schoolroom and give to each a large bending rattan cane about three feet long. He then ordered them to strike at each other with all their force while he presided with a similar weapon. Whenever there appeared to be a relaxation of activity by either of the unwilling combatants, he would compel them by his own violent strokes to renew theirs. "I have," declared George, "seen wales on the sides, ribs and arms of boys of the bigness of my finger."

From Reading George was sent to the Reverend Mr Fountain's at Marylebone, London, whose son, a doctor, was under-master. Located in the Manor House, which was demolished in 1791, the school was, so George says, the best for little boys that ever was. "They were treated with the utmost kindness and attention, and with proper correction, but only when it appeared to be absolutely necessary. Mrs Fountain was the best and most attentive of women to the small boys. She had them every morning in her own room and made them learn their lesson to her, which prepared them before they went into the schoolroom to the Doctor. She used to coax them to learn by giving them biscuits and milk and shewing them various other kindnesses. She might rather be considered as a mother than a schoolmistress to the children under her care. Whatever I learned was from kind and gentle treatment, for beating would not go down with me. A kind word and my lesson explained to me had more effect than all the sticks and rods in Christendom, for I was bold and daring even at that early age."

While there, George was involved in an amusing scene with Monsieur Laudomier, "the celebrated French tooth-drawer",

4

who used to attend at certain times of the year to examine the boys' teeth and extract those that were defective. "He had drawn out one of mine, which gave me great pain, and wanted to draw another, a ceremony which I did not approve, but the more teeth he drew, the more guineas in his pocket. Perceiving, however, that I was resolute and would not consent to a repetition of his operation, he endeavoured to play me a trick by concealing his instrument in his handkerchief. He accordingly prevailed on me to open my mouth that he might feel with his finger and thumb whether the tooth was loose or not, but the moment he got his thumb on my under jaw he attempted to hold my mouth open by force and had nearly fixed the instrument on my tooth. But I gave him a violent kick on the shins, which rather deranged him, and at the same instant caught his thumb fast between my teeth and gave him a small item to remember me as long as he lived. I then ran off, leaving him jumping about the room from excessive pain, and I shall probably be believed when I assert that he never after that attempted to draw any teeth of mine."

From Marylebone George went on to Eton College in 1764. Located in the small town of Eton on the opposite bank of the Thames to Windsor, it had been founded by Henry VI in 1440 and was by now the leading English boarding-school. Offering a rigorously classical syllabus, it provided advantages that were more social than educational.

While at the start of each term most boys came down by coach from the Swan with Two Necks tavern in London, George had only six miles to travel from his father's other country seat, Cannon Place, in the hamlet of Bray north-west of Eton. Unlike the King's Scholars, that is to say, some 70 poorer scholarship boys whose places were provided under the medieval statutes of the college, George belonged to the Oppidans, some 430 fee-paying boys who were the sons of the aristocracy, the church, the landed gentry, and other members of the Establishment. Whereas the King's Scholars slept in one huge dormitory, the Long Chamber, and were fed and clothed by the college, George as an Oppidan would live in a private boarding-house and be able to supplement his fare and provide for his clothing by purchases from the shopkeepers and publicans in the High Street.

On arriving at his boarding house George would have been sent to the college to collect sheets and bedding. Otherwise such abodes were run almost independently, though the college was of course responsible for schooling. Bedchambers commonly housed two to four boys. Next day George would have called at the college to be assigned a tutor, whose fees, like those of the headmaster, were not paid directly but formed part of the end-of-term accounts of the boarding house presented to his father. Purchases of provisions and liquor — not to mention clothing, which became a foppish and profligate interest of George — were included either in the account or in separate ones presented by shopkeepers and publicans in like manner. So began George's ruinous habit of shopping on tick, a practice that would land him in hot water later in life.

As George summarised his schooling, "I really made considerable progress in my learning and by the time I got into the fifth form I was a very tolerable Latin scholar and could construe most books with sufficient readiness. But I took a most decided aversion to the Greek language and never would learn it." Such a summary naturally falls far short of telling all. For instance, Eton began in George's day to encourage the performance and imitation of classical texts, including comic writing in ancient styles, so that the years spent by George in construing, writing and performing nurtured the wit for which he later became famous.

Outside school a high old time was had on free days with recreational pursuits ranging from dashing about town in small racing carriages, swimming in the Thames, and racing skiffs along it, to brawling with bargemen and local youths, attending cockfights or bull- or badger-baiting, and hunting water fowl. Boys also participated in cricket, "Eton Fives", and other obscure games too numerous to name. For those interested in real-tennis a court was available, and for those who were perhaps less active billiards could be played in Windsor. Betting — for example on horses, prizefighters, dogs, badgers, and games — was rife. A favourite winter pastime was rat-catching in infested older buildings. In later life George would publish "the rat-catching secret" and ever after be accorded the sobriquet "the rat-catcher".

Schooling eventually took a back seat in George's life. "My studies after some time had a different direction, for, from the moment I came into the fifth form, I studied everything but my book. My hours out of school in the day were employed in the sports of the field, being already fond of my dog and gun. By night game of another kind engrossed my whole attention. At that early period I had a most decided preference for female society and passed as much time in the company of women as I have ever done since. A carpenter's wife was the first object of my early affections nor can I well express the nature of my obligations to her. Frequently have I risked breaking my neck in getting over the roof of my boarding house at night to pass a few hours with some favourite grizette of Windsor. During the latter part of my time at Eton, *to perfect my education,* I became attached to and was much enamoured of the daughter of a vendor of cabbages."

Nor did George's early acquaintance with female society end there. "The big boys had a very wicked custom every Sunday of resorting to Castle prayers at Windsor, not to seek the Lord, but to seek the enamoratas who constantly and diligently attended to receive our devotions. Besides, in summer time it was our custom to walk in the public promenade in the [*Windsor*] Little Park. My father lived only six miles from Windsor and consequently I was as well known to every family in that town and neighbourhood as the King himself; but notwithstanding this, I constantly walked with some fair frail one arm in arm with as much sang-froid as I now would walk in Kensington Gardens with a beautiful woman."

During George's first year at college the Headmaster had been Dr Edward Barnard, a gifted administrator who, while not a profound scholar in any branch of literature, was imbued with a refined taste that instantly perceived the spirit and qualities of whatever author he was expounding. Charming, gentlemanly and dignified, with a natural tendency to joking and caricature, he is said to have had "that power of impressing his dictates and opinions on his scholars, which lessened the necessity of practising corporal correction. He knew how to awaken love and create fear with admirable address. Boys, who would have been hardened by the infliction of punishment, trembled at his rebuke." When, on his election to Provost, he took leave of the boys, many were moved to tears.

Dr Barnard's successor, Dr John Foster, had a quite contrasting personality. While infinitely superior to his predecessor in all points of classical scholarship, "he was," according to a writer of his day, "a strict disciplinarian, severe against all immoral conduct, inexorable when he discovered meditated deception, and he considered the deviation from truth to be an act of baseness which it would be equally wrong to pass without correction as to commit." Unlike Barnard, who was satisfied with grasping the ideas and characteristics of ancient texts, Foster was a pedant who insisted on ascertaining the exact force of every word. Even in outward appearance there was a great difference between the two, for, while the former was tall and dignified, the latter was described as small and insignificant. It would have been well for the college if the contrast had stopped there, but it soon became apparent that the new Headmaster was deficient in that kind of tact for which his predecessor had been so distinguished. Matters came to a head in the Great Eton Rebellion of 1768, in which George took part. It began with Foster's flogging of a praeposter.

Praeposters were part of a system of devolved power on which masters relied heavily to assert control. Sixth-formers, they exercised monitorial authority over their younger schoolfellows, flogging, for example, those who they met out of bounds or who as fags fell short of the mark. Fags, who acted as their servants in boarding houses, were a privilege accorded them in return for ruling there in place of adults.

Enforcing the bounds of the college exempted the praeposters by implication from observing them, but in autumn 1768 the masters claimed the right to send praeposters back to college, a claim which was strenuously resisted. All Foster's attempts at pacification proved in vain and affairs were brought to a crisis by a rencounter between a master and a praeposter in the main street of Eton one Saturday afternoon. No words passed at the time, but when next day the praeposter was performing his ordinary duty of keeping the lower boys quiet in church, he received a message that the master intended to complain of him for making a noise.

Feeling deeply aggrieved, the praeposter decided to find out whether the accusation was due to a misapprehension or to a mean spirit of revenge. Therefore, when the service was over, he lost no time in asking for an explanation. The master gave no reply, collared him, and dragged him round to Foster, who was about to administer punishment when the praeposters entered the room *en masse*, threatening to resign their duties if their privileges were to be thus abused. This bold device proved unsuccessful, their resignations were accepted, and their comrade was severely flogged.

One day later the ex-praeposters had an interview with the Headmaster at which they claimed that the masters should have no right to send them back to college unless they were found in taverns, billiard rooms, or other improper places, in which case they were willing to be sent back and even to be flogged. Foster refused to entertain their claim, leading the boys to vow that they would not take part in the forthcoming declamations — an oratorical event — on the ground that declaiming belonged to them as praeposters and not as members of the sixth form. Foster retorted that they must either declaim at the proper time or leave the college. And when a deputation of fifth-form Oppidans came to enquire whether the sixth-form boys had been expelled, he replied curtly, "Go and ask them."

A council of war was then held on the playing fields at which all of the sixth, many of the fifth, and even some of the fourth — a hundred and sixty in all — resolved to start at once for Maidenhead. It was the 2nd of November. A contemporary was later to record, "They marched with the greatest order and regularity, and ... during the whole time they were absent from Eton there was not one single act of riot, indecency, or intemperance committed."

The next morning the boys marched back to the playing fields and eighteen of them had a conference with the masters in the upper school. They offered to capitulate on condition that all should be treated alike, but Foster declared that he would make no conditions. This announcement caused a regular panic, and *sauve qui peut* became the order of the day. Three of the ringleaders made their peace, many of their comrades followed suit, while others more deeply implicated or more timid hastened away to their own homes — only to encounter the reproaches of their indignant parents.

Of George's part in the proceedings he has the following to say: "I made one in the great rebellion under Dr Foster, though only in the lower part of the fourth form. Foster was only a schoolmaster. In Dr Barnard's time such discontent never would have taken place; he was a gentleman as well as a scholar and knew well how to make the boys both obey and love him. He was well acquainted with human nature and governed, not by the rod, but by good sense and a knowledge of the passions. We marched to Maidenhead Bridge, when my father, who lived within one mile of that place, having heard of the business, sent his groom and a horse three different times in the day to take me home. I had pledged my honour to the boys not to leave them, of which I informed my father, and though he was much incensed against me, I steadily adhered to my promise and never deserted the cause, to support which I had so solemnly pledged myself. Some disgracefully forfeited their honour and were never after respected whilst at school, and it yet is an existing blot in their escutcheon."

When George left Eton in the summer of 1769, he did not go to either Oxford or Cambridge, as was customary with most young men of his ilk. "This was," he intimates, "a very fortunate circumstance in which my father shewed his superior judgment. As I had resolved on being a soldier, a German education was best suited to the profession I had chosen. Had I been placed at Oxford or Cambridge, not being of a studious disposition, my health might have suffered from every species of riot and dissipation, which is so prevalent at our universities, and my mind would have remained in the same uncultivated state at my departure as at my arrival, for it is a hundred to one if I had ever read any literary works except the *Sporting Calendar* and the newspaper. I was accordingly sent into Germany, to Göttingen, which is one of the most celebrated universities in the world."

George spent about twelve months at Göttingen, applying himself to mathematics, fortification, and the German language. In the town he found generally too many English, "who herd together and by always talking their own tongue never acquire a fluency in that of the country, which can only be obtained by associating with the natives." For its part the university was not entirely to his taste. Containing a reclusive set of learned professors whose knowledge extended no farther than the lectures they delivered to their students, it was no place for acquiring those elegant and polite manners so essential to an officer. Moreover, the society of women of the first manners, fashion and education, "without which no mind can be

11

polished," was wanting. So he moved on to the Courts of Hanover and Hesse-Cassel.

At Hanover George was patronised, "in every sense most flattering to my feelings," by Prinz Karl von Mecklenburg-Strelitz, a brother-in-law of George III, and was befriended by various officers, including Generals Freytag and Luckner, veterans of the Seven Years' War. While there he was introduced to the nobility, passed his time constantly in polite circles, and was instructed in the discipline of light cavalry. He attended all the Hanoverian reviews and even a Prussian one lasting four days near the town of Magdeburg.

From Hanover George carried letters of recommendation to the Court of Hesse-Cassel. The Hauptstadt, Cassel, was, he says, one of the cleanest and most delightful towns that he had ever beheld. "The new town is built entirely of stone and, on approaching it from a distance, has a very beautiful and grand appearance." Little did he imagine, when introduced at Court, that one day he would come to serve in the Landgrave's army.

From George's connections he could have gone in the suite of one of the young Princes of Brunswick to serve with the Russian army during the Russo-Turkish War of 1768-74, "but as this would have incurred an expence beyond the income my father allowed me, I wrote to him to request he would be so kind as to advance me a thousand pounds, with which he refused to comply, not I believe from want of generosity, but from the tender love my mother bore me."

Pyrmont was a spa resort in Lower Saxony ruled by the Prince of Waldeck. It had become a fashionable place for vacations in the 18th century and possessed a large spectacular park, a baroque castle, and an impressive complex of fortifications. George spent two successive summers there, patronised by the Prince, and has summarised its attractions. "The town and surrounding country is the most beautiful and romantic spot

I ever beheld." It abounded with a variety of amusements, and the walks and rides around it were delightful.

"No part of my life," George confides, "has been so pleasant and agreeable as the three years[3] I passed in Germany. I cannot help remarking with what elegance a person of small fortune may live in that country. In England, with a small income, one can scarcely procure necessaries of life. My father allowed me three hundred pounds per annum[4], which was fully sufficient for all my expences, and at the end of the year I had always an agreeable overplus."

George gives two instances of the cheapness of living and of servants' wages. "I had an extraordinary good servant, who came every morning at eight o'clock to my apartments and stayed as late at night as I wished. I only gave him one louis d'or per month[5] for wages, board wages, and clothes. While I remained in any great towns, I always dined at the public *table d'hôte*, over which some officer of distinction of the garrison presides. Many military gentlemen resort to it as well as travellers ... The dinner reckoning, exclusive of wine, was about fifteen pence[6], for which were provided two courses and a desert of pastry. Everything else was as cheap in proportion."

The hospitality and the open, honest character of the Germans so attached George to the country that when he was ordered home to join his regiment, he quit it with much reluctance and absolutely shed tears on his departure. He had been commissioned an ensign in the 1st (Grenadier) Regiment of Foot Guards on 31 January 1771, a rank which carried with it a captaincy in the rest of the army.

---

[3] In fact, three summers.
[4] Approximately £46,500 in today's money.
[5] The going monthly rate for a servant.
[6] Approximately £10 in today's money.

George has a few words to offer about his passage through Holland, "that most detestable of all countries, where a traveller is insulted by every species of extortion and where gold is worshipped more than the Deity. Whoever passes through this country, when they come to an inn, should always order dinner and supper at so much *per* head. Then they cannot be imposed on much as the price of wine is well known and lodging may be valued also. If you think you are charged too dear, you can have redress by applying to the burgomaster." At Delft, forgetful of this precaution and coming very late to an inn, he ordered supper and went in haste to bed so as to rise early in the morning and proceed on his way. There was nothing in the house but eggs and spinach, a few slices of dried bacon, and bread and cheese, to which lavish repast he added a pint of wine. "In the morning the landlady charged me above a pound sterling, and when I complained of the extravagance of the bill, she desired to look it over and returned it to me with about ten or twelve pence added to it, saying that she had omitted charging some articles." George went to complain to the burgomaster, who informed him that if he had made an agreement he would have punished the landlady, but as the case stood, it was not in his power.

Another precaution was highly necessary when unloading one's luggage on arrival at an inn. "If you have a trunk and two or three bundles, put them all into one wheelbarrow, for, if you are not on your guard when your trunk is in the wheelbarrow, the porters will take each one bundle and, if it be only so light a thing as an hat box, you must pay them the same as the man who wheels your trunk."

"I will," says George, "give another instance of the extortion and brutality of the people — I mean only of the lower orders. If you take a walk out from your inn and happen to lose your way, and you ask any common person in the street which is the way to such an inn, mentioning the sign of it, instead of telling you to turn either to the right or left, his reply is, 'I will go with you for a shilling.' In France, if you meet the meanest object in the street and ask him such a question, he is overstudious in describing the way. In Holland you must go into some reputable shop to inquire or address yourself to some well-dressed man, or you may walk round and round the town and never find your lodgings."

Despite George's low opinion of the people, there was one saving grace. "The laws in Holland are excellent, and if you are acquainted with the customs of the country, you can ever have redress. And one supreme blessing the inhabitants of this country enjoy: there is no imprisonment for debt, which, with all our boasted liberty, is the curse and disgrace of Old England."

As George took shipping for home, little did he know that events would soon take a marked turn affecting the entire course of his life.

CHAPTER 2

THE SPORTING ROVER

On his return to London in autumn 1771 George immediately joined his regiment and took up residence in St James's not far from his father's place in Pall Mall.

St James's was the most fashionable parish in London. It contained a great number of elegant houses belonging to persons of distinction and at its centre was St James's Square, pretty large and well paved, with a noble basin in the centre surrounded by a palisade. Bordering it on each side were fine houses inhabited mostly by the aristocracy. To the south lay St James's Palace, built by Henry VIII, and beyond it St James's Park, near a mile and a half in circumference. On all sides of the park were beautiful walks and in the centre, extending almost the whole length from east to west, was an imposing canal, at the east end of which was Horse Guards' Parade, where George and his regiment would muster and perform their exercises.

Of the time when he began his round of training, parades, and guard duty at the Royal Palaces, Tower of London and Windsor Castle George was later to observe, "I may with truth say that I knew my duty better than nine ensigns in ten at their debut on the [Horse Guards'] parade at Whitehall, for I not only was acquainted with the common parade duty but absolutely knew the manœuvre of a battalion, for I had made my profession my study and was devoutly attached to a military life."

George arrived in town as St James's was being transformed. Quiet streets were becoming crowded with servants and tradesmen as they prepared to receive the nobility with their

extended families and entourages, who would soon arrive from the country for "the season" — the period from November to June when Parliament most often sat. Together, the peers and their immediate relations comprised preponderantly London's high society — known in its day as the *beau monde*, an elite consisting of no more than a few hundred individuals of which George was a member. Marked by ostentatious consumption and fast living, it was an exclusive world which set the "tone" in fashion. Yet membership did not depend on being modish or trendy alone, but rather on pedigree, connections, manners, language, appearance and much else besides.

Despite its glittering public facade, the core business of the *beau monde* was in fact politics. Peers had a hereditary right to sit in the House of Lords and dominated the Cabinet. For its part the House of Commons was packed with members who boasted direct blood lines to the peerage, whereas ownership by peers of extensive acreage and property endowed them with sizable and direct control over numerous parliamentary seats. It is against this background that high society provided a forum in which parliamentary business could be discussed and political information exchanged.

It was not, however, politics which interested George so much as the pursuit and company of titled women, many of whom were irresistibly attracted by his combination of wit, immense charm, craggy features, fine physique, and larger-than-life personality. Whether it was daytime visits to private residences, balls, masquerades, salons, dinners or suppers, private social or gaming parties, outings to the theatre or opera, excursions to the pleasure gardens of Ranelagh or Vauxhall, and so on, the *beau monde* offered a mosaic of opportunities for social encounters.

It was not long before George's rake's progress through high society came to the attention of the press. According to one report, it is not believed "our hero is much disposed to attach himself for any length of time to a single mistress. *Universal benevolence to the Ladies* is his motto and he has fully approved himself worthy of the device." While he had always distinguished himself as a brave and judicious officer, "his amorous campaigns have been still more numerous and successful, and though he is too prudent a commander to glory in these conquests, some of them have been so manifest to the world that he could not conceal his victories. Valour and gallantry go hand in hand and the reason is in a great degree obvious: the ladies will not risque their reputation with a poltroon, who is too apt to boast of favours which he has never received and can neither defend himself or a lady's character if attacked, whereas the man of honour, who must be a man of spirit, carefully conceals his happiness and is ready to vindicate the character of his mistress at the price of his life. To this disposition we may chiefly ascribe the high reputation that Captain Hanger holds among the ladies, for ... no woman of taste disdains to rank him amongst the number of her admirers."

To the accuracy of the report we may attest George's own words: "I have held it as sacred as my creed that it was an excess of infamy either to betray or expose favours granted or confidence reposed, ... for, so help me God, I have never yet betrayed a woman nor ever intentionally injured one of the sex nor ever exposed their weakness or hurt their feelings." Yet despite George's discretion the names of several of his lovers did become public knowledge, as the press revealed.

There was, for example, Lady Sarah Bunbury, a daughter of the second Duke of Richmond and Lennox. Born in 1745, she was at one time widely spoken of as a possible match for the future George III, but it was as chief bridesmaid rather than bride that she eventually attended the royal wedding. In 1762 she broke a secret engagement to Lord Newbattle (later the fifth Marquess of Lothian) to marry Sir Charles Bunbury Bt, a Whig MP for Suffolk, but the marriage was not a success. Cold and reserved, Sir Charles was reputedly more attentive to his first love of horses than to his wife. Some five years later she became pregnant by her cousin Lord William Gordon, a son of the third Duke, and left the marital home never to return. Fleeing to Scotland, they co-habited for a short while, but by 1770 the affair was over. One of the foremost beauties of her day, she led the hyper-critical Horace Walpole to exclaim, "No Magdalene by Correggio was half so lovely or expressive!"

Then there were Harriet Lamb and Helen Kennedy. Harriet was a daughter of Sir Matthew Lamb Bt and a sister of Peniston Lamb, Lord Melbourne, whereas Helen was a second cousin of David Kennedy, the 10th Earl of Cassillis. And so George's progress continued, so that to his list of lovers, if the press is to be believed, "may be added almost all the first-rate women of spirit."

Nor were George's amorous adventures confined to St James's alone. As the season ended and spring turned to summer, members of the *beau monde* would return to the country, attend leisure towns such as Bath, Brighton and Scarborough, or take the waters at resorts abroad. One such resort visited by George and frequented by European nobility was Spa in the Prince-Bishopric of Liège, a territory which bisected the Austrian Netherlands. Lying in a wooded valley surrounded by undulating hills and countless rivers and springs, it was, besides the waters, noted for its casinos, one of which, the Casino de Spa, is the oldest in the world.

That George had been up to his old tricks was as usual related by the press: "When the Captain was at Spa, he there met the amiable Mrs Pitt, mother to Lady Ligonier. She was then still in her prime after having been a reigning toast for a succession of years. Her natural dispositions prevailed in favour of Mr Hanger, and as they lodged in the same house, they had frequent opportunities of testifying their mutual approbation. This lady has since retired to the south of France."

Penelope Pitt, a daughter of Sir Henry Atkins Bt, was in her early 50s, having married in 1746 George Pitt, the Tory MP for Dorset. In 1776 she would become Lady Rivers when her husband was elevated to the peerage. Theirs was not a happy marriage and in 1771 they separated. She went on to live mostly in France and Italy till her death in 1795, when she was buried in the Old English Cemetery at Livorno.

Almost inevitably George's conduct gave rise to scurrilous and unfounded rumours about him. He was, for example, accused of having an affair with the Hon Henrietta Wymondesold which led to the breakup of her marriage with Charles, a member of the landed gentry from Wanstead in Essex. Yet the breakup occurred in 1751, the year of George's birth! What in fact transpired was that Henrietta, the daughter of Robert Knight, Lord Luxborough, had begun a liaison with the Hon Josiah Child, a naval lieutenant and a brother of Earl Tylney. Charles discovered incriminating letters between them, divorced her in 1754, and was awarded damages of £2,500[7]. Unable to pay, the lovers married the same year and went into exile in France, where Josiah died in the winter of 1759-60, most probably of consumption. Soon after, Henrietta married Louis-Alexandre de Grimoard de Beauvoir, Comte de Roure, and died at Marseilles on 1 March 1763, aged 33, after giving birth to their son.

Despite his many relationships with ladies of distinction, George proceeded to cast his net wider, beginning with the demi-reps of the theatre. The demi-rep, or fashionable courtesan, was a woman whose sexual reputation had been compromised but who was able to maintain a position of sorts in fashionable circles due most often to the financial support of her lover. Into this class fell various actresses of the day. George's first liaison was with Mrs Maria Bailey, an actress at the Haymarket, who had recently been the mistress of Prince Henry Frederick, the Duke of Cumberland and Strathearn, a brother of George III. Before long he was also involved with Mrs Jane Lessingham, an actress at Covent Garden born in 1739. Again, the press did not fail to comment: "At the time Mrs Lessingham, an actress, was supported in a most splendid manner by Admiral Barrington. Whilst he was gaining laurels for himself and glory for his country abroad, the Captain most politely attended her at home to prevent her grief becoming too violent in the absence of her naval admirer." Insatiable, George moved on, as the press duly reported: "The amiable Mrs Saunders," another actress at the Haymarket, "whose character was for a long time equivocal and who in public never exceeded the bounds of a demi-rep, seemed

---

[7] Approximately £470,000 in today's money.

to have a peculiar predilection in favour of Captain Hanger. He was constantly in all her parties and their frequent *tête-à-tête* excursions made it suspected that even a woman of fortune might have strong partialities for a favourite admirer."

Of all the actresses with whom George dallied the most enchanting to him was Mrs Sophia Baddeley, a woman of exceptional beauty with a vivacious personality. A leading actress and singer at Covent Garden and Drury Lane, she was not averse to selling her sexual favours to a succession of admirers, among whom ranked the Duke of York, the Hon William Hanger (George's eldest brother), the Lords Grosvenor and Melbourne, Sir Cecil Bishop, Hananel Mendes da Costa, a wealthy merchant trading in copra with India, and George Garrick, the theatre manager.

During the 1771-72 season Sophia quit the stage. "During this recess," revealed the press, "Captain Hanger was introduced to her and so fervently pleaded the cause of love that our heroine yielded to his intreaties. The Captain still entertains a very great regard for her, accompanies her to all public places, and protects her with a spirit that does him honour. An instance of his behaviour will illustrate our observation. At the opening [*in January 1772*] of the Pantheon," a subscription venue offering fashionable entertainment such as balls, concerts and masquerades, "the proprietors endeavoured to exclude all women whose characters were suspicious, many of them having made their appearance on the first night, which greatly hurt the delicacy of some squeamish women of quality, whose reputations were as equivocal as those of the females they were desirous of expelling. Captain Hanger accompanied Mrs Baddeley on the second night, when the doorkeeper refused her admittance, saying he was authorised to reject what company he thought improper. Captain Hanger insisted upon knowing his authority, to which the doorkeeper replied he had the proprietors' orders for what he did. Captain Hanger then ordered the doorkeeper to bring the proprietors to him who had given these commands.

The servant excused himself by saying they were not present. Captain Hanger then bid him produce the master of the ceremonies as he was the ostensible manager. Captain Donnellan did not chuse to appear upon the occasion but gave orders for Mrs Baddeley's admission — and this resolute behaviour of Captain Hanger obliged the proprietors to lay aside all thoughts of requiring every female who desired admittance to the Pantheon to bring a certificate of her virtue in hand."

For a while George's progress came to an abrupt stand when he fell deeply in love with a Romany girl at Norwood, a village a few miles south of London on a high road to the coast. "If," George intimates, "the heart of this beautiful angel had been as fair as her countenance, we should have continued till this day, I make no doubt, mutually enjoying the delights of love. She had an enchanting voice, a pretty taste for music, and played charmingly on the dulcimer. By the light of the moon how her strains enchanted me! Amongst various other songs, she often used to sing with a considerable degree of sentiment and expression the following beautiful elegy on the accomplishments and trade of a tinker:

> Tom Tinker's my true love
> And I am his dear;
> And all the world over
> His budget I'll bear."

They were wed, but the ceremony was a curious affair conducted in accordance with Romany rites and attended by the first of three unpropitious omens. There was no one present but the couple, her parents and a black tomcat. "The old woman, " recalls George, "took the sagacious *feles* and placed him on a table. The old man, holding the black tom by the body, commanded me to take the cat's left forepaw into my right hand, at the same time directing the girl to take the cat's tail in her left hand, as we stood on opposite sides of the table, which was placed directly east and west. But whether the girl pressed the cat's tail too hard, so as to produce any comical sensation in the animal, I cannot determine; but whilst the old man was repeating a few sentences in the Romany language, which I judged to be a parental blessing, the cat began to swear and spit and shewed such discontent, either at his position on the table or at the nuptial ceremony, that it was with the utmost difficulty we could keep him on the table till the old man had finished his benediction. My mother (for so I always called her) shook her head and said to her husband, this forebodes no good."

The second omen came on the evening of the wedding. "As I sat chiding the night's delay in amorous dalliance with the lovely fair one and [in] conversation chaste, affectionate and instructive with her enlightened and aged parents, an *horned* owl of enormous size lighted on the tree which shaded our bower and hooted loudly. The father, addressing himself to me, said, 'Son,' for so the tender parent ever called me, 'behold, the bird of wisdom greets you and hails your nuptial day!' 'Poh,' said the old woman, putting her two forefingers up to her forehead and pointing them towards her husband, 'my dear, it is no such thing. You ought to know better.' At that very time I never heeded the old woman's sagacious foresight, though often since the remembrance of it has caused my heart to ache, and at this day, whenever I see an horned owl, or any owl, it brings to my mind my former misery and disgrace."

In the morning a final omen, equally unknown and unsuspected then by George, assailed his ears. "I was alarmed by the report of a gun. Rising from the bed where many hours, unnumbered in love's calendar, passed but as moments, I opened the door of my rural abode and asked who had been shooting in our peaceful habitations. The old man replied, 'It was me. I shot a cuckoo perched on the tree which shades your nuptial couch,' a bird whose notes I hate:

O bird of woe,
So fatal to the wedded state!

24

At that time I gave ear to none of these omens, but to my sorrow they were all shortly verified."

And so it transpired that on returning from a short absence George was informed by the parents that his wife had gone off with a travelling tinker of a neighbouring tribe, who wandered about the country mending pots and kettles. Seeking her, the parents "with the most persuasive kindness entreated her to return home and, with the fullest assurance of their protection, pardon and oblivion, to bury all past indiscretion in their hospitable but homely dwelling and look to better deeds and days. But no parental tears or supplication could prevail on her to quit the seducing tinker, for such magic powers did he possess, and he had so entranced her soul and fixed such a spell upon her actions, that she would listen to no persuasions and irrevocably resolved to share Tom Tinker's fate." In despair George reacted by descending into the depths of drunkenness, riot and dissipation.

A man of prolific sexual appetite, whose long nose seemed to confirm the old adage that men with great noses make great lovers, George began to cast his net even wider, resorting to prostitutes of every class. In his day London had more prostitutes plying their trade, whether on the open streets or not, than could be found anywhere else in Europe. The city was indeed the sex capital of Europe and perhaps of the world. There were the poor streetwalkers who slept rough and haunted the streets at all times of the day and night, many of whom were infected with venereal disease; the women who operated from rented rooms and solicited in the streets and taverns; the higher-class prostitutes who frequented fashionable bagnios, seraglios, "nunneries" or brothels under the protection of madams; and finally the demi-reps or high courtesans who were most often the kept mistresses of rich, influential or powerful men. None escaped George's attention.

Looking back, George was to admit, "I was early introduced into life and often kept both good and bad company, associated with men both good and bad, and with lewd women, and women not lewd, wicked and not wicked — in short, with men and women of every description and of every rank from the highest to the lowest, from St James's to St Giles's's[8], in palaces and night cellars, from the drawing room to the dust cart. The difficulties and misfortunes I have experienced, I am inclined to think, have proceeded from none of the above mentioned causes but from happening to come into life at a period of the greatest extravagance and profusion. Human nature is in general frail, and mine I confess has been wonderfully so. I could not stand the temptations of that age of extravagance, elegance and pleasure. Indeed, I am not the only sufferer, for most of my contemporaries and many of ten times my opulence have been ruined."

George "has made himself so very conspicuous upon the theatre of gallantry and dissipation," began an interesting article in July 1777, "that all our town readers will immediately know him, and it may seem extraordinary that he has so long escaped our observation. The truth is we have been lying in wait for him some time, but the eccentricity of his conduct and the variety of his amours prevented our tracing any particular attachment till the present; and as it may be of short duration, we have seized this opportunity of delineating his character and laying before our readers his extraordinary exploits.

"When at school," the article continued, "we find him much more addicted to plundering orchards than inclined to his studies. Indeed, he had an utter aversion to Greek and took more delight in the company of the pretty females in the neighbourhood than with either Homer or Virgil. He signalised himself very early in the service of the fair sex, and ere he was seventeen he had a child sworn to him by a maid servant and was flogged in school after being at least a nominal father for his *As in præsenti*.[9]"

---

[8] A haunt of thieves, vagabonds and common prostitutes.
[9] A reference to part of a work on Latin grammar written by William Lily (*c* 1468-1522) and used at Eton.

On repairing to the metropolis George "soon signalised himself in all public places as a buck of the first head. Having obtained a commission in the army, the Captain was well known about the gardens at Vauxhall and Marylebone [*frequented by prostitutes*] and the ladies of easy virtue found him a very good friend as his purse was constantly dilated to their wants and wishes. Such a career brought him to distress and he was obliged to have recourse to usurious Israelites to raise the necessary supplies as his guardian positively refused paying a number of superfluous debts which he had created. His pocket alone did not suffer by these debaucheries, but his health was much impaired and he found it necessary to make a temporary retreat."

On proposing to his guardian a tour upon the Continent George was advised, if he went to see the world, to take particular care the world should not see him. "The Captain either did not or would not understand Old Square-toes but set off for Paris to make a *figure*[10] in that capital. He had not been long there before he became the subject of public conversation, being constantly seen in the Tuileries, the Palais Royal, the guinguettes[11], and the rest of the public places, flushed with burgundy and champagne. He had, however, the luck to escape any *rencontres*[12], as, to do the French justice, they make great allowances for the behaviour of Englishmen, which they would not do in favour of their own countrymen."

George became enamoured of a poor *figurante*[13] who had been hackneyed in the *sérails*[14] and upon the pavements of Paris. "It is true," observed the article, "he found her an easy conquest

---

[10] Name for himself.
[11] Popular drinking establishments outside the centre of Paris, which also served food and catered for dances.
[12] Duels.
[13] Bit player
[14] Seraglios

as she found him an easy dupe, and he enabled her to assist a corporal of dragoons who was her *cher ami* to the summit of his wishes. In a word, as poor a *figurante* as she was upon the stage, he was in her opinion a poorer *figurant* upon the theatre of love, where he seldom appeared but when intoxicated.

"Having exhausted his letter of credit, it was time for him to think of returning home, which he did with regret at leaving his fond and faithful mistress. Upon his appearance in England, *much improved, no doubt, by his travels*, he renewed his former acquaintance and, being now in full possession of his fortune, gave an ample scope to his disposition and genius.

"He shone with uncommon *éclat* at all the masquerades," the article went on, "where he was generally noisy and riotous from inebriation, whereby he obtained the title of Captain Toper. His exploits in King's Place[15] are registered in Charlotte Hayes's annals of dissipation and riot, and her bills for broken looking glasses, china and the like amounted in one week to a very considerable sum. The Captain's dexterity in this kind of destruction was not confined to this lady's house only. Every nunnery in that neighbourhood as well as the New Buildings can evince his extraordinary feats. His prowess he also testified in many other ways, and tho', unlike Don Quixote, he never tilted with a windmill, he has often attacked, sword in hand, those innocent and useful vehicles called sedan chairs; and to his skill and courage, be it spoken, he has often vanquished a whole phalanx united. Their wounds, though not *mortal*, have often created a great *mortification* in their masters when they discovered the fatal effects of the preceding night.

"In his intrigues he has oftentimes been unlucky. His ambition has ever excited him to have amours with women of some consequence in a certain line, but his constant state of intoxication,

---

[15] A court running between Pall Mall and King Street, St James's. Virtually all its houses were high-class brothels, including Charlotte Hayes' nunnery.

added to his natural disposition for riot and confusion, has frequently precluded him from the arms of those desirable females whom he has so ardently wished for. The waiters at Lovejoy's and the other houses of modest recreation knew it was in vain to send for these ladies in his name as they would never come."

By some accident George became acquainted with Mary Frederick, wife of John (1750-1825), the MP for Newport, Cornwall, who would succeed to a baronetcy in 1783. "This lady," the article reported, "agreed to keep him company on condition that he would never call upon her but when he was in a perfect state of sobriety. To these terms the Captain agreed and for a few days fulfilled the contract. But one morning returning from Vauxhall overcharged with claret, he called upon her before the servants were stirring, and not obtaining immediate entrance, he broke all the windows and raised so great an uproar that the watchmen took him to the round house, where he was confined till he recovered his senses. This outrage broke off the connection as Mrs Frederick would not keep up a correspondence with a man of such a violent disposition."

George then crossed the path of Lady Grosvenor, wife of Richard, the first Baron, who in 1769 had caught her *in flagrante delicto* with Prince Henry Frederick, the Duke of Cumberland and Strathearn. They separated. According to the article, "The Captain made an attempt one night upon Lady Grosvenor at the Pantheon, and as he was masked and tolerably sober the beginning of the evening, he probably might have prevailed as he was one of the best dressed masks in the place and had a very handsome diamond ring upon his finger which greatly attracted her ladyship's attention; but before morning he applied so often to the bottle to drink libations to his *angelic mistress* that he lost her for want of recollecting her dress. The Captain met her ladyship the next masquerade night at Conelys'[16] when

---

[16] Carlisle House in Soho Square, a risqué venue for concerts, gambling and exotic masquerades.

he renewed his addresses, but she treated him with the greatest coolness, considering his former behaviour as an intended affront. He now had recourse to the bottle to dissipate his melancholy for the loss of his *angelic mistress* and once more got most compleatly intoxicated upon her ladyship's account.

"This was," the article concludes, "the state of Captain Toper's amours when he made an acquaintance with 'the Hibernian Thais'[17]", the daughter of a tradesman in Dublin who had run away rather than marry. "Her temporary wants induced her to yield to the Captain; a pressing mercer may be said to have been his Mercury upon this occasion. The Captain's purse quieted the urgent trader and promoted his suit. It is somewhat singular that the Captain since this connection has only broken two of her pier-glasses and one set of china. He has, however, replaced them and promises never to be guilty of a like offence. How long he will keep his promise cannot be ascertained, but this is certain, if the Captain breaks a favourite set of china which she doats upon, she will certainly break with him."

"I must," claimed George, "have been more than a man, or, more properly speaking, less than a man, not to have indulged in the pleasures of the gay world, which I could not partake of without being at a very considerable expence, by far more than my income could afford." His estate in Berkshire, bequeathed to him by his aunt, Lady Coleraine of the first creation, brought in a rent of £200[18] a year; otherwise all he possessed was £3,000 in cash as a youngest son's fortune. Yet his outlay on clothes alone was immense. "I was," he admits, "extremely extravagant in my dress. For one winter's dress-clothes only, it cost me nine hundred pounds. I employed other tailors to furnish servants' clothes and morning and hunting frocks etc for myself."

---

[17] Thais was the name of a Greek courtesan who became the wife of Ptolemy I of Egypt *c* 335 BC.

[18] To transpose this and later sums in this chapter into present-day values multiply by a factor of 140.

In particular he always made a point of being handsomely dressed at each celebration of the King's birthday, but for one especially, he put himself to very great expense, having two suits for the day. "My morning vestments cost me near eighty pounds and those for the ball above one hundred and eighty. It was a satin coat *brodé en plain et sur les coutures* and the first satin coat that had ever made its appearance in this country. Shortly after, satin-dress clothes became common amongst well dressed men."

"I never was fond of cards or dice," asserts George, "nor ever played for any considerable sum of money — at least no further than the fashion of the times compelled me. I claim, however, no merit whatever for abstaining from play, as it afforded me no pleasure. If it had, I certainly should have gratified that passion as I have done some others." Nevertheless, cards did feature in a press report about him that appeared in May 1772. "The Captain is lately returned from a tour in Ireland, where the Hibernian beauties paid him a regard not inferior to the English toasts. An anecdote has transpired that does great honour to his humanity and generosity. Whilst he was in the capital of that kingdom, being one evening in Lucas's coffee house, he met with a young gentleman who lodged in the same house with him and who was in possession of a sum of money given him by his relations as his fortune to purchase a commission, and was accordingly upon the point of embarking for England. A party at piquet was proposed and Captain Hanger was so very successful that he won all the young gentleman's cash. Upon their return home together Mr Hanger perceived his late antagonist extremely gloomy, and after he had retired to his own apartment, the Captain had the charitable curiosity to listen to a very extraordinary soliloquy which concluded with, 'Since all hopes are vanished, this pistol shall do its office.' The Captain immediately rushed in, prevented the execution of this rash sentence, and insisted upon his coming down into his lodging and drinking a bottle. By plying him plentifully with the crimson juice he diverted his thoughts till morning, when the Captain contrived to remit him his money in notes by letter supposed to be sent by a lady who entertained a very high opinion of his merit. The young gentleman did not discover the kind and genteel imposition till after he had arrived in England. He has since purchased a cornetcy of dragoons and now relates this adventure so greatly to the Captain's advantage."

Before the age of twenty George had fought three duels, but whether with the épée or pistol he does not say. "In those days," he relates, "I was in great habits of fencing, having a person to attend me three times a week to perfect me in that science. Being very strong in the arm and wrist, I was ever prepossessed with an idea that if I could, unobserved, change from the one side of my adversary's blade to the other and beat on it, I should be certain of hitting the very best fencer. This was a favourite coup of mine."

Like much of the populace, George in his younger days had a romantic admiration for the highwayman and has left an account of his involvement with a famous one, William Hawkes — a latter-day Robin Hood, who in 1774 was awaiting sentence of death at Newgate. Of opinion that Hawkes was brave, charitable, honourable and humane, George began to seek a series of interviews with him. "Returning from Newmarket to London after a very wet and dirty ride, very much in dishabille, being in dirty boots, surtout coat and round hat, which no gentleman in those days wore in London — in short, just as I was when I dismounted from my horse, I went to Newgate and desired to see Mr Hawkes, but without telling the turnkey who I was. The turnkey called him out to the taproom and I heard him tell him that an acquaintance wanted to speak to him. After calling for a bottle of wine and condoling with him on his situation, I entered on my business with him, telling him I knew he had a famous mare. I then made him a present of two or three guineas and told him that as the mare was to be sold for the benefit of the captors, I hoped he would not deceive me but tell me whether he would recommend me to buy her or not. 'Sir,' answered he, 'it is not likely that a man so near his latter end as I am, for there is hardly any chance of my escaping, should deceive anyone. Therefore, sir, pray tell me for what purpose do you want her.' I replied, 'For *the road* and *only* for the road.' 'Then, sir, I will fairly tell you that I recommend you not to purchase her, for I do not think she will suit you as *it was with the greatest difficulty I could ever get her up to a carriage.*'"

George took such a particular liking to the man that he made himself known to him and used to go and see him at least three times a week till he was executed. George assured him that there was nothing in his power that he would not do to save his life and in fact entered into a plan with him for his safety, requesting that he would point out any means by which he might be saved. "There is nothing but money, sir," said he, "can save me but that I have not, and even if I had it, I fear it is now too late, for the person I robbed is bound over to prosecute me at the ensuing sessions." George immediately put a £50 note in his hand, asking him if it was sufficient for the purpose. He threw himself on his knees and blessed George a hundred times. "Oh, dear sir, had I known you when first confined and before I was committed to take my trial, you could have saved my life. However, I will try what can be done and be assured, sir, I will not make an improper or dishonest use of your money." A few days afterwards, as George sat at breakfast, his servant told him that a woman wanted to speak to him. George ordered her to be shown up, and who should it be but the wife of Hawkes, who came with her husband's best gratitude and respects. She returned the £50 note, saying that Hawkes had tried every means to no purpose and that die he must.

George went constantly to see "this brave fellow" at Newgate till the day of his execution, when he placed himself on horseback close to the tail of the cart on its passage to Tyburn. "Just before he was turned off," adds George, "prayers being ended, he fixed his eyes on me, smiled, nodded his head to me, and then looking up to heaven, I am confident from the signs he made to me that he prayed to God, before whom he was shortly to appear, to bless me for my intended kindness. Then, not waiting for the driving on of the cart, with a manly exertion he sprang out of it, which launched him into eternity.

"I will tell you my opinion of him. I would rather have had the prayers of this man than of all the church-going hypocrites of the age or of any sanctified Methodist who reads prayers in his own family twice a day."

It was during his years in London that George began to gain a reputation for eccentricity, centred as much on the singularity of his widely expressed opinions as on his untoward behaviour. He was, for example, a firm advocate of polygamy, not in general, but in severely restricted circumstances. In short, a man should not be entitled to take a second wife "merely from caprice or fancy but only in case of some mental or corporeal defect which renders his cohabiting with his former wife impossible."

Never one to deny himself the pleasures of the flesh, George was also keenly interested in the sports of the turf and field. "The turf," he confesses, "I was passionately fond of and indulged that pleasure to a very great extent. I once stood three thousand guineas on one race, Shark against Leviathan, and won it; my confederate, Mr Robert Pigott, stood five thousand on the event. I was a considerable gainer by the turf notwithstanding the enormous expence of keeping running horses in those days, as every horse in training at Newmarket cost the owner between eighty and ninety pounds a year if not moved from that place, but if he travelled the country, it was computed, to clear himself, he must win three fifty-pound plates during the summer. To use the idea, but not the precise words, of Macheath[19], I can with truth say the turf has done me justice."

---

[19] A character in John Gay's *The Beggar's Opera*.

A published subscriber to the *Racing Calendar* and the *Sporting Calendar*, George was a member of the Jockey Club and involved in making the matches, sweepstakes etc to be run at Ascot, Bath, Newmarket, York and many other places. He also at times took part in races, for example riding Lord Clermont's Rapid Roan in a Newmarket sweepstake at the second spring meeting in May 1775.

A crack shot, reputedly the best in the land, George was very knowledgeable about the field, publishing in 1814 his *Colonel Hanger to all Sportsmen, and particularly to Farmers and Gamekeepers*, a work that has stood the test of time and been recently reprinted. In it he provides useful tips on shooting a wide variety of game besides addressing the care of dogs and horses, ways to catch vermin etc.

As far as George's career in the Guards was concerned, the wheels came off the waggon in early 1776. Promoted to lieutenant on 20 February, he resigned his commission one month later. "It is," he explains, "sufficient to say that I conceived myself most unjustly treated relative to a promotion that took place in the First Regiment of Foot Guards. Great parliamentary interest was the cause of it to the entire destruction of my promotion in a service to which I was most devoutly attached and of which I resolved to experience the substance, not the disgraceful empty shadow of parading about the streets of London with the outward flimsy insignia of a soldier — a cockade and red coat. All my friends advised me to remain in the regiment and my worthy friend, that enlightened commander Sir William Draper, in particular advised me to do so. I never shall forget his words, 'You are used very ill but you cannot contend against power. Put up with it and use it at some future period as a plea to be served.' But I was too young to take advice and too haughty and high in blood tamely to brook an injury without resenting it or shewing all the indignation I felt on the occasion. Deaf to all advice and blind to my own interest, vexed, heated, and agitated with an honest consciousness of the wrongs I had suffered, I resolved on quitting the Guards and of serving in the Hessian troops in America.

"I should," he goes on, "be guilty of ingratitude if I did not acknowledge the singular kindness which Lord North shewed me when I first resolved on quitting the British service. I had the honour of being as well acquainted with him as his high rank as minister of the country and my inferior situation could admit, for I was accustomed to meet him oftentimes in many of the first and gayest circles in London, for this able statesman, the best of private characters, the most pleasant, engaging and amiable of mankind, did not bury himself in the inaccessible retreats of Downing Street but, when affairs of state did not require his attention, relaxed himself in the fashionable assemblies, which he never failed to enliven by that incomparable flow of wit and good humour which he possessed.

"It was," continues George, "absolutely necessary that I should, if not recommended by the minister, have his permission — or at least that he should acknowledge me as an officer and a gentleman. On my relating to this liberal and friendly nobleman how I had been treated and merely requesting him to recommend me as a gentleman to the Hessian minister, he replied, 'My dear Mr Hanger, however displeased you may be from the history you have related to me, surely you do not prefer any foreign service to your own; and there will be several new regiments raised in which you from your situation are entitled to serve with an advanced rank.' 'My Lord, I understand your meaning and return you my most sincere thanks for your kind intention, and I assure you on my honour I shall be as grateful for your intended goodness as if I accepted it, but I find myself so vexed, grieved and injured that nothing on earth can make me remain in the British Army.' He then said, 'I am sorry you are so determined, Mr Hanger, but if you will bring the Hessian minister to me any morning, I will give orders that you shall be admitted and will say anything you shall please to the Hessian minister.' 'My Lord, I most gratefully acknowledge my obligations to you. I wish you only to recommend me to His Serene Highness the Landgrave's protection.' 'It shall be done, sir,' and of course it was and in the most friendly and handsome manner."

George learned of the outcome while in the country. "In my way down to Andover in Hampshire, where I kept my hunters, I called on my old and intimate friend, Lord Spencer Hamilton, and imparted to him what I had done, in confidence of his secrecy. I kept this design of mine so profound a secret that it was not in the least known or suspected till one day, after hunting, while I was at dinner with my friend Lord Egmont and some other gentlemen at the Castle Inn, Marlborough, the waiter informed me that an express was arrived to me from the Hessian minister. After reading the contents, that he had received a dispatch from Hesse-Cassel in which His Serene Highness the Landgrave had appointed me a captain in His Corps of Jägers and had sent my commission to him, I threw the letter on the table for the company to peruse, which they did with the utmost astonishment. I set off for London the next day." His commission — in fact as a staff captain — was dated 18 January 1778.

After being presented at Court as a Hessian officer, George two months later joined up with a convoy of Hessian troops bound for America. Escorted by naval ships under Rear Admiral Gambier, they sailed from Portsmouth on 15 March.

CHAPTER 3

PHILADELPHIA TO RHODE ISLAND

George reached New York City on 26 May 1778 and three days later set sail for Philadelphia to join the Jäger Corps there. He was not unduly surprised to find the two-day voyage up the Delaware fraught with danger, for the revolutionaries controlled the riverbanks, eagerly taking pot shots at passing vessels. He arrived in the city on 6 June only to discover that it was about to be evacuated by the British and Hessians.

By now the war had been running for over three years but had hardly affected the revolutionaries' control of the revolted colonies, though East and West Florida remained loyal. By the beginning of 1777 the British had been forced to abandon Boston — their last toehold in New England, had captured New York City, Long Island and Newport, Rhode Island, but, after initially occupying New Jersey, had had to withdraw from it in the face of reverses at Trenton and Princeton. It was then that the plan for the Philadelphia campaign was devised.

If Philadelphia was threatened, then, according to Sir William Howe, the British commander-in-chief, it would be incumbent on George Washington, the revolutionary commander, to risk a battle to protect the capital of the confederacy. "My opinion," said he," has always been that the defeat of the rebel regular [Continental] army was the surest road to peace." If it was crushed, not only one province but three would be the certain and immediate prize, for, he claimed, the destinies of New York and New Jersey were bound up in the fate of Pennsylvania, a combined region in which political inclinations were nearly balanced. From such a secure and conveniently situated base the British army could then proceed to subjugate, first Virginia and the Carolinas, and eventually Connecticut and Massachusetts. It was a plan which he was confident would win Britain the war.

Unfortunately for the British events did not turn out as expected. They did indeed occupy Philadelphia, but despite the Battles of Brandywine and Germantown, the Continental army remained an ever present threat, confining the British to occupation of the city. Apart from that post and those gained on the eastern seaboard, the British Army held not one single acre of soil on the mainland north of East Florida — and to make matters worse, an army had been lost in the province of New York when Burgoyne capitulated at Saratoga. All in all, the revolutionaries remained clearly in the ascendancy.

It was at this juncture that France entered the war on the side of the revolutionaries. Every consideration now pointed to the desirability of concentrating British forces as far as possible. So when Sir Henry Clinton arrived in Philadelphia on 8 May to supersede Howe, he brought with him orders to evacuate the city and, should he reach New York, to embark 8,000 men with artillery and stores for the West Indies and East and West Florida.

On reporting for duty, George would have expected to command a jäger company, but his commanding officer, Lt Colonel Ludwig Johann Adolph von Wurmb, had other ideas. Despite George's assertions in later life to the contrary, he was never formally entrusted with the command of jägers but had in due course to make do with another arrangement as we shall see later.

At the start of the Philadelphia campaign the Jäger Corps had comprised four companies of foot jägers — three Hessian and one Anspach — and one mounted company, in all 865 men. As their name implies, most were huntsmen and all were crack shots. While at Philadelphia the Corps had been augmented by two newly arrived companies from Germany, increasing the total complement to 1,200, but had suffered materially by attrition. For example, in the Battle of Brandywine two officers and six men were killed, whereas three sergeants and 35 privates were seriously wounded, the former of whom and many of the latter died. And so the losses continued during the numerous minor actions in which the Corps was engaged. The élite of the Hessian troops, the jägers were employed to great advantage in leading the van of a marching army or protecting its rear, covering a withdrawal, reconnoitring, and conducting partisan warfare, particularly ambuscades.

A distressing scene had met George's eyes when he landed. Convinced the British were about to leave, many loyalists were placing their furniture and personal possessions on the pavement by their homes and frantically searching for means to convey them and their persons to transports off shore. In the words of a lady who observed the chaos, "Her head grew dizzy with the bustle and confusion: ... carts, drays and waggons laden with dry goods and household furniture, dragged by men through the streets to the wharfs for want of horses; beds, boxes, trunks, chairs, tables etc turned out in the utmost confusion and haste." Waiting in the river were some 300 ships to transport them, surplus army supplies, sick or wounded soldiers, and enemy prisoners to New York.

Yet the deplorable fate of the loyalists was a mere sideshow to one of the trickiest of military problems: how to evacuate an occupied city in the face of the enemy. Clinton's answer was to continue improving certain defensive works as a blind while destroying others and disposing of a mass of ordnance, firearms and military hardware, whether by taking it on board ship, burning it, or sinking it in the river. Almost inevitably the utmost confusion was sown in the minds of the enemy, as evinced by the following report of 10th June: "The enemy at Philadelphia for three weeks past have been doing and undoing, one day extremely busy in fortifying and the next in demolishing. In short, their manœuvres are so various as to render it utterly impossible to guess what measures they mean finally to pursue."

Most of the occupying troops, some 17,000 or more men, evacuated the city on the 15th and 16th, crossing the Delaware to

New Jersey at Cooper's Ferry. Only the Jäger Corps and a few other detachments remained. The night was clear and very pleasant, the air balmy and still, becoming "lazy" as the morning of the 17th broke hot. It was then that they left, crossing to Gloucester Point on the New Jersey shore. "They made no noise in evacuating the city but at the last moment left in the greatest haste, fearing perhaps that the Americans had heard of their intended departure and would attack them. A lady who saw them leave said, 'They did not go away — they vanished.'"

NEW JERSEY

The army began its march to New York in two columns: one consisting of a baggage train of 1,500 waggons that extended for more than eight miles, and another composed of troops not needed for its protection. The former was commanded by General Freiherr Wilhelm von Knyphausen, the GOC in charge of the Hessian forces, and the latter by Lt General Earl Cornwallis. At times the columns united. Walking beside the waggons were countless camp followers, predominantly women.

Almost immediately the New Jersey revolutionary militia began to swarm around the columns, continually sniping at them, destroying bridges, and felling trees across the roads in their path. Later, as Washington crossed the Delaware in pursuit, detachments of Continental troops joined in.

Most often the Jäger Corps formed the van of a column or its rear, but occasionally protected its flanks. By 27 June, when Knyphausen's leading column had come to rest on a beautiful plain just beyond Monmouth Court House, the Jäger Corps found itself posted in a large, very pleasant wood on the Trenton road, where after dark it was menaced by revolutionary militia. George was later to recall, "I shall never forget the night before the Battle of Monmouth Court House. It was uncommonly dark with frequent thunderstorms and rain. It fell to my lot that night to have the outermost picket. Never could man pass a more anxious time: the fires all put out, the enemy's patroles feeling us and firing every half hour and oftener at the advanced sentries; our men on sentry firing sometimes at the enemy's patroles and sometimes at cattle in the woods, as soldiers will do when they hear a noise in the bushes, challenge, and gain no reply; the night so dark (taking it by turns every half hour with two lieutenants to visit the sentries) as not to be able to perceive our own men until we came close upon them and in danger of being fired at by our own men. Such a night of anxiety and danger I never since passed, and blessed my God when the day began to dawn."

Shortly afterwards Knyphausen's column moved off bound for Middletown. Thrown on to its left flank, the Jäger Corps had to skirmish with the enemy throughout the day as the column pushed ever deeper into the very difficult defiles of the area. At times the situation became pretty desperate, as Captain Johann Ewald in his journal makes clear: "... the terrain was so difficult to cross, because of the sunken roads, impassable underbrush, marshes, and many brooks which cut through the country here, that the greater part of the Jäger Corps more than once found itself in the dilemma of being cut off from the army, which happened to me several times today. I thought that I was connected with the division and ran into whole swarms of Americans not over twenty to thirty paces away. But since we took up the favourite cry of the great Frederick — "*Allons! Allons!*" — and our jägers knew nothing else, we constantly got out of this business with honor. Indeed, large groups of Americans penetrated several times between the intervals of the jäger platoons up to the waggons, killing men and horses. Then, when they were driven back by the infantry escorting the waggons, they ran against the jägers and we were forced to fire on all sides."

In the meantime Washington attacked in force Cornwallis's column, which followed behind, precipitating the Battle of Monmouth. It was a bloody affair in which Clinton, who was with the column, drove back the enemy across three ravines before continuing his march. The enemy for propaganda purposes claimed victory — a specious claim that has nevertheless percolated down in American history to the present day.

By 1 July the army had passed through Middletown and encamped on the heights of Navesink beside the sea. While there the jägers, who were guarding the entrance to the heights, had two skirmishes with the enemy before crossing a pontoon bridge to Sandy Hook and moving into camp at Morris's House on York[20] Island. By the 7th the entire army had passed either to New York or Long Island.

---

[20] Now Manhattan.

The march had been a most trying affair. Conducted in almost unbearable heat, with temperatures reaching 96° F in the shade, it had seen many men die of sunstroke, no less than 59 during the Battle of Monmouth. The Jäger Corps too was affected, as recorded, for example, in its journal on 26 June: "We lost three men on account of the dreadful heat. The march was very fatiguing. Being the last troops, we had constantly to deal with the enemy and suffered from a great shortage of water due to the exhausted or spoiled wells. Consequently many of the jägers collapsed on the road and were dragged away on the officers' horses, for we could not procure any waggons. This happened very often during the withdrawal across Jersey." Moreover, when encamped, the entire army did not have a single tent, so that there was no protection from the heat of the sun or from the insects, which were a constant problem. "We were," says Ewald, "so terribly bitten at night by the mosquitoes and other kinds of vermin that we could not open our eyes for the swelling in our faces. Many men were made almost unrecognisable, and our bodies looked like those of people who have been suddenly attacked by measles or smallpox." Nevertheless, a few moments of light relief occurred on the 24th when there was a total eclipse of the sun lasting four minutes from 9 am. Despite all the difficulties faced by the troops, they still found many opportunities for undertaking unauthorised and widespread pillage, which, when New Jersey was briefly occupied in 1776, had done much to turn it against the Crown.

On 21 July the arrangement for George began to take shape. In general orders volunteers were sought from the Hessian regiments to form a company of chasseurs to be commanded by him. Comprising four officers, twelve non-commissioned officers, three drummers and 100 privates, they reported for duty four days later at Morris's House before going into camp on Spuyten Duyvil Hill, the base for their operations till November. One of the volunteers was a serjeant, Johann Carl Philip von Krafft, a soldier of fortune who has left a most interesting journal of his part in the war. Born in Dresden in 1752, he had served as a lieutenant in the Prussian army, but tiring of garrison duty, he resigned in May 1776 and sought advancement in a more active role elsewhere. After a series of adventures in which he crossed the Atlantic twice, he made his way to Valley Forge but was unable to obtain a commission in the Continental army as a captain. Passing on to Philadelphia, he settled on becoming a Hessian serjeant in the Regiment von Donop.

Now reporting for duty as a volunteer, von Krafft records that he brought from his regiment "a very good letter of recommendation to the new captain of the chasseurs, who was an Englishman by birth and of the highest rank. He had studied at Göttingen and was called George von Hanger."

Spuyten Duyvil Hill lay between the Hudson River and King's Bridge, which connected the northern tip of York Island with the mainland of Westchester County. Encamped beside the chasseurs was the Jäger Corps. From then till the troops moved into winter quarters all were involved in patrols and small-scale warfare protecting York Island from incursions by the enemy, whose main force under Washington occupied White Plains to the north with its advanced posts at Valentine's Hill and Philipse's House, four miles from the outposts of George's encampment. Typical of what went on is described in the following entries in von Krafft's journal:

1 August. Saturday. At daybreak we and all the jägers who were not on watch or picket had to patrol. We chasseurs had the middle of the corps. We marched a distance of about four English miles, when we arrived at an elevation where out of the near lying bushes three musket shots were fired. The bullets killed the horse of a jäger who was riding on our flank. We immediately marched up to the place and several more shots were fired. Standing a little lower down now we could hear the bullets whistle over our heads. We could see nothing. It was very hazy and we could not see fifty steps ahead. Some mounted jägers who had been sent forward came back and brought news that a considerable number of rebels had made a stand on another height and had field-pieces with them. At this news we retreated in good order without firing a shot. Our corps consisted of five foot and one mounted jägers, our chasseur company, and two three-pounder amusettes which had been given to the corps by the British. Around these several jägers constantly remained with muskets and bayonets.

2 August. Sunday. Towards evening a loud alarm was given in our camp because some rebels showed themselves near the outposts. We all had to turn out, but only to advance to the front of the camp. Nor did we stay there long, for it soon grew quiet again.

The next afternoon the camp had a view of a second conflagration in New York City, the first having occurred in 1776. "We saw from our camp a great fire which reduced nearly

64 houses in York to ashes, among them provision and bake houses." The day after, at two o'clock in the afternoon, "a terrible thunderstorm with heavy rain again came up. The lightning struck a schooner lying off New York, set fire to it, and was the cause of its blowing up with 260 barrels of powder."

As during the march across New Jersey, insects began to be a persistent problem in August. For several days, Ewald relates, mosquitoes had arrived in vast swarms with the south wind, "which torment us extremely. Moreover, all the bushes are full of large gray beetles, which because of their great numbers make such a loud hissing sound that one cannot hear during the night." By day they were plagued with swarms of flies.

On 23 September, as part of a movement forward by Knyphausen, a detachment of some 30 chasseurs and jägers began advancing at 6 am to Philipse's House in driving rain, opening the pretty church there and quartering themselves in it. "Finally," von Krafft reveals, "a search was begun and a large potato field was cleaned out and many other luxuries brought in. Fowls, pigs and cattle were slaughtered, although everything had to be done secretly. As usual when on the march, we received nothing but salt pork, biscuit and rum for rations. In short we led, as the Hessians term it, a hussar life. The rain continued with surprising violence so that we were glad to have got into such nice dry quarters. We gathered hay and straw and made ourselves good beds. For a mattress I had a cushion covered with green cloth, the covering of which I took with me when we marched away ... Constant complaints were made to the jägers and to us that cattle had been slaughtered, but the matter was not very closely investigated by the staff and other officers. So we had good night quarters here. The rain stopped during the night and it became clear again."

The next day the detachment advanced farther to the 20-mile-stone, keeping to the right of it and ascending a height. There they built huts in which to encamp till further orders. "The foraging," says von Krafft, "commenced again immediately, during which some of the soldiers began to plunder. Many of the houses, which I saw afterwards, had been left in a deplorable state and the soldiers had made a good haul. We were not forbidden to get provisions but very strictly admonished not to take anything from the people in their houses. However, even when they were caught in the act, the punishment was not equal to the crime. For a few days we had an abundance of good food and this was my only booty."

By the 30th the whole of George's chasseur company and the entire Jäger Corps had come up. On that day he was involved in the aftermath of an action graphically described by Ewald in which a detachment of jägers was worsted by Major "Light Horse Harry" Lee of the enemy:

On the 30th at daybreak I made a patrol with 60 jägers and twelve horse towards Dobbs Ferry in order to obtain information whether an enemy detachment had approached past Tarrytown, as was rumoured. I went still farther than I was ordered since I risked nothing and had covered my rear in echelon, but could not collect the slightest news from the country people and returned safely.

A little over halfway back I met Captain Donop with a party just as strong which Lt Colonel Wurmb had sent out after me. I assured the good Donop that I had discovered no trace of the enemy, but begged him to be careful to cover his rear and flanks and to let only a few men go past the defile up to the heights of Post's plantation. Here again, the good man followed his nose and let Lieutenant Bickell and 30 men cross the defile. When several shots rang out there, he lost his presence of mind and sent Lieutenant Mertz with his twelve horsemen past the defile to rush support to the foot jägers. But Donop himself took flight with the rest of his men when he caught sight of several troops of enemy horsemen on his right who threatened to cut him off, although they could not have done him any harm if he had withdrawn only 150 paces, where there was an inaccessible cliff.

Lieutenant Bickell realised that he and his foot jägers were completely surrounded by the enemy. Nevertheless, he withdrew

48

through three ambuscades along the steep cliffs to Saw Mill Creek. He lost only one corporal and eight jägers of his advanced guard and seven skirmishers. But Lieutenant Mertz, who was supposed to save Bickell, found himself cut off on all sides as soon as he had passed the defile, partly by horsemen and partly by infantry. He therefore chose the shortest way to cut through the enemy horsemen, but was overcome by the superior force. He was severely wounded by two sabre cuts and the remaining twelve mounted jägers, including the quartermaster, were all hacked to pieces, except for the latter and another man. Lt Colonel Wurmb and the Corps hastened to their aid but found nothing but the corpses of these brave men. This misfortune was attributable to nothing other than the carelessness and weakness of Captain Donop.

"Captain Hanger," adds Baurmeister, "was sent after the rebels with a flag of truce to take equipage and servants to Lieutenant Mertz. However, Major Lee procured the lieutenant's release because he had so gallantly defended himself .., and he returned with Captain Hanger. His wounds, which are across the nose and on both cheeks, are not dangerous. He has already been exchanged for another lieutenant."

It was at this point that the Peace Commissioners, who had been dispatched by Britain to seek an accommodation, published a proclamation. Dated 3 October, it was their last despairing act in the face of Congress's refusal to entertain negotiations short of independence. Offering, *inter alia*, freedom for ever from taxation by Britain, it conceded everything that the revolted colonies had sought before the war began — only matters had irretrievably moved on.

For form's sake it was judged proper for Clinton to forward the proclamation to Congress by land from the outposts of the army and to dispatch a vessel with it to Philadelphia. Accordingly copies were sent to the outposts of the Jäger Corps with orders to Lt Colonel von Wurmb to deliver them to the most contiguous advanced post of the opposing army.

"I was," says George, "the only Englishman in that corps. Colonel von Wurmb therefore requested me as a favour (it not being my turn for duty) to go out with these proclamations and assigned as his reason that, as the other officers did not understand the English language, some mistake might take place from their not being able to explain matters and converse with the American officers. Colonel von Wurmb certainly could have commanded me on this service, but to comply with a request or even a hint from him was but a small tribute of gratitude for me to pay to so good and amiable a man as well as so kind a friend. It was therefore with the greater pleasure that I undertook this duty, but not without foreseeing the disagreeable consequences attendant on it, by which I might have lost my life and in the most unpleasant manner for a soldier and a gentleman."

George concedes that he was perfectly aware of the temper of the revolutionaries, elated as they were by the reinforcements that their ally France was sending. Already a French fleet was off the coast and French troops were in prospect. Therefore "it was most natural to imagine that [Congress] would reject all proposals from the British Government, not only with scorn but contempt." So, on taking his leave of von Wurmb, George told him that he would endeavour to stay as short a time at the revolutionary outpost as possible, merely to demand a receipt, and push back with all expedition, for he was convinced that, if he remained a sufficient time for them to deliberate, he would be stopped and made a prisoner. "The event," he claims, "proved the truth of my conjectures."

George here observes that the trumpeter and mounted jäger who accompanied him carried several hundred printed copies of the proclamation for him to distribute, as he went along, at the countrymen's houses and in the towns through which he passed. In Tarrytown, situated fourteen miles from the Hessian outposts, he distributed some hundreds. About three or four miles farther beyond Tarrytown he fell in with a patrol of light dragoons who carried him to their officer at a house close by. He commanded about 50 men. "I gave him," recounts George, "thirteen packets, one addressed to every State, and one to General Washington. On reading a printed copy, he told me he did not know whether it was proper for him to receive such papers and that it was necessary for him to send to know the commands of General Scott[21] on that subject, who lay at the distance of about four miles. I told him I was commanded to leave them at the first American outpost that I should fall in with, and with an air of nonchalance I added that, if he did not choose to receive them, I should leave them with the landlord of the house, but that it was but common politeness from one officer to another to give me an acknowledgement under his hand that I had left them at the house, merely to shew my commanding officer that I had done my duty, as I might otherwise be very severely reprimanded on my return to the British army and perhaps put under arrest. In short, after a good deal of persuasion and telling him that the proclamation, whatever it contained, was nothing to him or to me as it came from the British Commissioners, and that certainly I should in a similar case not hesitate one moment in giving him a receipt, I procured a receipt from him and, taking a polite leave of him, rode off for our army with no small degree of speed and pleasure. A few minutes after, he dispatched an officer with the proclamations to General Scott, but not before I had given every soldier who came round me one of them."

On George's return through Tarrytown there were above 200 persons collected together and he was under some apprehension that they would stop him, as a few armed militia among them said that they knew not what business he had to deliver printed papers inviting the citizens of America to desert Congress. He told them that he was under the sanction of a flag or truce and had done nothing but what the inhabitants

---

[21] Charles Scott (c 1739-1813) was a brigadier general in the Continental line. He had taken a prominent part in the New Jersey, Philadelphia and Monmouth campaigns and would be taken prisoner in the Capitulation of Charlestown. In later life he became Governor of Kentucky.

requested. "The populace," writes George, "were nearly all in favour of me and requested me to continue my distribution of the papers, which I did and absolutely went so far at their request as to read one to the people as I sat on my horse and nailed one up against the public house before I departed. I knew very well, from the distance General Scott was, that I could not be easily overtaken and that I had near an hour to spare. I then made the best of my way home and met with a strong patrole of our corps within two miles of the town, when I returned without further interruption to the camp."

As George correctly states, the very day of his excursion the admiral dispatched a cutter to Philadelphia with counterparts of the same packets that he had carried. The moment the cutter cast anchor in the Delaware its lieutenant and his whole crew were made prisoner. The lieutenant remained above a year in Philadelphia jail. "I should," George adds, "have been sent there also and have kept him company had I waited to receive General Scott's commands, who, as I learned from the communication we held at the outposts, had sent orders to detain me — but fortunately the bird was flown."

On 10 October Knyphausen's troops marched back to New York City and George's chasseurs re-occupied their old camp on Spuyten Duyvil Hill. As before, their time was spent in frequent patrols and in turning out in response to the many alarms. While there von Krafft, who was involved in various clerical duties, was rewarded by George and on 5 November paid tribute to his generosity: "Captain von Hanger, being pleased with my writing, gave me two guineas for my pains and half a guinea regularly each month for the future in addition." On the 15th, a very cold and snowy day, the chasseurs were disbanded and the men returned to their regiments to take up winter quarters. The Jäger Corps moved to Flushing on Long Island.

It was then that Clinton appointed George as one of his aides-de-camp, presumably to facilitate liaison with Knyphausen and his staff in view of George's fluency in German. He would serve as such till the close of 1779, affording him ample opportunities to continue with his womanising ways.

George had not been above two months in America when he received distressing news from England. By the time of his departure from there he had contracted a mortgage on his Berkshire estate of £13,000 and for some time had been resolved to sell it and take a general view of his financial affairs. Little acquainted with them, he had been constantly raising money from time to time as he needed it. Preparatory to a sale a survey of the estate had been conducted.

As his departure approached, George had been in company with a gentleman named Wyatt, "the great land surveyor", with whom he was on terms of the greatest intimacy. Wyatt said to him, "George Hanger, you have had your estate surveyed and, as I am informed, intend to sell it. I have been in your neighbourhood lately and know, I believe, rather more of your estate than you do yourself." — to which, says George, he readily assented, or Wyatt must have known very little of it indeed. "Then," his friend went on, "as I have a regard for you, I request, if you have any faith in my knowledge of estates, that you will put it into my hands to dispose of it — but upon one condition, to which you must, before this company, pledge me your honour." Knowing his man, George promised on his honour to assent to whatever was proposed. "I have," his friend continued, "a very good estate of my own and besides I am paid very liberally by several noblemen and gentlemen for the management of their estates and do not want to make any money of you. You must therefore promise me that you will never request my acceptance of one farthing for my trouble. My expences I will charge you, and nothing more, as my design and wish is to serve you as a friend." Such, George remarks, was the generous and noble manner in which his friend acted by him. "Your estate," said he, "is very valuable, far more so than you imagine. I have been acquainted with all the particulars of it by a skilful man, a surveyor who lives near you, who advised me to buy it, but I have just bought an estate or I would have purchased it. That is now out of the question as I have no more money."

George considered himself inexpressibly fortunate to have met a man of such integrity and rejoiced in leaving his affairs in so capable hands on his departure for America. By then the estate had been resurveyed and George had given his friend full power of attorney to dispose of it. When asked to calculate its value, Wyatt had replied, "It is honestly worth £24,000 and I give you my honour that if I had not lately bought an estate, I would myself give you that sum for it."

On completing his march through New Jersey in July, George had received a letter from his mother advising him that Wyatt had been seized with a paralytic stroke before he could parcel out George's estate and that he might shortly die. At the same time the mortgagee was endeavouring to foreclose the mortgage on the estate and sell it. She sought a fresh power of attorney to enable her and some friend jointly to transact George's business as she was fearful that Wyatt would never recover. George forwarded it by the first packet. In the meantime his friend did recover a little and, the moment that he was able to go down to the estate, did not neglect to arrange everything for sale. Unfortunately, at this point a second stroke ended his life.

During the interval between Wyatt's death and the arrival of the fresh power of attorney the mortgagee foreclosed the mortgage and the estate was sold at public auction for little more than half its real value. The mistake that George had made was not to put the name of some other person in the original power of attorney that he gave to Wyatt. "Had I done so, as I have been informed from the best authority, it would not have been practicable to have foreclosed the mortgage. But I never dreamed of Mr Wyatt being struck with a fit of apoplexy, for he was a hale, hearty man and by no means advanced in years, though he was of a corpulent habit." Affected by a fall in land values arising from the war with France, the estate had realised some £16,500, though, claims George, if he could have kept it till the peace, it would have fetched between £20,000 and £30,000.

Besides the bad news about his estate, his mother informed him that some outstanding debts amounting to several hundred pounds remained unpaid — despite the security that Wyatt had given for George, and that executions had been effected in his house after his friend's death due to the great deficiency in the sale of the estate. "Thus I at once found myself several hundreds worse than nothing instead of not owing a shilling and having £8,000 or £10,000 in hand, as Mr Wyatt assured me, and which he certainly would have accomplished had not the French war broke out or a legal compulsion forced me to sell my estate during that period. I now indeed and in truth became a soldier of fortune, for I was stripped and plundered of everything and, which was worse, left encumbered with debts."

The year 1779 was free of campaigning in the northern and central theatres of the war, being marked by desultory operations such as the Connecticut coast raid too inconsequential to describe. In the south, however, British arms had fared well. Savannah had been captured, a siege of it by the French and revolutionaries had been broken, and a tenuous hold had been gained on lower Georgia. Together with reports of considerable support for the Crown in the southern colonies, these events led the British to conclude that a strategy of pursuing the war from south to north offered the best chance of success. To facilitate an expedition there while retaining sufficient troops at New York City Clinton ordered the evacuation of Newport, Rhode Island, which took place on 25 October. He subsequently had second thoughts and, in making a desperate attempt to retrieve the situation, involved George in what proved to be a very risky venture indeed, as George related many years later.

"The commander-in-chief, after having given orders to General Prescott to evacuate Rhode Island, destroy the works, and repair with the troops to New York, was induced, a few days after he had sent those instructions, from certain events that took place, to countermand these orders and sent me to Rhode Island for that purpose, giving me instructions to examine two particular works, and if I found them not destroyed, or capable by a few days' labour of being put in their former state, General Prescott was by no means to evacuate the place. I sailed in the *Delaware* frigate, Captain Mason[22], and although it is not above 180 miles from Sandy Hook, I was seven days on my passage, being forced to work up close under Long Island in the very teeth of the wind, as it blew very fresh throughout the whole course of it."

At dusk on the evening of the seventh day the frigate cast anchor about a mile and a half from Newport harbour. On her approach, there were two small armed sloops working out of it but on seeing the frigate they immediately put back, arousing strong suspicions that they were enemies and that the place had been evacuated. There were, however, small rivers and creeks on the opposite shore of Connecticut and it was possible that they might have come from there and not from Rhode Island. George consulted his friend Mason, who was clearly of opinion that from the length of their passage they had arrived too late and that the place had indeed been evacuated. George was of the same sentiment, yet there was a chance that it might not be so, for, when frigates arrived, they always sent their boat in and the general might not have thought it necessary to send a boat from shore till the next morning. George suggested to Mason how absurd he would appear were he to return to New York and

---

[22] The *Delaware* had been a revolutionary frigate that was captured on 27 September 1777 when she ran on to sand while fiercely cannonading Philadelphia. She struck after being raked by fire from four cannon of the Hessian grenadier battalions. Now serving in the Royal Navy, she had a complement of 200 men, an armament of 28 British 9-pounders, and was commanded by Captain Christopher Mason (*c* 1740-1801), who would die a vice admiral of the white.

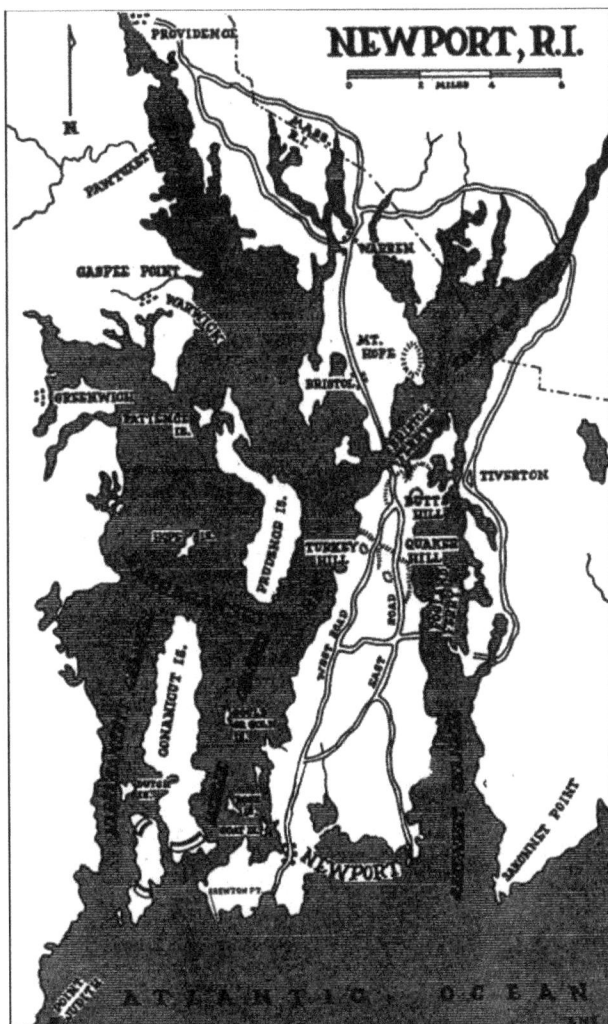

find there that the troops had not left Newport at the time when he arrived. At the same time he stated the magnitude of the business in which he was engaged and that he would never dare to show his face again to Clinton if he did not do everything that depended on himself. He was therefore anxious to risk any danger in order to investigate the object of his mission. He accordingly requested Mason to give him an armed boat, being determined to land in the dark and gain intelligence.

Complying with the earnest request, Mason gave George his ten-oared barge, two marines, a coxswain, and one of his lieutenants, making in all a party of fifteen men. George timed it so as to enter the harbour at the end of the flood tide that they might have the tide with them on returning. On their departure from the ship Mason enjoined the lieutenant strictly to obey George's orders. At the same time, being sensible of the imminent danger they would encounter, he requested George to act with the utmost prudence and circumspection, saying that he would not, for ten thousand guineas, have the boat's crew lost or taken prisoner as they had attended him as bargemen throughout the war. The boat was well armed; each man had a musket and bayonet, with cutlass, pistols, etc etc and plenty of ammunition. With oars muffled the party approached the harbour in silence, keeping close under the shade thrown on the water by the high craggy rocks on the right, which, with the darkness of the night, made the party so concealed from sight that when a sloop from the harbour tacked and came about not above 150 yards away, she was quite unable to perceive them. They lay on their oars till she had completely tacked and stood half way over to the other side, when they proceeded to bring the boat to shore directly under the high bluff of Brenton Point, not far from the battery. A boat might have passed within 30 yards and not have seen them. George then landed with the two marines only, who wore sailors' blue jackets to cover and conceal their red and white uniforms. He ordered them to proceed when he proceeded and to lie down when he fell to the ground. They then crawled up the precipice so as to be able to look just above the summit, where they remained some time to observe while George determined how they were to proceed. He heard the sentinels challenge every now and then and cry, "All is well," for they were quite on the alert, having spotted, as he was later informed, a man of war anchor off the harbour. At last a patrol from the nearest picket, which from the fire George judged was not above 300 yards away, passed so near that he could distinctly hear them speak, and he heard two sentinels challenge the patrol, one on his right, the other on his left.

When the patrol passed, he knew that he had little to fear and that from the darkness of the night he could easily pass between them. He accordingly ran across the road that they went down and, when over in the next field, which was very rough and bushy, he laid the marines down in order to set the position of their boat by the Pole Star, "which is immovable. This every officer, especially of light troops, should be well acquainted with. If I had not known it, I might have been easily taken prisoner in wandering along the cliff in search of the boat on my return."

Looking about for a house from which he might take some person to gain intelligence, George fixed his eyes on two which, as far as he could judge by the lights in them, were about a mile away and quite at a distance from any others. There were several nearer him, but they were too close to the pickets and patrols along the shore to suit his purpose. With great caution and always lying down whenever he heard anything, he approached them. They were about 200 yards apart. In one he saw two lights, in the other only one. He therefore made up to the latter and, laying the two marines down among the cabbages in the garden, he stood about ten yards from the door at the garden gate and hallooed out, whereupon an old woman came to the door and asked what he wanted and who he was. George replied, "I am an officer come from town and am ordered over to Connecticut by the general on business. I have lost my way in the dark and want to be put into the path to Brenton Point. Pray send someone to the end of the garden to put me into it." She replied, "One of our family is gone to town and the other is gone to bed, but if he is not undressed, I will send him to show you." George had previously determined with his two faithful marines that, if he could not entice any one person out of the house, they would enter it and take someone away by force, but he dreaded the consequences, knowing that if resistance was made, they would be obliged to shed blood in their own defence. His stratagem worked completely. Out came "a fine young fellow, as straight and as tall as a poplar tree". The moment George saw him on the steps, he said, "Come along, my good man, just put me into the path to Brenton Point, and I will give you a dollar."

Retiring a few yards from the garden gate, which the young man passed, and when at a sufficient distance from the house, George took him fast by the coat and, putting his pistol to his head, told him to look behind at the two marines, who had their bayonets pointed within two feet of his body. He then charged him not to speak, pledged his honour that he would not hurt him, but that if he uttered a word, should he hear any soldiers passing, he would be killed and they would endeavour to make their escape through the darkness. George took him into a rough place close by and made him sit down. He then told him that he was a British, not a revolutionary, officer and had landed from the frigate off the harbour to gain intelligence. He now gave him a half-joe[23] and repeated his assurance that he would treat him well, but that he must come along with them. The young man's fears at length subsided and he told George that the day before he arrived the British had evacuated the place and that a revolutionary force of 3,000 men now occupied it.

Judging with the marines that the ebb tide had begun and that the moon would rise in about an hour, George proceeded to the boat, walking alongside the young man with his hand fast in his right-hand jacket pocket, "for I knew too well to trust a New Englander's promises. Had he got a yard start of us, he would have alarmed the whole country."

When they arrived within about 400 yards of the rock from where they had landed, they had the same road to cross on which they had seen the patrol pass. As they lay down on one side of it, waiting for the passing of a patrol that they might hear where the sentinels were, their guide attempted to betray them, saying there was no danger if they went up the path. "I knew

---

[23] A Portuguese gold coin in common circulation in North America. It was worth about $8.

better", says George, "and now no longer trusted him but put it out of his power to do any mischief by taking my pocket handkerchief and stuffing the greatest part of it into his mouth that he should not call out. At the same time I made one of the marines hold him fast by the left hand whilst I held him fast by the right." When the patrol had passed, they crossed the path and, on arriving at the brink of the precipice, George had, by keeping his eyes constantly on the Pole Star, set the boat with such precision that when he hallooed, "Mason, ahoy!" he was answered directly beneath where he stood, "Hanger, ahoy!" which were the signals fixed on before their departure. They got the young man into the boat and rowed out of the harbour, the moon not rising before they were quite clear of it. Summing up, George concludes, "Everything turned out well. The tide and rising of the moon was well timed and with no inconsiderable degree of pleasure I arrived on board the *Delaware* frigate to the great joy of my friend Captain Mason."

Unfortunately it was not possible to land the young man on the opposite shore or to send him back to Newport. Mason therefore proposed putting him next day on the shore of Block Island, a few leagues away, but the fog proved so thick that they could not make it with safety. They therefore stood out to sea and George was compelled to take him to New York. On arrival there he provided him with quarters, drew provisions for him, and supplied him with necessaries. It was intended to send him by the first flag of truce to Rhode Island or by the first boat to New London or some town contiguous to his home in New England, but he had not been six days in New York when he sickened of the smallpox and died.

The sudden disappearance of the young man, George admits, was certainly suspicious and it gave rise to many scurrilous reports in the Connecticut and Philadelphia newspapers grossly aspersing George's character as an officer and a gentleman. At first it was stated that the man had been murdered at Newport and thrown overboard at sea. Later, when it became publicly known at New York that George had necessarily brought him there and treated him with kindness, a more just account was published, but one still adding that the man had been thrown into prison and had died there of jail fever.

From his being absent from New York for so many days, indeed above double the time usually required to make the passage, for the wind was foul nearly the whole way there and back, George had been given over for lost. Some imagined that the frigate had sailed at night into the harbour and been captured, "though such croakers[24] little knew the abilities and judgement of Captain Mason," while others supposed that George had landed and been taken prisoner. Setting aside all such conjectures, he arrived just as Clinton was at dinner with fourteen or fifteen officers. After relating the whole affair at table to Clinton and receiving his thanks in the kindest manner, George would never forget to the last day of his life a very singular remark of Clinton's: "I commend your prowess much, but at the same time I am sorry you risked so much, as it was not my wish you should venture so far, for upon my word, my dear Hanger, I believe if they had taken you at Rhode Island, they would have hanged you directly." George replied, "My dear general, that never entered into my head, it being totally impossible for the Americans to commit such an outrage on an officer sent by you in character of an aide-de-camp with orders to our commanding officer at Rhode Island. I could be subjected to no other danger but of being imprisoned. They could not surely be guilty of such an act." "You may think so, Hanger, " replied the general, "but I give you my word I do not, for I know not what they would not do, and I am happy to see you returned safe." Sitting at the table was George's "worthy and intimate friend", Major John André, another of Clinton's aides-de-camp, who in 1780 would be captured by the revolutionaries when on a secret mission and hanged as a spy.

---

[24] Croakers: a now archaic expression denoting persons who habitually prophecy evil or misfortune unjustifiably to the irritation of others.

As the year 1779 came to a close, George received even worse news on the financial front: "Fortune, that fickle goddess, not satisfied with having already turned her wheel from me and my interests, again destined me to be the object of her caprice and neglect. I received a letter from my sister, Mrs Vansittart[25], whose tender love and regard for me is deeply imprinted in my breast, informing me that the Duchess of St Albans, my godmother, was dead. She had made a will in my favour that was witnessed by my mother in which she made me heir to her whole property to a very considerable amount. Within the last twelve months of her death a Mr Roberts came over from Ireland. She had never seen him before or ever heard of him. He, however, proved to her Grace's satisfaction that he was related to her, so that she reversed her intentions, made a new will, and left everything to him. Her second will only bore date six months prior to her death. Had she died seven months sooner, I should have inherited a considerable property and a great addition after the Duke's death, who was then living. The Duchess of St Albans was a Miss Roberts, a rich heiress. Her parents and her near relations dying when she was very young, my father received her into his family, educated and protected her. Out of his family she married the Duke of St Albans. She stood godmother to me and lived in the strictest intimacy and friendship with our family. It was but natural to believe that she would have left some part of her property to our family, but thus she in gratitude repaid my father and mother for their tender care and attention to her for many years by leaving her whole property to a gentleman with whom she never had any acquaintance till about a year before her death. But fate had decreed this, together with many other mortifications, miseries and distresses which I was destined to suffer. Doomed as I was to a life chequered with misfortunes by a Supreme Power, that same Power gave to me a vigorous constitution and a bold and undaunted mind to stem the current of adversity and bear up against a sea of troubles."

---

[25] On 7 August 1773 the Hon Anne Hanger had married Arthur Vansittart of Shottesbrook and Clewes, the MP for Berkshire.

CHAPTER 4

THE CHARLESTOWN CAMPAIGN

Beginning with the siege of Charlestown, the southern campaigns would prove to be Britain's last throw of the dice in the American Revolutionary War.

By the close of 1779 the situation on the ground remained pretty much the same as three years earlier, except that Newport, Rhode Island, had been evacuated, Penobscot, Maine, occupied, and lower Georgia tenuously regained. East and West Florida still remained loyal, but West Florida was threatened by Spain, which had now entered the war. Otherwise, apart from New York City and Long Island, the revolutionaries remained firmly in control of the revolted colonies.

Britain was losing the war.

To turn the tide the British high command had directed its attention, as we have seen, to the south. A bold strategy was evolved. By a series of campaigns beginning at Charlestown the British would move north through the Carolinas into Virginia and form the numerous loyalists of the Carolinas into militia as they progressed. Material reliance would be placed on the militia to maintain control of the territory that had been conquered, freeing regular and British American troops for the onward advance. If all went well, the south would be recovered and civil government eventually reinstated there under the Crown.

A most important factor in the equation was the paucity of available troops. Clinton had at his disposal an entire force which at most amounted to only 27,000 rank and file fit for duty, including the troops in Georgia and the Floridas. Of these 12,000 to 15,000 men were required to maintain the posts at New York and Long Island, so that only a dangerously small balance remained for service in other quarters.

SOUTHERN THEATRE

65

If the strategy were to succeed, a new base — Charlestown — had first to be taken and held. As the troops advanced into the interior, posts had to be established to support the militia in maintaining control of conquered territory, and lines of communication sufficiently guarded. In short, two complete armies were really required: one in the south; and another at New York to hold the forces of New England in check and to deter an offensive against Canada. It would be Clinton's task to make one army do the work of two by relying on the sea for communication between the different parts of his force. If command of the sea were kept, the troops detached to the south could if necessary be supported and might succeed; if command of the sea were lost, they or part of them ran the risk of defeat in detail.

As preparations for the campaign got under way, Hessian general orders on 10 December 1779 again sought volunteers for a chasseur company to accompany it under George's command. By the 19th they and the rest of the troops had embarked in a fleet of 80 transports to be escorted by five ships of the line and five frigates under the naval commander-in-chief, Vice Admiral Marriot Arbuthnot. On the 24th the ships fell down to Sandy Hook. According to George, it was at this point that a circumstance occurred which nearly cost him his life.

> The commander-in-chief had fallen down to Sandy Hook preparatory to his sailing with the army and had desired me to remain in New York till the next day to bring some papers of consequence to him from his secretary which were not then finished, and having received them, I thought of the best means of proceeding to the Hook myself. The transports had all dropped down and I could not, even in all the river, find a sloop or schooner for my purpose. I therefore pressed a strong rowboat with two men from the Flymarket stairs and proceeded on my way to the Hook. The frost had set in intensely severe for two or three days, so that vast sheets of ice floated up and down the channel with the tide. Before I had got half way to Staten Island, the eddy tide from round the back point of it drove several large sheets of ice into the channel in which my boat got completely entangled, and we could

66

find no way out, the ice approaching nearer to us every moment. At this instant Mr Hamilton, a gentleman in the quartermaster and transport service, was fortunately going down from the dockyard in a very strong large sloop. Mr Hamilton, seeing a boat in distress, surrounded by the ice and endeavouring to find her way out, knowing the danger we were exposed to, very humanely bore down upon us, breaking by the force of his vessel through the flakes of ice. I was on a very intimate footing with Mr Hamilton but knew not who my deliverer was until I came within 50 or 60 yards of him. He was astonished how I could have been so imprudent as to attempt passing down the river amongst the ice in a rowboat. I told him I had been warned of the danger and knew it at my departure but I could get no sloop or schooner, and as the papers were of consequence to the commander-in-chief, it was necessary he should have them as the fleet was to sail that night. Besides, I thought, as the tide of ebb ran very strong down to the Hook, I should not meet any ice in my way sufficient to block me up as it would go the same way with me and therefore would not greatly endanger me. Indeed I never dreamed of the shoals of ice that are hurried round the point of Staten Island by the eddy tide meeting the other bodies of ice going down to the island with the ebb tide, which completely hemmed me in between them.

Myself and one of the watermen had not stepped on board the sloop above two or three minutes when, as the other waterman and my servant were handing a favourite spaniel and my portmanteau out of the boat, a sheet of ice stove her nearly in two. My servant jumped on board but the waterman slipped down and would have been crushed between the vessel and the ice if we had not thrown a rope to his assistance and hauled him up. Thus I providentially escaped from a most miserable death, as I was above three miles from any shore and must evidently have foreseen my death approaching without any chance whatever of escaping. I arrived, however, safe at the Hook, delivered the papers to the commander-in-chief, and sailed at daybreak the next morning. This happened on Christmas Eve.

Had the expedition been delayed 48 hours longer, the whole fleet of transports would have been frozen fast in the river, as the frost that winter was more intense than the oldest American had ever known. Incredible as it may appear, it is an absolute fact that in a few days it froze so intensely that a regiment of cavalry, cannon and waggons passed from Long Island to Staten Island on the ice over a channel so deep as to admit the largest ships in the British navy to sail up to New York.

The rendezvous for the fleet was the isle of Tybee near the mouth of the Savannah River, Georgia. Despite a harrowing passage, almost all the 8,700 troops arrived safely by the end of January, but few horses survived and much of the artillery was lost together with many valuable supplies. Embarked on the *Anna*, George's chasseurs did not fare so well, as he relates: "In the violent gale of wind which arose about five days after we quit the harbour of New York, the ship ran foul of another in the night, which carried away both her main and mizzen masts. Of course, having but the foremast remaining, she was compelled to put before the wind and make every wind a fair one. She found herself unable to make either the American coast or bear down upon the West Indies. Therefore, putting the troops and crew to a shorter allowance, she bore away right before the wind, it then blowing hard at north-west, and the first port she made was St Ives in Cornwall. The oldest navigator must acknowledge this as a most singular event — a ship dismasted, bound for Georgia, and driven to England." Yet George's account does not adequately describe the full horrors of the voyage. Provisioned for one month for only 100 men, the transport was in fact carrying 250 and famine soon set in. The dogs were eaten; bones were ground up and boiled with shavings from salt-beef barrels; and the master even went so far as to propose that they should cannibalise each other, beginning with the female camp followers — a proposal rejected with disgust. Having struck a rock off the Irish coast and sprung a leak, the vessel eventually reached St Ives, where, in answer to her signals of distress, two boats with a pilot and a carpenter put out to her assistance. The carpenter was so frightened at the sight of the famished Hessians that he started off again for the shore as fast as his oars would take him. The pilot succeeded in beaching the ship just as she was about to founder.

Fortunately for George he did not take passage in the *Anna* but in the *John*, having been requested by Clinton to see that proper attention was paid to three of his favourite horses. After a tedious voyage beset by contrary winds and the most violent storms, he arrived safely off Tybee. Forlornly waiting for his chasseurs, he remained at Savannah as Clinton, Cornwallis and the bulk of the troops sailed on 10 February for Simmons (now Seabrook) Island, South Carolina, to begin their march on Charlestown.

While at Savannah, George had an opportunity to see about 600 native Americans of the Cherokee and Creek nations preparing and training themselves for war. The sight was very pleasing to him as he had never seen any large body of native Americans before.

"The Indians," states George, "abstain from women, take physic, and prepare their bodies for war by frequently running and using other manly exercises. In one, not unlike the game we call *goff*[26], they shew great skill and activity. They were a very fine race of men. One of their chiefs came to pay his respects to the commanding officer at Savannah. He was mounted on a small, mean Chickesaw horse about twelve hands and an half high. His dress consisted of a linen shirt, a pair of blue cloth trousers with yellow and scarlet flaps sewed down the outward seams. Over this he had on an old full-dress uniform of the English foot guards, the lace very much tarnished; a very large tye-wig on his head; an old gold-laced uniform hat, Cumberland-cocked; a large gorget round his neck; a sword in a belt hung over his shoulder; a tomahawk and scalping knife in his girdle; rings in his nose and ears; his face and breast, which was quite open, painted various colours; and a musket on his shoulder. He was one of the most distinguished chiefs amongst the whole Indian nations and was called the *Mad Dog*. I took him for a madman and never laughed more heartily in my life than when I first saw him."

---

[26] An alternative 18th-century spelling of "golf".

George was particularly struck by the beautiful red birds of Georgia known as Virginia nightingales, which were as plentiful there as sparrows in England. He was offered a dozen caught in a trap for a York shilling. "I might have had them, I dare say, for sixpence, and the cock birds are sold in London by the bird fanciers for three guineas apiece."

Meanwhile Clinton, who had been cautiously advancing with 6,000 men, called for a reinforcement of 1,500 more from Savannah, a corps that had been otherwise intended for a diversionary move on Augusta. Quitting Savannah on 5 March, it joined up with Clinton shortly before the 29th, when he established himself on Charlestown Neck, breaking ground three days later within 800 yards of the town's defences. With the reinforcement came George.

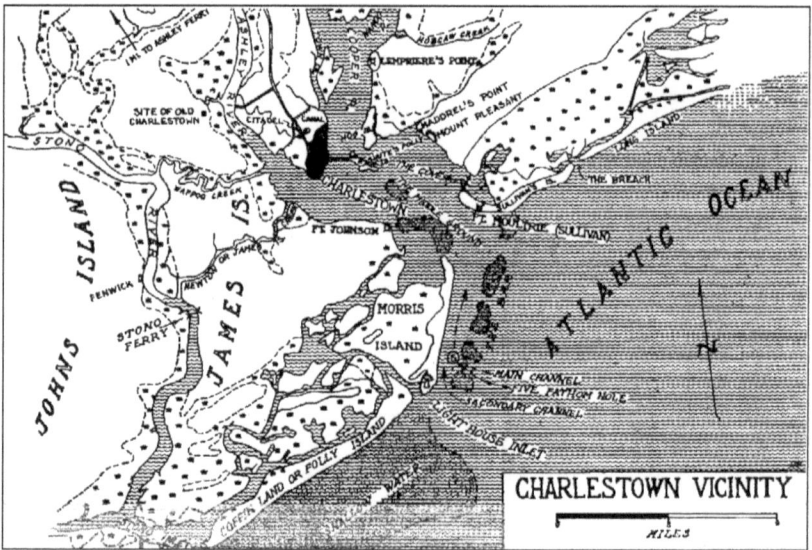

CHARLESTOWN VICINITY

Charlestown lay at the tip of a peninsular ("the Neck") bounded on the west by the Ashley River, on the east by the Cooper, and on the south and south-east by the harbour. Occupying it was a combined force of Continental troops and militia commanded by Major General Benjamin Lincoln. At the capitulation it would have been augmented to almost 5,500 men.

Not the sharpest tool in the box, Lincoln had been seduced by Clinton's leisurely advance into concluding that he might strengthen Charlestown's defences in time to withstand a siege. It would prove a fatal mistake. Not only would he lose the garrison and town but by concentrating his available force there he would open the whole of South Carolina to control by the British.

About his involvement in ensuing events George is not specific, commenting only briefly: "My worthy friend Sir Henry Clinton, until an opportunity presented itself of employing me more actively, honoured me during the siege of Charlestown by continuing me in his family as one of his aides-de-camp." However, other sources reveal in part what he got up to. He began, for example, to act as an emissary between Clinton, who was commanding the siege, and Cornwallis, who had been detached to the east of the Cooper River, but as the situation on the Neck became critical for the defenders, with the prospect that the town would soon be stormed, George came into his own. He was ordered by Clinton to spy out the defences and recommend the point of attack. Having studied fortification at Göttingen, he was considered eminently suitable for the job. Very risky it proved to be, for, inevitably, he had to enter the advanced works, occupied by the jägers, amid a continuing barrage of cannon and musket fire from the enemy. Men were being constantly killed or wounded around him.

It was at this point that a terrifying bombardment of the town and the threat of an imminent assault broke the will of the inhabitants, who petitioned Lincoln, the revolutionary commander, to capitulate. He did so. On 12 May the defenders marched out and delivered up the town together with a mass of ordnance, shot, powder, firearms and ammunition. It was the greatest victory so far gained by the British in the war.

The Union Jack was raised on the ramparts and again flew over Charlestown.

CHAPTER 5

BRITISH ASCENDANCY
IN SOUTH CAROLINA

Before sailing back to New York in early June with a large proportion of the troops who had come with him, Clinton rapidly settled the preliminary arrangements for the consolidation of British authority in South Carolina and Georgia.

On 19 May Cornwallis, having been appointed by Clinton as GOC in the south, began to march with some 2,500 men for Camden in the Backcountry. Crossing the Santee at Lenud's Ferry[27] with part of his corps, he marched up the eastern side of the river while Lord Rawdon with the rest proceeded by way of Monck's Corner and Nelson's Ferry. Camden was reached on 1 June.

At first named Pine Tree Hill, the village lay to the east of the Wateree River about 35 miles north of its confluence with the Congaree. Settled about 1750 and laid out in plots and streets around a square, it was now inhabited mostly by Scotch-Irish Presbyterians, whose meeting house and that of the Quakers were features of the place. Besides Joseph Kershaw's country store, it was home to saw- and grist-mills, one or more taverns, breweries, distilleries, a pottery, and various other artisan shops. Nine years earlier a courthouse had been built. All in all, trade was brisk and by now the village had become a principal entrepôt for the back settlements.

Politically, occupation of Camden was of course inevitable, but militarily its location left much to be desired. As Rawdon

---

[27] Pronounced "Lenew's".

remarked many years later,[28] "Camden had always been reprobated by me as a station, not merely from the extraordinary disadvantages which attended it as an individual position, but from its being on the wrong side of the river and covering nothing, while it was constantly liable to have its communication with the interior district cut off."

Headquarters at Camden was established in Joseph Kershaw's mansion. He was a leading incendiary.

Meanwhile George was for a time in limbo, waiting for a decision on his part in the arrangements, and so took time out to go fire-hunting for deer at night. "I was," he tells us, "an eyewitness to this amusement when I first went about 30 miles up the country just after the siege of Charlestown with my old, intimate and worthy friend, Colonel Simcoe, then commanding the Queen's Rangers and undoubtedly one of the very best officers in our service."

Two backwoodsmen went with him, all three of them on horseback lest, creeping along the edge of swamps, they might tread on a rattlesnake, of which there were plenty nearby. It is a fact, he notes, that "the rattlesnake, when he hears the stamp of a horse's foot, flies away, for divine nature has so ordained it that this deadly animal avoids you as much as you wish to avoid it, and no person is bitten by a rattlesnake excepting he come on it when it lies coiled up asleep and basking in the sun."

One of the backwoodsmen brought with him a large frying pan with a very long iron handle and put in it about half a dozen middling-sized knots of pine, which were full of turpentine. When he lit them, they gave off a great and very strong light. Placing the pan over his left shoulder so that the light was

---

[28] Francis Lord Rawdon (1755-1826) was Colonel of the Volunteers of Ireland, a British American regiment, and would soon command at Camden. In later life he became Governor General of India.

carried behind his head, he mounted his horse with a musket in his right hand loaded with buckshot, having first put strong, thick sacks over the horse's rump to prevent any fire falling down and burning the animal. The other man followed about 70 or 100 yards behind with a bag of turpentine knots to replenish the fire in the pan. Close after him came George on horseback. The effect was twofold. First, as far off as 200 yards the eyes of any deer appeared just like two balls of fire. Second, the deer, astonished and surprised at so strange a light, would stand stock-still, terrified, and, gazing at it, would permit the huntsman to approach very near.

"We had not been out long," says George, "walking our horses very gently by the side of a swamp, where the deer at night feed, when we found one. Before we came within 100 yards of him, he ran away. To the best of my recollection one of our horses snorted. We had not gone a quarter of a mile further ere we found another. The backwoodsman did not go directly up to him but took his way about 30 yards on one side of the deer. The animal, I am certain, let him come within less than 40 yards of him. He then pulled up his horse, which was going only at a very slow walk, laid his arm over the handle of the frying pan, supported his musket with his left hand, fired, and shot the deer. The deer was standing rather sideways to him with his head turned round to the light, so that he shot him in the forequarters just behind the fore elbow. The animal did not run five yards. We threw him over his horse and returned home."

George was aware that an Act of the South Carolina Assembly had been passed[29] imposing a fine on any person convicted of fire-hunting by night, "for some persons, not approaching near enough to distinguish plainly that it was a deer and no other animal, have shot young colts, oxen and

---

[29] Dated 23 August 1769, it expired five years later, but would be revived in the mid 1780s.

heifers," whose eyes at night appeared just the same as those of a deer.

Back In Charlestown George became acquainted with the South Carolina planters, being of opinion that that "in all America there are not better educated or better bred men. Indeed, Charlestown is celebrated for the splendour, luxury and education of its inhabitants." Yet beneath the planters' veneer of sophistication was their condonation of, and involvement in, that most bestial of institutions, slavery. Nowhere in George's writings does he ever comment on it. In fact, in the social life of the town, so another visitor wrote, "the general topics of conversation, when cards and the bottle" did not intervene, were "of negroes and the price of indigo and rice."

There were no more than 2,000 planters, but till now they had controlled both houses of the legislature, and society took its pattern exclusively from them. More often than not, they overcame the isolation of plantation life by leaving their estates to the management of overseers and settling in Charlestown, where, according to Dr Alexander Garden, they "are absolutely above every occupation but eating, drinking, lolling, smoking, and sleeping, which five modes constitute the essence of their life." Unsurprisingly, most lacked questing curiosity, energy, and perseverance. Nevertheless, they did find time for their balls and genteel dances, hunting, gaming, the turf, opera and theatre, not forgetting the endemic vice of the Carolinas — the excessive consumption of alcoholic liquor. Although there is no evidence whatever of a highly developed cultural life, this never-numerous gentry did display to a marked degree what they called *taste* and managed to impart to the town's social life a surface brilliance and blithe insouciance that never failed to inspire strangers to superlatives. Charlestown to Crèvecœur was the Lima of the north: "The inhabitants are the gayest in America. It is the centre of our *beau monde*." As to the courtesy of the planters, it was legendary even then. Yet many were not present throughout the year, for, as the sickly seasons began, they would quit the town and sail to the north, most often to Rhode Island, bearing in mind that "Carolina is in the spring a paradise, in the summer a hell, and in the autumn a hospital."

At last George's part in ensuing operations was settled, but sadly not much to his liking. He was appointed deputy, with the rank of major, to Patrick Ferguson, the newly appointed Inspector General of Militia, an officer who was destined to play a prominent but ultimately tragic part in the events of the coming months. Of his appointment George has the following to say: "When the siege of Charlestown was finished and the town taken, Sir Henry Clinton gave me a warrant in conjunction with my old friend Colonel Ferguson either jointly or separately, throughout the Provinces of South and North Carolina, to regulate, inspect, muster, etc all volunteer corps, loyal militia, and others; to inspect the quantity of corn, cattle, etc belonging to the inhabitants; and to report thereon to Lord Cornwallis, who commanded in the southern provinces. The power and command vested in me by this warrant was very extensive. It extended even so far as to empower me to join the race of Carolinians together in holy matrimony." His principal task, however, would be to assist Ferguson in forming the loyalists, predominantly those of the Backcountry, into companies or battalions of royal militia. The younger men unencumbered with large families were to be liable for offensive operations, whereas the rest were to undertake domestic duties.

George joined up with Ferguson and his men on 25 May as they marched through Charlestown after crossing the harbour from Fort Arbuthnot (formerly Moultrie) on Sullivan's Island. Next day, as part of a mixed corps of some 600 men commanded by Lt Colonel Nisbet Balfour,[30] they got in motion about three

---

[30] Balfour (1743-1823) was Lt Colonel of the 23rd Regiment (the Royal Welch Fusiliers), now stationed at Camden. He would soon be appointed Commandant of Charlestown. He died a full general.

o'clock in the morning on their way to Ninety Six,[31] a village which lay to the south of the Saluda River some 60 miles west of its confluence with the Broad. In the Backcountry it was second in importance to Camden.

Advancing along what was once an Indian trading path, they marched by stages in the early mornings to avoid the excessive heat and thunderstorms of a Carolina day. By 4 June they had covered 70 miles and lay at rest in the shade of woodland to the north of Nelson's Ferry, where, it being the King's birthday, they drank His health in captured wine. By the 7th, as they were about to enter the Backcountry, they had reached Thomson's plantation a little to the south of the Congaree River and not far from its confluence with the Santee. It was here that George came to a determination that was to affect his entire involvement in the war. If, however, his future involvement is to be placed in its proper context, we first need to draw a brief sketch of the Backcountry, its inhabitants — including George's comments on them, and those developments which had led many to remain loyal to the Crown.

The Backcountry, in so far as it relates to South Carolina, is an amorphous expression describing the vast swathe of territory now to be entered by the British. Though other interpretations are wider or more restrictive, it is used in this work to refer to the then Districts of Camden and Ninety Six. In the east the outer boundary began at the confluence of the Congaree and Wateree, extended northwards to the North Carolina line, continued westwards along that line to the Cherokee nation, and followed the Georgia line to a point just below Augusta. From there it

---

[31] Ninety Six was so named because it lay within 96 miles of Fort Prince George on the Keowee River, a fort constructed in 1753 above and opposite to the Cherokee town of Keowee. Situated on an eminence it was at this time, before its fortification by the British, a village containing about twelve dwelling houses, a courthouse, and a jail. Around it the land had been cleared for a mile.

proceeded in the south to a point on the Saluda midway between the village of Ninety Six and the Broad River before following the Saluda and Congaree eastwards.

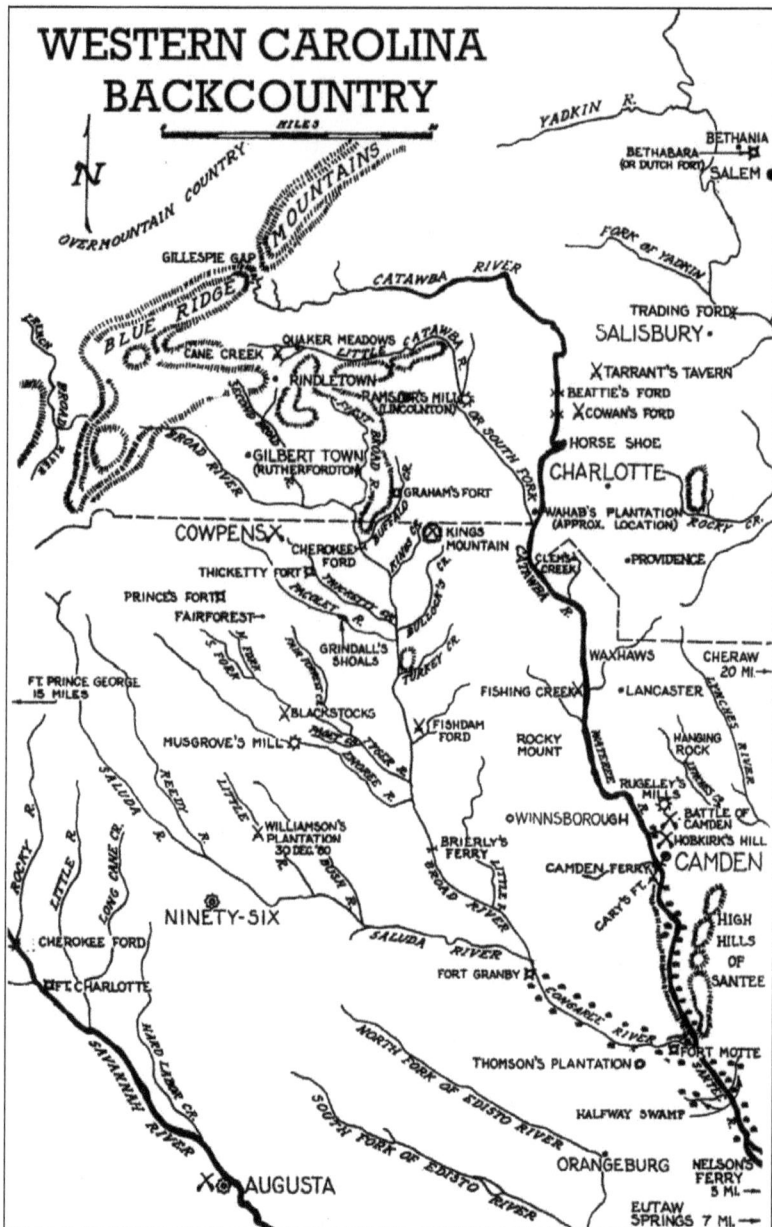

WESTERN CAROLINA BACKCOUNTRY

Today the South Carolina Backcountry presents a very different aspect from that encountered by the first white settlers in the middle of the eighteenth century. It was then a region interspersed with extensive plains widely covered by cane; with open forests of elm, hickory, oak, pine, poplar and walnut, between which lay a rich carpet of peavine; and with numerous ponds, rivers and streams, along which stretched vast cane-brakes. It was partly flat, partly undulating, and partly hilly terrain, which rose to the Great Smoky Mountains in the distance. It abounded in many species of game ranging from bison, deer and elk to turkeys and other wildfowl. Common were the beaver, muskrat, opossum, raccoon, and squirrel. Among beasts of prey, the bear, polecat, puma, wildcat, and wolf were numerous, while the rattlesnake was widely to be found. Edible fish such as the shad were prolific.

By 1780 the Backcountry had become dotted with small farms and settlements, but much of the landscape remained as it was thirty years earlier. The bison and elk had been hunted to extinction there, but the other wild animals were still to be found, though in diminished numbers.

The Backcountry had yet to evolve into a uniform society. Of the national groups the Scotch-Irish were the most numerous. Disliked by others, they were aggressive, courageous, emotional, fiercely intolerant, hard-drinking, and in many cases inclined to indolence. Of the other groups the Germans from the Palatinate, who had settled mostly in the Dutch Fork, predominated. Better farmers, they were pacific, law-abiding, temperate, and devoted to the ideal of a well-ordered society. The rest were composed of other immigrants from the Old World or their descendants, a number of whom — less than ten per cent of the back inhabitants — were slaves. Clannishness, through which many clung tenaciously to their cultural heritage, was the order of the day, while mutual dislike or suspicion more often than not triumphed over brotherhood and charity. Not a melting pot, the Backcountry was more akin to the Tower of Babel.

By 1776 the proportion of South Carolina's population living above the fall line had soared to some 83,000, 50 per cent of its entire population and 79 per cent of its white inhabitants. By the opening of the seventies the small farm had become the means by which 95 per cent of the Backcountry settlers made a living. Nevertheless, clearing land and developing a farm involved too much backbreaking toil for some, who contented themselves with a small corn patch and hunting. Overall, the Backcountry had begun to produce an amazing amount of grain and meat, and towards the end of the colonial era as many as 3,000 waggons per year were being sent down from there to Charlestown.

Living in log cabins or primitive shelters on the edge of western civilisation, very many Backcountry settlers no longer conformed to accepted standards of behaviour. Criminality, immorality, and irreligion were rife, accentuated by the severe shortage of clergymen and the lack of education. Admittedly, odd meeting houses were to be found, for example at Bush River, Camden, the Dutch Fork, Fair Forest, Fishing Creek, Turkey Creek, and the Waxhaws; itinerant preachers came and went; but in general the vast majority of the population caught neither sight nor sound of a minister. "In the back parts of Carolina," recalled George many years later, "you may search after an angel with as much chance of finding one as a parson; there is no such thing — I mean when I was there. What they are now, I know not. It is not impossible, but they may have become more religious, moral, and virtuous since the great affection they have imbibed for the French. In my time you might travel 60 or 70 miles and not see a church or even a schism shop[32]. I have often called at a dog-house in the woods, inhabited by eight or ten persons, merely from curiosity. I have asked the master of the house: 'Pray, my friend, of what religion are you?' 'Of what religion, sir?' 'Yes, my friend, of what religion are you — or to what sect do you belong?' 'Oh! now I understand you; why, for

---

[32] meeting house.

the matter of that, *religion does not trouble us much in these parts.*'" As to honesty, Cornwallis would soon observe, "I will not be godfather to any man's honesty in this province."

The ignorance and illiteracy of most Backcountry settlers went hand in hand with a lack of intellectual curiosity. According to the Reverend Charles Woodmason, "Few or no books are to be found in all this vast country," besides a few religious works. "Nor do they delight in historical books or in having them read to them .., for these people despise knowledge, and instead of honouring a learned person or any one of wit or knowledge, be it in the arts, sciences or languages, they despise and ill treat them."

Quite a few of the settlers would once have been the orphaned or neglected children who swarmed over the Backcountry on the eve of the revolution. Described as then living "expos'd in a state of nature," they had been "oblig'd almost to associate with villains and vagabonds for subsistence."

Of the few meeting houses most were attended by Scotch-Irish Presbyterians, who surpassed all other sects in bigotry and fierce denominationalism, going to lengths which are almost unbelievable. Men of God, their ministers brought politics into the pulpit, exhorted rebellion, and in some cases — for example the Reverend John Simpson of Fishing Creek — took up arms themselves.

Scattered among the Backcountry population was a body of hardy, illiterate and lawless backwoodsmen whom the British came to fear more than most. They tended to have no settled habitation and lived partly by hunting and partly by preying on their neighbours. "This distinguished race of men," declares George, "are more savage than the Indians and possess every one of their vices but not one of their virtues. I have known one of these fellows travel two hundred miles through the woods, never keeping any road or path, guided by the sun by day and the stars by night, to kill a particular person belonging to the

81

opposite party. He would shoot him before his own door and ride away to boast of what he had done on his return ... I speak ... of that heathen race known by the name of *crackers*."

Despite the vaunted levelling spirit of the Backcountry, a gentry of sorts had arisen composed of the wealthy who had acquired extensive land holdings, merchants, surveyors, lawyers, and men of status in other fields. Few though they were, their influence was profound, but sadly for the British almost all were of the revolutionary persuasion.

As in the rest of South Carolina, an endemic vice in all ranks was the excessive consumption of alcoholic liquor. Rough cider and peach or apple brandy were common beverages, rum was consumed in large quantities, but rye whiskey, favoured in particular by the Scotch-Irish, was the grand elixir. Except the temperate Germans, who preferred their beer, almost every-one drank to excess: the morning bevvy, the dinner dram, the evening nightcap, and the more or less frequent tipple in between times. Taverns, still houses, and drinking cabins did a roaring trade, whereas stores commonly held among their stock a pretty liberal quantity of something to keep the spirits up.

Amid the hardships of Backcountry life a high old time was had with recreational pursuits. From the simple pleasures of hunting and fishing they extended to horse racing and shooting matches, but more often than not they centred around the tavern, where drunkenness, gaming, cheating, quarrelling, and brawling were commonplace, particularly on days when court or other public business was transacted. Completing the picture were communal harvest days, dances, and occasions such as musters and vendues, all of which gave ample rein to the wild frolicking common on the frontier.

Of the factors that had led many Backcountry settlers to remain loyal to the Crown, a combination of three predominated. Partly it was a sense of belonging to a wider British community besides being Americans; partly it was a feeling of gratitude to the Crown for the grant of land; and partly it was antagonism to the Lowcountry élite, whose gross neglect of the Backcountry only a few years earlier had turned many settlers against them and the revolutionary cause which they came to espouse. Admittedly, a framework of local government had recently been established, representation in the legislature was lately secured, but memories of past grievances were long.

Now divided politically as well as in other ways, the Backcountry was a place where emotions often ran free, unrestrained by concepts of civilised behaviour. A powder keg waiting to explode, it would be ignited by the coming of the British.

When we last left George, he was at Thomson's plantation to the south of the Congaree. Dismayed by the civil nature of much of his duties and sharing to some extent the regular army's contempt for militia, he decided to seek the relinquishment of his office. On 7 June he took leave of Ferguson's men and rode over to Camden, where, supported by his good friends Rawdon and Tarleton, he persuaded Cornwallis to appoint him major in Tarleton's British Legion[33] in succession to the Hon Charles Cochrane, who was returning home on personal business. Although Cornwallis had no delegated authority to make the appointment, he did so until Clinton's pleasure be known, having earlier given George an assurance that he would be prepared to assist him if he could. As George relates it, "Lord Cornwallis most kindly told me that, although I was separated from my old friend and protector Sir Henry Clinton, if it was in his power to make my situation pleasant, I had but to command him. To serve under the command of so good-natured and brave a soldier could not but be pleasing to me and to every other officer who is acquainted with his goodness of heart.

---

[33] The Legion was a composite regiment of cavalry and infantry raised on the British American establishment. The men were American loyalists, whereas the principal officers were British.

I should be wanting in common justice if I did not testify his kindness and protection towards me, which, from that day to this moment, he has never withheld from me."

Aware that Cornwallis would be writing to Clinton for confirmation of the appointment, George penned the following letter, pressing his case, to Major John André, now Clinton's adjutant general:

21 June 1780

Dear André

I hope Sir Henry Clinton will not imagine me ungrateful or dissatisfyed after so generous a provision made for me by my writing to you upon the following subject, but the hopes I have had given me by my friends Lord Rawdon and Tarleton, who both spoak to the general concerning my being appointed to the Legion and that agreable service, induce me to entreat you to make mention concerning it to His Excellency. Major Cocheran has gott Lord Cornwallis's leave to go to New York, for which place he setts off by the first convoy and intends from there for England. Whatever his intentions or views may be, should I be appointed to the cavalry, which is of all things in the world what I wish, I shall not at all interfere with him. I shall not doubt of your proposing this to His Excellency the very first oportunitie and receiving his answer. Be so kind as to send two or three duplicates to inform me of His Excellency's decision. I beg leave to conclude, and believe me to be with the highest gratitude and attention to Sir Henry Clinton and love and affection to you

Your ever sincere friend

GEORGE HANGER

[*Subscribed*:]

The post I now am appointed to I shall be happy, though appointed to the Legion, to do every thing in it that can in any [way], I hope, forward Sir Henry Clinton's wishes without requiring or deserving the smallest emolument.

On meeting up with George, Tarleton would have told him of his rout of Colonel Abraham Buford and 3 to 400 Virginia revolutionaries on 29 May.

If we look to George's *Life, Adventures, and Opinions*, we seek in vain his reasons for eagerly desiring to join the British Legion, a regiment noted for its severity. "I am not," he declares, "going to fight over again the American War. It is as much forgotten as the Trojan war and the recital of one would be full as interesting as the other." So we need to look elsewhere for clues. Both he and Tarleton were good friends, having first met when both frequented London high society in the early 1770s, both were womanisers, and both in their private lives had much in common. They were on the same wavelength. As to their approach to the war, it must inevitably be assumed that George, humane as he was, agreed with Tarleton that severity was the surest means of ending the bloodshed — otherwise why join the Legion?

For two months after the capture of Charlestown a false calm prevailed in South Carolina, broken only by the actions at Mobley's Meeting House, Alexander's and Beckham's Old Fields, and Hill's Iron Works. Revolutionaries in great numbers allowed that the game was up and came in to submit. All in all, the outlook could not have seemed brighter for consolidating and furthering British success in the south.

On 21 June, having left the command at Camden to Rawdon, Cornwallis set out for Charlestown, where he arrived four days later. Accompanying him were Tarleton and George.

CHAPTER 6

INCIPIENT UNREST AND
A THREAT FROM THE NORTH

As George set foot again in Charlestown, he would have found a town whose social life was gradually regaining some of its former glitter. Although neither horse racing nor the theatre was resumed, subscription balls and concerts would again be held, while gentlemen's clubs — of which there were many — provided for men a favourite venue for wining, dining, and convivial conversation. One of the most brilliant was the St Patrick's Society, to which George, the son of an Irish peer, would have almost certainly been invited. In all of them a sea change had occurred. Now the higher echelons of society were dominated by loyalists, who had replaced those of the revolutionary persuasion, not only as officers in clubs and societies, but also as officials in the government of the town and in the established church.

George and Tarleton were billeted in the town houses of revolutionary families, who were excluded or confined to only one or two rooms. According to Alexander Garden Jr,[34] "A lady of the highest respectability writing to Colonel Tarleton requesting the liberty of using one or two apartments in her house immediately occupied by him, as they would essentially contribute to her comfort, he concisely replied:

---

[34] He was a turncoat who, having taken protection and sworn allegiance to the Crown, later joined the enemy to save the confiscation of his and his father's estates.

Madam

After mature deliberation my eyes are so opened, and senses convinced, that the enemies of my country should not enjoy every convenience that I hold it an act of propriety to retain the house in Broad Street given me by the commander-in-chief for my sole accommodation.

B TARLETON.

Brief as his sojourn in town was, George left a lasting impression on Charlestonians. Playing fast and loose, he reverted to his womanising ways, ever mindful that for many of his calling life was short. While, says Garden, ladies supporting the revolution kept their distance, "among those who, favouring opposite principles, became the intimate associates of the successful invaders there was a wide distinction of conduct and character: mirth, revelry, and scenes of pleasure and dissipation" became the order of the day. Of George's conduct Garden provides the following critique, tainted as it is by political partiality: "Where the exercise of peculiar severity was contemplated and the prevailing authorities wished to bend the haughty spirit of patriotism to submission or humble the constancy that bid defiance to oppression, the ready instrument of tyranny was at hand. Who could hear of the wanton insults of Major Hanger, without the slightest regard either to decency or cleanliness, introducing into the best apartments of the most respectable families his cats, his dogs and his monkeys while revelling himself in every species of sensuality under the eyes of the unprotected females on whom he was billeted, and not lament that heaven had not spared some chosen bolt to punish his atrocity. I cannot be more particular, for —

'T would fill each generous breast with wild amazement
To hear the story told.'"

A favourite resort of British officers, to which George would have repaired, was a farmhouse some two miles from town called Dewees' Tavern. It was often the scene of entertainments and splendid balls attended by large and elegant assemblies of officers and their partners.

Meanwhile, as George lingered in Charlestown and July progressed into August, British ascendancy in the rest of South Carolina began so soon to unravel in the face of internal uprisings and an external threat. Among other things the communication between Charlestown and Camden soon became a matter of concern. As Cornwallis observed to Rawdon, "The great difficulty of our communication is that we can have no fixt posts on any of the rivers, or indeed in any part of the lower country. No way occurs to me but sending some of those loose corps to make incursions and intimidate." Accordingly Tarleton and George with 30 of the British Legion cavalry were placed under orders to march for this purpose, though ultimately bound for Camden.

In the late evening of 31 July the detachment set off, passing through the great gate of Charlestown covered by a strong hornwork of masonry constructed by the besieged and now being improved by Major James Moncrief as part of his strengthening of the lines.[35] On they marched past the Quarter House, five and a half miles distant, a place of festivity and refreshment frequented by George and his lovers, before passing by the Eight-Mile-House, a tavern on the Goose Creek Road. From there they began to make very slow progress indeed. Battered by violent winds and heavy rains which had been raging for the past eight days, the low country was so completely flooded that the detachment, joined by a party of militia, did not cross the Santee at Lenud's Ferry until 6 August. Before crossing, Tarleton reported to Cornwallis:

---

[35] Moncrief (1744-1793) was a Scot who was a major, and soon to be a lt colonel, in the Corps of Engineers. An extraordinarily gifted military engineer, he gained fame in 1779 in the defence of Savannah, in 1780 in the siege of Charlestown, and subsequently in the formidable fortification of that place.

Lenew's Ferry
August 5th 1780

Earl Cornwallis etc etc etc
Charles Town

My Lord

I have the honor to inform you of my reaching this place this morning. The incessant rains having rais'd the water and destroyed the small bridges render'd the journey hitherto tedious.

Colonel Ball is here. His militia are not *numerous*. He will, I believe, be able to furnish me with about 25 young men to assist in allaying this commotion near Black River and intermediate to Lenew's and Murray's Ferrys. They likewise will be able to point out the instruments of disaffection.

I cannot ascertain whether Major Wemyss is marched from George Town. I shall if possible communicate with him. For that purpose I shall dispatch a man to him this afternoon.

The country, my Lord, I found *scared*. I prais'd the militia, tho' not large, for their alacrity in turning out.

They talked of the enemy crossing to this side the Santee. Their fears multiplied their dangers. A man is just come in who informs me that they lye in bodies of 30 and 40. Many of the insurgents, having taken certificates and paroles, don't deserve lenity. None shall they experience. I have promis'd the young men who chuse to assist me in this expedition the plunder of the leaders of the faction. If warfare allows me, I shall give these disturbers of the peace no quarter. If humanity obliges me to spare their lives, I shall convey them close prisoners to Camden. Fire and confiscation must take place on their effects etc. I must discriminate with severity.

I shall cross the ferry tomorrow, my Lord, and make use of every exertion and precaution in my power. I send all my baggage to Nelson's under the escort of the old militia on this side.

My Lord, I have the honor to be with the greatest respect
Your Lordship's devoted servant

BANASTRE TARLETON

Advancing to Black River, they began to punish those in that quarter who had revolted. The detachment, but not the militia, then moved on to Camden, which they reached by the 10th. There George found that the situation for the British was becoming critical.

Preparations had long been afoot for the autumn campaign in North Carolina, but by now all were at risk as Major General Horatio Gates with Continental and militia troops menaced Camden. Meanwhile Rawdon had concentrated his force and fallen back to the town, towards which Gates advanced from Rugeley's Mills in the late evening of the 15th. It lay only fifteen miles to the south.

As the British hold on South Carolina gradually weakened, Cornwallis was preoccupied in Charlestown with regulating the civil and commercial affairs of the town and country, endeavouring to form a militia in the lower districts, and forwarding the preparations for the autumn campaign. After handing over the business to Balfour, who arrived as Commandant on 3 August, he set out for Camden one week later. In the night between the 13th and 14th he arrived there with a fixed resolution to attack Gates at all hazards.

Coincidentally, as Gates advanced south towards Camden, Cornwallis marched north to meet him.

CHAPTER 7

THE GLORIOUS SIXTEENTH[36] AND THE ACTION AT FISHING CREEK

About two o'clock in the morning of 16 August, as Gates and Cornwallis advanced towards each other, their vans collided nine miles north of Camden.

Forming Cornwallis's van was a party of the British Legion's cavalry and mounted infantry amounting in all to 40 men, but whether George was in command of them or of the rest of the cavalry forming the rear guard we do not know. Musketry was kept up for fifteen minutes or so, and then, as if by common consent, the firing ceased. There was no moon, the air was sultry with the heat and humidity of an early morning in late summer, and neither side wanted to fight in the dark.

Gates's army was not in the best of shape. On the march from Coxe's Mill in North Carolina his men had traversed a barren country abounding in sandy plains, intersected by swamps, very thinly inhabited, and largely destitute of provisions and forage. They had had to subsist on precarious supplies of corn meal and lean beef, of which they often did not receive a half ration. At times the crop of grain had been new and unfit for use, but out of necessity many had plucked the green ears, which, when boiled with beef and eaten with green

---

[36] The Glorious Sixteenth is an apt description of a momentous day in the annals of the British Army. First used in *The Cornwallis Papers* by Balfour, the expression began falling into disuse as considerations of political correctness sadly intruded. Yet militarily it remains from a British perspective as accurate as ever, and in this sense it is high time that we saw its revival.

peaches instead of bread, provided a seemingly palatable repast, but one found to have painful effects. On the 15th, as they were about to march from Rugeley's towards Camden, the men were issued with a full ration of corn meal and meat. There being no rum in camp — the customary heart warmer and stimulant for unusual exertion, Gates had the bright idea of issuing to each man one gill of molasses from the hospital store, brought down by Stevens from Virginia. It proved to be a medicine indeed, an untimely physic. As the night progressed, the men prepared hasty meals of quick-baked bread and meat with a dessert of mush or dumplings mixed with the molasses. It operated so cathartically that, in the words of Otho Williams, Gates's Deputy Adjutant General, "very many of the men ... were breaking the ranks all night and were certainly much debilitated before the action commenced in the morning."

According to Williams, Gates had with him 3,052 rank and file fit for duty, of whom more than two thirds were militia. If we allow for officers, NCOs and drummers, his total force came to some 3,500 men. Cornwallis had had to leave behind at Camden near 800 men who were sick, so that his rank and file, and total force, amounted to some 1,850 and 2,170 respectively.

As the battle got underway, George remained in the rear with the Legion cavalry, formed in a column due to the thickness of the woods, their left flank to the right of the high road leading from Camden. Apart from the sounds of battle, there was a dead calm with a little haziness in the air, which, preventing the smoke rising from the musketry and cannon, occasioned such thick darkness that the action ahead was obscured. Hidden from view was the rout of Gates's left, centre and reserve, leaving only the Continental brigade forming his right on the field of battle. As the British right and left wings engaged it, Cornwallis ordered George and his men to charge its flank in order to complete the rout, which, according to Cornwallis, was performed with their usual promptitude and gallantry, great execution being done. And so, despite the Continental troops displaying the utmost bravery, Gates's army was demolished within the hour.

Yet for George and the Legion cavalry the action had not yet ended. They were ordered by Cornwallis to continue the pursuit to Hanging Rock, twenty-two miles north of the battlefield, "during which many of the enemy were slain, a number of prisoners, near 150 waggons, a considerable quantity of military stores, and all the baggage and camp equipage of the rebel army fell into our hands." Charles Stedman, a British commissary at Camden, relates that the road for some miles was strewn with the wounded and killed who had been overtaken by the Legion in their pursuit. "The number of dead horses, broken waggons and baggage scattered on the road formed a perfect scene of horror and confusion. Arms, knapsacks and accoutrements found were innumerable, such was the terror and dismay of the Americans."

As ever Garden has something to say about George's involvement: "A person requiring of this unfeeling man the particulars of Gates' defeat, he replied, 'Flushed with victory and eager in pursuit, my arm was too well employed to allow much time for observation, but overtaking the waggon of de Kalb[37] on which was seated a monkey fantastically dressed, I ceased to destroy and, addressing the affrighted animal, exclaimed, 'You, monsieur, I perceive are a Frenchman and a gentleman. *Je vous donne la parole.*'

> 'Where were thy terrors, conscience? Where thy justice?
> That this bad man dare boldly own his crimes,
> Insult thy sacred power, and glory in it.'
> FRANCIS."

---

[37] A German, Major General Johann Kalb had acted for many years in the service of the King of France. Where his ultimate loyalty lay, whether to the King or to the revolutionaries, has never been satisfactorily determined. He had commanded Gates's right wing, being mortally wounded in the battle.

Exhausted by the previous night's march and by their part in the battle and pursuit, the Legion were only briefly spared from further exertions. Cornwallis ordered Tarleton to move early next morning, the 17th, in quest of Brigadier General Thomas Sumter, who was leisurely returning from a foray down the west bank of the Catawba and Wateree, having captured Cary's redoubt and a number of British troops. Reinforced by a detachment of the 71st's light troops, making 350 men in all, Tarleton and George marched up the east bank through the woods till at dusk they came to the ferry near Rocky Mount, a slight eminence on the opposite side evacuated only a few days earlier by Turnbull's New York Volunteers. In its vicinity, about a mile from the river, the enemy's fires could be perceived. Immediate care was taken to secure the boats and instant orders were given to pass the night without fires. No alarm happened but at daybreak it was apparent that the enemy had decamped. Captain Charles Campbell, who commanded the 71st's detachment, was instantly dispatched across the river with a small party and instructed to hold out a white handkerchief if Sumter was continuing his march. In the meantime preparations were made for passing the river. On arriving at Rocky Mount, Campbell displayed the appointed signal, whereupon the boats with the infantry at once pushed off while the cavalry crossed by swimming.

Dogging Sumter's tracks, the troops at midday reached Fishing Creek, where Tarleton found that a large part of them simply could not continue, overpowered as they were by the fatigue of the last two days and the intense heat. He therefore selected some 100 cavalry and 60 infantry best able to bear further hardship and marched on, leaving the rest posted on advantageous ground to refresh themselves and cover the retreat in case of accident. A few miles distant they came upon Sumter and his men in camp.

During the march up the west bank an incident occurred which exemplified the skill of American riflemen. It was described by George many years later: "Colonel Tarleton and myself were standing a few yards out of a wood, observing the situation of a part of the enemy which we intended to attack. There was a rivulet in the enemy's front, and a mill on it, to which we stood directly with our horses' heads fronting, observing their motions. It was an absolute plain field between us and the mill, not so much as a single bush on it. Our orderly-bugle stood behind us, about three yards, but with his horse's side to our horses' tails. A rifleman passed over the mill-dam, evidently observing two officers, and laid himself down on his belly, for in such positions they always lie to take a good shot at a long distance. He took a deliberate and cool shot at my friend, at me, and the bugle-horn man.[38] Now observe how well this fellow shot. It was in the month of August and not a breath of wind was stirring. Colonel Tarleton's horse and mine, I am certain, were not anything like two feet apart, for we were in close consultation how we should attack with our troops, which laid 300 yards in the wood and could not be perceived by the enemy. A rifle ball passed between him and me. Looking directly to the mill, I evidently observed the flash of the powder. I directly said to my friend, 'I think we had better move or we shall have two or three of these gentlemen shortly amusing themselves at our expence.' The words were hardly out of my mouth when the bugle-horn man behind us, and directly central, jumped off his horse and said, 'Sir, my horse is shot.' The horse staggered, fell down, and died."[39]

---

[38] "I have," adds George, "passed several times over this ground and ever observed it with the greatest attention, and I can positively assert that the distance he fired from at us was full four hundred yards."

[39] George provides several clues as to the date and location of this incident, being almost certainly on the 18th at White's Mill on Fishing Creek: the month was August; August in 1780 was the only one in which George and Tarleton were serving together in the Legion; they were preparing to attack on ground which George traversed on more than one occasion; and he traversed this particular ground, not only now, but perhaps on his return and on the Legion's advance into North Carolina. In no other circumstances did this conjunction of events occur, preparatory as they were to an attack. By contrast George's march from Charlestown to Camden had covered ground over which he passed only once.

George is emphatic that never in his life did he see better rifles (or men who shot better) than those made in America. "They are made," he says, "in Lancaster and two or three neighbouring towns in that vicinity in Pennsylvania. The barrels weigh about six pounds two or three ounces, carry a ball no larger than thirty-six to the pound, and are three feet three inches long. I have often asked what was the most they thought they could do with their rifle. They have replied that they thought they were generally sure of splitting a man's head at 200 yards, for so they termed their hitting the head. I have also asked several whether they could hit a man at 400 yards. They have replied certainly, or shoot very near him," as indeed is evinced by George's anecdote.

George contrasts the American rifle with the British Brown Bess: "I do maintain that no man was ever killed at 200 yards by a common soldier's musket *by the person who aimed at him*. A soldier's musket, if not exceeding badly bored and very crooked as many are, will strike the figure of a man at 80 yards; it may even at 100 yards; but a soldier must be very unfortunate indeed who shall be wounded by a common musket at 150 yards, *provided his antagonist aims at him*; and as to firing at a man at 200 yards with a common musket, you may just as well fire at the moon and have the same hopes of hitting your object."

Nor does George have much respect for the marksmanship of the British soldier, offering "some remarks respecting the training of a raw countryman, or a mechanic from Birmingham, perfectly awkward and generally very ignorant. He is consigned to the superintendence of the drill serjeant. He is first taught to walk, next to march, and hold himself tolerably erect. Then a firelock is placed in his hands, which he handles at first as awkwardly as a bear would a plumb cake. When he is taught the manual exercise and fit to do regimental duty, they then take him to fire powder. Whilst the drill serjeant is teaching him to fire either by files or by platoons, the serjeant says to him, laying his cane along the barrels of the firelocks, 'Lower the muzzles of your pieces, my lads, otherwise when you come into action, you will fire over the enemy.' After this the recruit is taken to fire ball at a target. How is he taught? Thus he is spoken to: 'Take steady aim, my lad, at the bull's eye of the target; hold your piece fast to the shoulder that it may not hurt you in the recoil; when you get your sight, pull smartly.' This is the general way in which I believe they are taught, and in the name of truth and common sense permit me to ask you how a drill serjeant who is no marksman himself can teach an ignorant countryman or a low order of a mechanic to be a good marksman. In my humble opinion, excellent in their way as they are to discipline the soldier and form him for parade and actual service in the line, the serjeant is just as capable of teaching him how to solve one of Sir Isaac Newton's problems as to teach him to be a marksman."

When we left Tarleton, he had pushed on with part of his corps to Sumter's camp. Whether George accompanied him or was left a few miles behind in command of those too fatigued to continue we do not know. From the brow of a hill Tarleton saw Sumter's men below resting on well protected ground. Informed that the firing of his vedettes, and perhaps of the rifleman described by George, was due to militia shooting beeves, Sumter lay under a waggon in the shade with his horse nearby. Weary from marching and four nights with little or no sleep, his men were drowsing in the heat or cooling themselves in the river.

With a shout Tarleton's troops fell upon them. Sumter cut loose his horse and tried to rally his corps, but pandemonium reigned and a brief defence from behind the waggons was soon over. Of the men in the river some were drowned, "floating down like the corks of a fishing seine," while those not killed or captured fled into the bushes until clothes could be borrowed from the country people.

Tarleton released all Sumter's prisoners and burned what stores he could not carry. Losing only sixteen men and 20 horses killed or wounded, he secured some 350 prisoners, 800 horses,

1,000 stand of arms, 44 waggons loaded with baggage and stores, two ammunition waggons, and two 3-pounders. 150 of the enemy were killed or wounded, but the chief prize, Sumter himself, escaped unharmed. Sadly, among the British dead was Charles Campbell, a young officer, "whose conduct and abilities", in Tarleton's own words, "afforded the most flattering prospect that he would be an honour to his country," a view echoed by Cornwallis.

The crushing effect of the British successes was unaffected by a setback at Musgrove's Mill on Enoree. While commanding there a mixed force of British American troops and militia, Lt Colonel Alexander Innes was defeated on the 19th by a party of enemy irregulars, who, on hearing of the disaster at Camden, promptly retreated over the border.

All in all, the way now appeared open — superficially — for the invasion of North Carolina.

CHAPTER 8

THE ABORTED INVASION
OF NORTH CAROLINA

As events would prove, the autumn campaign was a very risky venture indeed, yet despite the operational difficulties attending it Cornwallis saw no option but to go on to the offensive.

Throughout the campaign a pressing concern would be the sickliness of the troops, whether they were those who marched with Cornwallis or those who were intended to join him later from Camden.

An immediate problem, which delayed the march, was the formation of supply trains. Waggons there were aplenty, what with those taken in the recent engagements and others pressed from Orangeburg and Ninety Six, but horses, gear, conductors and drivers were wanting.

Another cause of delay was the severe lack of provision at Camden, exacerbated by additional mouths to feed after the Battle. On 31 August Cornwallis remarked to Balfour, "Hitherto, so far from being able to get a few days' [*provision*] beforehand, which is absolutely necessary for our march, we are this day without either flour or meal and Tarleton's horses have had no forage since the action."

Against all the odds Cornwallis managed to assemble a proviant train of 38 waggons by 7 September, twenty of which were loaded with a puncheon of rum in each and the rest with flour and salt. At daybreak, accompanied by two 3-pounders, he marched towards Charlotte with the 23rd, 33rd and Volunteers of Ireland, leaving behind material numbers of their dead, sick and wounded. Two days later he reached the border settlement at the Waxhaws and was joined by Samuel Bryan's North Carolina militia. The troops soon set up camp on Waxhaw Creek, living on wheat collected and ground from the plantations in the neighbourhood, most of which were owned by Scotch-Irish revolutionaries who had fled.

On 8 September Tarleton and George crossed the Wateree at Camden Ferry and advanced with the British Legion and a detachment of the 71st's light troops towards White's Mill on Fishing Creek. While there on the 17th, Tarleton fell ill of a violent attack of yellow fever. His entire corps, the command of which had devolved on George, was now needed to protect him. Fearful that they would be attacked by enemy militia, Cornwallis dispatched his aide-de-camp, Lt John Money, on the 22nd to report back. Money noted in his journal, "The post was such that the cavalry in case of attack could not act. Those who had carbines were dismounted and took post in a wood to the right, and every other precaution taken to strengthen the post and prevent a surprise." The next day, much to everyone's relief, Tarleton had become well enough to be moved by litter to Blair's Mill on the east side of the Catawba. Crossing with him at the ford there, which was 600 yards wide and three and a half feet deep, George and the Legion joined Cornwallis. All in all, Tarleton's illness was one of the main reasons for setting back the entry into Charlotte.

On the 24th the Legion marched at four in the afternoon towards Charlotte, accompanied by the 23rd, 33rd and Volunteers of Ireland. Halting at Twelve Mile Creek, they waited till the moon rose before proceeding towards Sugar Creek on the Charlotte road. No certain intelligence having been received that Sumter had passed the Catawba, Rawdon was detached with the Legion and the flank companies of the Volunteers of Ireland to attack him. On arriving at Bigger's Ferry, they discovered that Sumter had passed the evening before and that Brigadier Generals Jethro Sumner and William Lee Davidson of the North Carolina revolutionary militia had retired from McAlpine's Creek. After taking post at the ferry, the detachment marched at daybreak on the 26th and joined the rest of the troops at the cross roads within four miles of Charlotte.

Assigned to form the van with the Legion, George says, "Earl Cornwallis ordered me to be very cautious how I advanced as he expected a very large body of militia to be either in the neighbourhood or ... Charlotte." Skirmishing with a small party of the enemy along the Steele Creek Road, George halted within sight of the village that the rest of the troops might close up, and in the meantime he endeavoured to reconnoitre.

Charlotte lay on rising ground and contained about twenty houses built on two wide streets which crossed each other at right angles. At their intersection stood the court house, a frame building raised on eight brick pillars ten feet from the ground. Between them a stone wall had been erected three and a half feet high, the open basement serving as a market house. On the left of the village as George faced it was an open common while on the right were one or two houses with gardens. "Determined to give his Lordship some earnest of what he might expect in North Carolina," Lt Colonel William Richardson Davie occupied the village with his corps of 150 men and a few revolutionary militia commanded by Major Joseph Graham. One company was posted in three lines under the court house behind the stone wall whereas the rest were drawn up on either side of it or advanced behind the houses and gardens on George's right.

The Legion cavalry under George's immediate command were the first to enter the village. It was now about ten in the morning. Proceeding at a slow pace till fired on by an advanced party of the enemy, they then came on at a brisk trot to within fifty yards of the court house. There the enemy's first line moved up to the stone wall and fired, wheeling outwards and down the flanks of the second line as it advanced. Believing the enemy was retreating, the Legion cavalry rushed up to the court house only to be met with a full fire from the enemy posted on either side of it. Immediately they wheeled about and retreated back from where they came, being fired on by the second line at the court house, but at rather too great a distance to have much effect. George freely admits that militarily it was not his greatest day: "I acknowledge that I was guilty of an error in judgment in entering the town at all with the cavalry before I had previously searched it well with infantry, after the precaution Earl Cornwallis had given me."

Yet George did manage to retrieve the situation, as he himself explains: "We had a part of the Legion infantry mounted on inferior horses to enable them to march with the cavalry, ready to dismount and support the dragoons. These infantry of their own accord very properly had dismounted and formed before the cavalry were near out of the town. I ordered them to take possession of the houses to the right, which was executed before the light infantry and the remainder of the Legion infantry came up, who were left behind with Earl Cornwallis to march at the head of his column."

Reinforced, the Legion infantry pressed ahead under cover of the houses and gardens, exchanging a hot fire with the enemy, whose advanced parties had been withdrawn. Eventually the enemy's position became untenable and Davie ordered a retreat by the Salisbury road. Ordered by Cornwallis to pursue with the Legion cavalry and infantry, George declares, "This service they performed with spirit, alacrity, and success. We had not moved above one mile in search of the foe when we fell in with them, attacked them instantly whilst they were attempting to form, dispersed them with some loss, and drove them for six miles, forcing them even through the very pickets of a numerous corps of militia commanded by General Sumner, who, supposing a large part of the army to be near at hand, broke up his camp and marched that evening sixteen miles." From the enemy's standpoint Joseph Graham has one or two words to offer that would have been undoubtedly pleasing to George's ear: "The enemy seemed to understand this Parthian kind of warfare and manœuvred with great skill, the cavalry and infantry supporting each other alternately as the nature of the ground or opposition seemed to require. They taught us a lesson of the kind which in several instances was practised against them before the end of the war. During the whole day they committed nothing to hazard, except when the cavalry first charged up to the court house."

Returning at sunset to Charlotte, the Legion encamped across the street by which they had first entered the village. The rest of the troops encamped to the east, south-east and west of the court house. A veritable hornet's nest of opposition was now stirred up, as Tarleton makes clear:

Charlotte town afforded some conveniencies blended with great disadvantages. The mills in its neighbourhood were supposed of sufficient consequence to render it for the present an eligible position, and in future a necessary post when the army advanced, but the aptness of its intermediate situation between Camden and Salisbury and the quantity of its mills did not counterbalance its defects. The town and environs abounded with inveterate enemies; the plantations in the neighbourhood were small and uncultivated; the roads narrow and crossed in every direction; and the whole face of the country covered with close and thick woods. In addition to these disadvantages no estimation could be made of the sentiments of half the inhabitants of North Carolina whilst the royal army remained at Charlotte town. It was evident, and it had been frequently mentioned to the King's officers, that the counties of Mecklenburg and Rowan were more hostile to England than any others in America. The vigilance and animosity of these surrounding districts checked the exertions of the well affected and totally destroyed all communication between the King's troops and the loyalists in the other parts of the province. No British commander could obtain any information in that position which would facilitate his designs or guide his future conduct.

The foraging parties were every day harassed by the inhabitants, who did not remain at home to receive payment for the produce of their plantations, but generally fired from covert places to annoy the British detachments. Ineffectual attempts were made upon convoys coming from Camden and the intermediate post at Blair's Mill, but individuals with expresses were frequently murdered ... Notwithstanding the different checks and losses sustained by the militia of the district, they continued their hostilities with unwearied perseverance, and the British troops were so effectually blockaded in their present position that very few out of a great number of messengers could reach Charlotte town in the beginning of October to give intelligence of Ferguson's situation.

Matters were so bad that according to Charles Stedman, who was there, one half of the entire army one day, and the other the next, was needed to protect the foraging parties and cattle drivers. George himself states that the foraging parties were attacked by the enemy so frequently that it became necessary never to send a small detachment on that service. "Colonel Tarleton, just then recovered from a violent attack of the yellow fever, judged it necessary to go in person, with his whole corps or above two-thirds, when he had not detachments from the rest of the army. I will aver that when collecting forage I myself have seen situations near that town where the woods were so intricate and so thick with underwood (which is not common in the southern parts of America) that it was totally impossible to see our videttes or our sentries from the main body. In one instance particularly, where Lieutenant Oldfield of the Quartermaster General's Department was wounded, the enemy under cover of impervious thickets, impenetrable to any troops except those well acquainted with the private paths, approached so near to the whole line of the British infantry as to give them their fire before ever they were perceived. Charlotte town itself, on one side most particularly, where the light and Legion infantry camp lay, was enveloped with woods. Earl Cornwallis himself, visiting the pickets of these corps (which from Tarleton's sickness I had the honour of commanding at that time) ordered me to advance them considerably further than usually is the custom and connect them more closely one with the other ... As to the disposition of the inhabitants, they totally deserted the town on our approach. Not three or four men remained in the whole town."

When asked by a journalist what would throw his administration off course, the British Prime Minister Harold Macmillan replied, "Events, my dear boy, events." It was now at Charlotte that unforeseen events conspired to terminate the autumn campaign.

The first of these was — as we have seen — the entirely unexpected ferocity with which the inhabitants of the locality continued resolutely to oppose the occupation of Charlotte itself. On 3 October Cornwallis commented to Balfour, "This County of Mecklenburg is the most rebellious and inveterate that I have met with in this country, not excepting any part of the Jerseys." It soon became apparent that the village was completely unsuitable for a small intermediate post, so effectually would it have been blockaded and so high would have been the risk of its being taken out in detail. Preoccupied with defending itself, the post would have exerted no control over the surrounding territory and afforded no protection to messengers coming to and from Cornwallis as he pursued his onward march. Extraordinarily difficult as it already was to communicate with South Carolina (almost all of the messengers being waylaid), Cornwallis faced the prospect of totally losing the communication if he proceeded farther. He nevertheless contemplated advancing as late as the 11th, but as Rawdon explained to Balfour, the lack of communication with South Carolina brought about by the inveteracy of the Mecklenburg inhabitants, the uncertainty of cooperation with a diversionary force intended for the Chesapeake, and the possible consequences of a second event of calamitous proportions convinced him that he had to turn back. He quit Charlotte at sunset on the 14th.

The second event was the defeat of Ferguson. Why, as he became increasingly aware of the formidable force gathering to oppose him, he did not press ahead to join Cornwallis has long remained a puzzle. The answer may at first have lain partly in his having ideas beyond his station, that is to say, in his reluctance to forego a separate command, which he had previously exercised on more than one occasion, and partly, as evinced by *The Cornwallis Papers*, in his belief that he could take on and defeat his opponents himself. If initially the answer, it was eventually over-taken by another as Ferguson began to realise that his hopes of success were doubtful. Taking post on 6 October at King's Mountain, "where I do not think that I can be forced by a stronger enemy than that against us," he called for 2 or 300 of Colonel Matthew Floyd's militia to join him the following evening unless they were destined for another service. With such a reinforcement "we do not think ourselves inferior to the enemy if you are pleas'd to order us forward; but help so near at hand, it appear'd to me improper of myself to commit any thing to hasard." It soon became clear that he was egregiously mistaken in believing that the risks of advancing outweighed for the time being those of remaining where he was. The terrain at King's Mountain proved ideal for an onslaught by revolutionary irregulars and he was totally defeated in the afternoon of the 7th. Ferguson was killed and his entire party consisting of the American Volunteers and some 800 militia was captured or killed.

Cornwallis for his part was not free of blame for the disaster. The war had shown the fatal effects of detachments such as Ferguson's and their ruinous consequences. While, admittedly, having sound reasons for not reinforcing Ferguson offensively, Cornwallis appears to have taken no account — at least in the short term — of the need to support him for defence. "Certain it is," asserts George, "that he was defeated for this plain reason: he was *beyond the reach of support*. He was too far advanced on the left of the British army to retire on the approach of a very superior force. Detachments have been the ruin both of modern and ancient armies and will be again. They must sometimes be risked but they are ever attended with danger. Every detachment employed at such a distance that it cannot fall back safely on the main army or be supported from it must ever be looked upon *as in the air.* King's Mountain, where Ferguson halted and fought, was fifty miles in a direct line from Charlotte town."

Nothing is so certain as the unexpected, and it was the unexpected, magnifying the risks of losing territory to the south, that ultimately put paid to the northward invasion.

On 8 or 9 October Cornwallis had fallen ill with a feverish cold and the command had now devolved on Rawdon. His mettle was soon tested during the harrowing withdrawal from Charlotte. The troops began by taking the road leading to the Old Nation Ford on the Catawba and were guided by William McCafferty, a Scotch-Irish merchant in Charlotte who had remained behind in an endeavour to save his property. According to Joseph Graham, "McCafferty led them the road to the right about two miles below Charlotte, which goes to Park's Mill. When they got near that place, he suggested that they were on the wrong road and that he must ride a little out of the way to the left to find the right one. When he got a short distance from them, he wheeled about, as he well knew the country, and left them. The scene of confusion and disorder which succeeded among them is not easily described. They were two miles to the right of the road they intended to go, the night was dark, and being near Cedar Creek, they were intercepted by high hills and deep ravines. They attempted at different places to file to their left along byways in order to reach the main road; but finally most of them got into the woods, were separated into parties, and kept halooing to find which way their comrades had gone. By midnight they were three or four miles apart and appeared to be panic-struck lest the Americans should come upon them in that situation. They did not concentrate until noon the next day about seven miles from Charlotte. Owing to the difficult passes they took, the darkness of the night, and the scare upon them they left behind them forty wagons and considerable booty which was found dispersed for the most part near Park's Mill." Completing the picture are the remarks of Charles Stedman, who was present, as stated earlier:

"In this retreat the King's troops suffered much, encountered the greatest difficulties; the soldiers had no tents; it rained for several days without intermission; the roads were over their shoes in water and mud. At night, when the army took up its ground, it encamped in the woods in a most unhealthy climate, for many days without rum. Sometimes the army had beef and no bread; at other times bread and no beef. For five days it was supported upon indian corn, which was collected as it stood in the field, five ears of which were the allowance for two soldiers for twenty-four hours ... The water that the army drank was frequently as thick as puddle. Few armies ever encountered greater difficulties and hardships; the soldiers bore them with great patience and without a murmur. Their attachment to their commander supported them in the day of adversity, knowing, as they did, that their officers' and even Lords Cornwallis and Rawdon's fare was not better than their own. Yet, with all their resolution and patience, they could not have proceeded but for the personal exertions of the militia, who, with a zeal that did them infinite honour, rendered the most important services [*in obtaining provisions*]." It was only on the 21st, when the Catawba was passed at Lands Ford, that matters began to take a turn for the better.

The troops arrived at Winnsborough on the 29th, less the 7th Regiment and the sick, who had been sent to Camden. Among the sick was George, as he recounts: "I caught the yellow fever at Charlottebourg. Tarleton was just recovering from it as I sickened. When the army marched from that town, myself and five officers who had the same disorder were put into waggons and carried with the army. They all died in the first week of our march and were buried in the woods as the army moved on. My sickness happened in the autumn, at which time the rainy season sets in, when small rivulets, which generally the soldier may walk through and not wet him above the ankles, swell in a few hours to such an height as to take a man up to the neck and oftentimes for some hours impede the march of an army. In passing several of these small brooks the straw on which I lay in the waggon was often wetted. Kind nature had endowed me with a constitution much stronger than the generality of mankind, or the damps I encountered must have killed me. The fatigue of travelling alone brought the other five officers in a very short time to their graves. I took the advantage of the escort of a regiment which was ordered to leave the army and march down out of North Carolina to Camden in South Carolina, where I arrived safe and all but dead. I had travelled over a great extent of country in a waggon, so that from the roughness of the roads and the general debility of my whole frame I was reduced to something very like a skeleton." George would never see active service again.

CHAPTER 9

RECUPERATION FROM YELLOW FEVER — TERMINATION OF THE AMERICAN WAR

Prostrate at Camden, George began very slowly to recover. "I was," he says, "so weak that I could not turn myself but was forced to be moved by my attendants when I wanted for ease to change my posture. In this miserable situation I lay so long, first on one side, then on the other, and then on my back, that the bones of my back and each hip came fairly or rather freely through the skin. I then had no other posture to lay in but on my stomach with pillows to support me." It may be thought "that I exaggerate the miseries I suffered, for surely no man ever endured more, but I pledge my honour that all I relate is strictly true. I will give additional testimony to my own, for, having the honour to dine at Lord Moira's house[40] in St James's Place about two years after my arrival in England, where His Royal Highness the Prince of Wales, Sir Henry Clinton, General Vaughan, General Crosbie and many other officers who had served in America were present, his Lordship could not refrain from observing how surprising it was that a man should be sitting in that company whose bones he had absolutely seen at Camden come through his skin. The disorder at last fell down into my legs, which I am of opinion saved my life, as that moment I began to recover. Till that circumstance I had taken nothing to support me but opium and port wine for three weeks as nothing else would stay on my stomach. I now began to have an appetite

---

[40] At this time Rawdon had not in fact succeeded to the Earldom of Moira, but would do so in 1793.

and by degrees I recovered but for a long time could not walk without the assistance of one crutch. If I do not actually owe my life to Earl Moira, I certainly am indebted to him for the more speedy recovery of my health from the many comfortable and nourishing things he sent me every day from his own table, which my servants could not make and were not to be purchased; and the butcher's meat killed at that time of the year is absolutely little better than carrion at Camden."

Elsewhere events began to turn markedly in the revolution-aries' favour after Major General Nathanael Greene superseded Gates on 4 December 1780. Moving with the bulk of his troops from Charlotte to the Pee Dee, he detached Brigadier General Daniel Morgan and a combined force of Continentals and militia to South Carolina's Backcountry beyond the Broad River. As evinced by Ferguson, the war had shown that distant detach-ments beyond the reach of support were fraught with danger, but in Morgan's case the risk would pay off. He defeated Tarleton at the Cowpens on 17 January 1781, killing or capturing all of Tarleton's men except 200 of the British Legion cavalry who fled. Cornwallis nevertheless continued with the winter campaign in North Carolina, gaining a pyrrhic victory over Greene at Guilford, but was so crippled that by early April he had had to retire to Wilmington to refit.

For a time, as Cornwallis advanced, Rawdon maintained the British position in South Carolina and Georgia. He was first tested in mid February 1781 when he frustrated an attempt by Sumter to excite a revolt along the Congaree. He was next tested by Greene's arrival before Camden on 19 April. Unable to detach and protect the country or draw supplies from it, Rawdon saw the necessity of retiring within the Santee, but it was no longer in his power to do so. "I therefore conceived some immediate effort necessary," he observed, "and indeed I did not think that the disparity of numbers was such as should justify a bare defence." He therefore proceeded to attack Greene on the 25th and defeated him at the Battle of Hobkirk's Hill. He then evacuated Camden on

10 May and passed the Santee on the 13th and 14th. Accompanying him was George, who pays him the following tribute: "I was witness to the arduous task to which this nobleman, young in years but a veteran in abilities and military science, was appointed and from which he extricated himself with so much honour to his talents and advantage to his country."

"From Camden," says George, "I went down to Charlestown, where I found my old friend Doctor Hayes, physician general to our army, who assured me that, notwithstanding the great debility I laboured under, my stamina was sound and unimpaired and that if I would go to sea for two or three months and take my passage to the northward so as to quit for a short time that baneful climate, I should be as good a man as I ever was in respect to health. Captain George Montague, an intimate friend of mine, who commanded the *Pearl* frigate, was ordered by the Admiral with the *Iris* frigate, Captain Dawson, to cruise off the Bermuda islands and he kindly took me on board."

George set sail on 25 May, the two frigates escorting off coast a fleet of transports carrying revolutionary prisoners who had enlisted for service under Lord Charles Montagu on the Spanish Main. Parting with the transports on 8 June, the frigates made land at Bermuda on the 17th and 29th. Later, bearing away, they captured two vessels, the *Betsey* bound from Philadelphia for Hispaniola and a French poleacre out of Cape François[41] on its way to Marseilles. On 16 July they called at Sandy Hook, where the *Pearl* replenished her supplies before sailing on 8 August for Cape Sable and Nantucket, arriving back at New York on 5 September. Many years later George recalled his excursion:

> I remained at sea above three months and so beneficial was the sea voyage, and bathing every morning in salt water, that before three weeks were passed I had laid aside my crutch.

---

[41] Now renamed Cape Haitien.

During our voyage I had the pleasure of landing at Bermudas, a beautiful spot and the most healthy climate on the face of the whole earth. Sick persons from the West Indies and the Carolinas resort to this island for the recovery of their health. Being situated a great distance from any land, it feels not the heat of summer from the perpetual refreshing breezes of the ocean. There are here two species of fish, uncommonly fine and of a very luscious quality, called grouper and porgy, the one equal to a john dory, the other superior in flavour to a carp. This island swarms with poultry and yields the finest onions, both which are sent to the West Indies. Cedar wood is in great plenty on this island, so much so that all the schooners and sloops are built with it. They are very light and buoyant and sail faster than any vessels.

The time for our cruise being expired, Captain George Montague bore away for the Chesapeake Bay. We made the Capes about two o'clock pm and were standing into the bay. It was my intent to land at the first British port and proceed to join my regiment, the British Legion, commanded by Colonel Tarleton. A privateer, however, fortunately bore down to us and informed us that the Count de Grasse with a French fleet lay at anchor up the bay. If it had not been for this intelligence, we should have anchored at night in the middle of the French fleet, as we imagined we should find the British fleet there.

We stood out a great distance to sea that night in order to avoid the track of another French fleet coming from Rhode Island to join Count de Grasse and then made the best of our way to New York.

Cornwallis in the meantime had entered Virginia and, as now discovered by George, had become entrapped at Yorktown. Besieged by the revolutionaries and the French, he capitulated on 19 October 1781. "I sailed from New York," states George, "in my friend Montague's frigate with that fleet of men of war which took on board ten thousand chosen troops, the prime of the British and Hessian forces, under the command of Sir Henry Clinton with the intent to relieve Lord Cornwallis's army. This force unfortunately arrived three or four days after Lord

Cornwallis's army had capitulated. The fleet returned to New York. This misfortune drew the war to a conclusion."

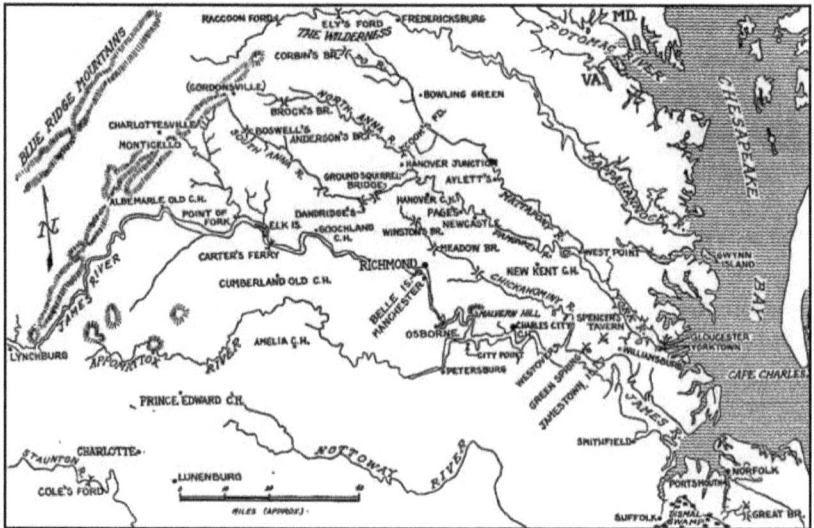

As to the cause of the catastrophe, George takes issue with the view that the destruction of the British interest in the southern parts of America was greatly attributable to the defeats of Ferguson and Tarleton at King's Mountain and Cowpens. Dismissing them as only partial misfortunes, he continues, "I will be so bold as to assert that these misfortunes did not in any degree contribute to the loss of America nor could many such misfortunes have produced that calamity. Our ruin was completed by permitting *a superior French fleet* to ride triumphant on the American seas the autumn of 1781. That, and that only, ruined our cause in America and disgracefully put an end to the war. There the nail was clinched!"

Would that the cause have been so simple! In fact there were several. If Cornwallis's light troops had not been lost at Cowpens, there might well have been a more favourable outcome to the disastrous winter campaign in North Carolina. In that event Cornwallis would not have felt impelled by specious reasoning to march into Virginia, so that Yorktown and the loss of South Carolina and Georgia would have been averted. Even so, Yorktown was not due to that decision alone. There were other factors in the equation: the occupation of Yorktown in compliance with Clinton's wishes but against Cornwallis's better judgement, its coincidence with the arrival of de Grasse and the French fleet, the failure of the Royal Navy to cater adequately for command of North American waters, Cornwallis's decision not to break out at once from Yorktown in the light of Clinton's assurances of relief, and ultimately the squall which put paid to his doing so at the close of the siege.

As far as George Washington is concerned, he emerges from his campaign as a decisive, resolute commander with keen strategic awareness, but his success was due less to concentrating his forces in an exemplary way than preponderantly to a combination of those chance circumstances we have described. "*Est-il heureux?*" Napoleon was wont to ask of a prospective general. "Is he lucky?" In Washington's case the answer, incontrovertibly, is "Yes, in spades!"

Writing of Yorktown in 1902, Fortescue concluded, "The blow was, on the whole, perhaps the heaviest that has fallen on the British Army." It would have been difficult at that time to disagree.

As peace negotiations progressed towards a treaty in which the independence of the United States would be recognised by Britain, George assumed command of the British Legion, including the now freed Legion troops captured at Cowpens and Yorktown, Tarleton having returned home.

In May 1782 Clinton was superseded by Sir Guy Carleton. "I lost," says George, "my kind protector and friend, and the army the best of men and a most gallant soldier." Of Carleton he adds, "The manner in which this gallant and distinguished veteran received me, after all those officers under whose auspices I had served the whole war were departed for England, was highly gratifying to my feelings, and the assurance he made me, on his arrival at New York, of employing me in a very active line, provided the war had continued, deserves my warmest thanks."

George continues by "relating a ludicrous conversation which took place between Sir Guy Carleton and myself one day when I had the honour of dining at headquarters immediately after his arrival, which strongly evinced his good humour and affability. The great skill which from years of practice I had acquired in the knowledge of a rifle gun, and the precision and perfection to which I had brought the art of shooting with a rifle, was well known to the army and Sir Guy Carleton had been informed of it. At dinner he said to me, sitting opposite to him, 'Major Hanger, I have been told that you are a most skilful marksman with a rifle gun. I have heard of astonishing feats that you have performed in shooting!' Thanking him for the compliment, I told his Excellency that I was vain enough to say with truth that many officers in the army had witnessed my adroitness. I then began to inform Sir Guy how my old deceased friend, Colonel Ferguson, and myself had practised together, who for skill and knowledge of that weapon had been so celebrated, and that Ferguson had ever acknowledged the superiority of my skill to his after one particular day's practice when I had shot three balls running into one hole. Sir Guy replied to this, 'I know you are very expert in this art.' Now had I been quiet and satisfied with the compliment the commander-in-chief paid me and not pushed this affair farther, it had been well for me, but I replied, 'Yes, Sir Guy, I really have reduced the art of shooting with a rifle to such a nicety that at a moderate distance I can *kill a flea* with a single ball.' At this Sir Guy began to stare not a little and seemed to indicate from the smile on his countenance that he thought I had rather outstepped my usual outdoings in the art. Observing this, I respectfully replied, 'I see by your Excellency's countenance that you seem doubtful of the singularity and perfection of my art, but if I may presume so much as to dare offer a wager to my commander-in-chief, I will bet your Excellency five guineas that I kill a flea with a single ball once in eight shots at eight yards.' Sir Guy replied, 'My dear Major, I am not given to lay wagers but for once I will bet you five guineas provided you will *let the flea hop*.' A loud laugh ensued at the table, and after laughing heartily myself, I placed my knuckle under the table and, striking the table, said, 'Sir Guy, I knock under and will never speak of my skill in shooting with a rifle gun again before you.'"

George states that peace took place soon after, presumably referring to the arrival of news that provisional articles of a treaty had been concluded in Paris on 30 November 1782. He then obtained a passport from Congress and the French ambassador at Philadelphia to repair there to visit his old acquaintance the Duc de Lauzun. He confesses that, although he had a passport, he was rather doubtful and diffident how he should journey across the ferries to Philadelphia in the character of major to the British Legion, a corps not much esteemed by the revolutionaries, but his friend Mr Church, who resided many years after the war in England, and Colonel Wadsworth, who had acted with him as joint commissaries to the French army, kindly took him under their protection on the journey. "These two gentlemen," recalls George, "in great good humour but not without some degree of fear and displeasure on my part, when they arrived at Princetown, invited the celebrated, pious and well-known character Doctor Witherspoon. To this pious man they exhibited me in such characters that, although the peace was concluded, I truly believe the doctor thought his head in danger that night, and certain I am, if he had heard that I had been within ten miles of his pious and sanctified domain, he would have buried the last silver teaspoon he was possessed of ten feet underground. Thus did my friend Church and Wadsworth amuse themselves at my expense, and what is more, all they told the doctor in good humour and in fun, playing me off before him, the pious divine took for gospel."

George records that he was treated with the greatest civility, not only by the French ambassador and officers, but also with the most perfect respect, attention and politeness by the leading families in Philadelphia, particularly by Robert Morris, "The Financier of the Revolution", and by Gouverneur Morris, the assistant to his namesake, whose understanding, "though he had by some misfortune lost one leg," was not in the least impaired, "for he was one of the most sensible, the best informed, and most agreeable of men I ever knew." Above all George expresses his gratitude to Major General Philemon Dickinson, who as head of the New Jersey revolutionary militia had seen much distinguished service, "for the uncommon civility and attention he showed to me. His house, replete with the truest hospitality, was open to me by night and by day. His mind was too noble, too enlightened, too expanded to think ill of, or harbour any rancour against, me or any other officer who by any active services might have made themselves obnoxious to the generality of Americans. I am convinced from my heart that had I been of ten times more detriment to the Americans, his respect would in proportion have increased, for he had from an early period of the war served his country with distinction and alacrity and honoured those British officers who had endeavoured to the utmost of their abilities to serve their King and country."

George then relates a conversation that took place at Dickinson's table before a large company, a conversation in which George, a percipient and farsighted political observer, expressed an opinion on the future destiny of the government of the Unites States. "At that time, when peace had been concluded but a few weeks, I remember well, when General Dickinson asked me my opinion of the government and of its stability, I communicated my thoughts nearly in the following words: 'Sir, as long as General Washington and the other principal military characters and leading men in Congress who have brought about this revolution are alive, the government will remain as it is, united, but when all of you are in your graves there will be wars and rumours of wars in this country. There are too many different interests in it for them to be united under one government. Just as this war commenced, you were going to fight amongst yourselves

118

and would have fought had the British not interfered. You then, one and all, united against us as your common enemy, but one of these days the northern and southern powers will fight as vigorously against each other as they both have united to do against the British.'" Less than eighty years later the civil war came to pass. It was a remarkable prophecy, one that is justly remembered to this day. Nor did George end there. He went on to anticipate the Mexican-American War and concluded, "I anxiously hope and trust I shall live to see the day when an alliance offensive and defensive will be formed between the two countries," namely the UK and the USA, as now in effect obtains.

"I claim," adds George, "no greater merit for my opinions relative to America than is due to Mother Shipton, who prophesied that London would go to Hampstead, and we all know that it is already arrived within a few hundred yards of it."

"Before I quit Philadelphia," George goes on, "I cannot refrain from mentioning the toasts which were always given after dinner at the tables of the most distinguished characters. I was invited by the President of Congress to dinner, when he gave the following in rotation: The Congress — Our great and good ally the King of France — The King of England — General Washington — Sir Guy Carleton. These were the standing toasts, after which many convivial and polite ones were given. At the time that these gentlemen were toasting the King of France as their great and good ally, poor Louis never dreamed that they were drinking a separation to his head from his body, but it is well known now that the revolution which he favoured in America brought on his destruction and the revolution in France."

In September 1783 we find George in Nova Scotia, arranging for lands to be allotted to those soldiers of the British Legion who had chosen to remain and settle in North America. All but 80 of the regiment accompanied him, the rest taking passage for England. "I landed," says George, "at Halifax and from thence sailed to Port Roseway[42] and the River Jordan as well as to many other places." On the 20th John Parr, the Governor, reported to Carleton, "Hanger seemed very happy to have Port Mouton allotted for the Legion." On 10 October the corps was disbanded.

Of Nova Scotia George has little complimentary to relate: "This country may be described in a few words: there is seven months' intense hard winter; during the other five the inhabitants live without any intermission in a thick fog. One happiness the poor settlers enjoy, and I know of no other — in one day they can catch enough codfish to salt, without going above four or five miles from the shore, to supply two or three families for a twelvemonth. With a small patch of potatoes, therefore, they can never starve. I saw nothing here worthy of observation excepting a perpetual continuation of rocks and stony mountains and an iron-bound coast frightful and dangerous to the mariner. I was very near being cast away on making Port Roseway harbour. If the fog had not cleared up a little, in half an hour more we should have been driven by the current on the breakers, for then we were lying to, having had a faint view of the land through the fog early that morning. From Halifax I returned to New York on board a frigate commanded by my old friend Captain Hawkins, now Admiral Witshead."

George remained at New York until it was evacuated by Carleton on 25 November. "With that fleet I took my passage for England and arrived in the Downs after near seven years' absence.[43]"

---

[42] Soon to be renamed Shelburne.
[43] George was in fact in North America for only 5½ years.

CHAPTER 10

EQUERRY TO THE PRINCE OF WALES — THE WESTMINSTER ELECTION OF 1784 AND AFTER

Some months before George quit America he gave joint power of attorney to his friends John McMahon, who was taking passage before him, and Tarleton to endeavour at an arrangement of his affairs prior to his arrival in Europe.

It was agreed that George would go to Calais and remain there until he knew how the land lay. So that he should not be in want, McMahon generously gave him a credit for £500 on his banker in London. "To this friend," avers George, "I certainly owe all the happiness and misfortunes I have undergone, for, had it not been for his exertions, I never should have come to England but gone to Germany, where I am certain the Landgrave of Hesse-Cassel would have requited my services in a far more satisfactory manner than this country has done. Would to God I had never to this hour placed my foot on British ground! I had then my half pay as major in the British service, which I could have received abroad, and besides this I had about two hundred and forty pounds per annum left me by my kind mother, which sum was then totally unimpaired. With my employment and pay as a Hessian officer in his Serene Highness's service I could have lived most magnificently and never have known distress or have been subjected to a prison in a land of liberty."

George then testifies his gratitude to Richard Tattersall, a very old and intimate friend, for "a liberality and generosity of conduct that stands unrivalled.[44]   When he heard that Captain McMahon was deputed by me to endeavour to arrange my shattered and plundered circumstances so as to enable me to live in my native country, my dear and worthy friend, old Richard, waited on Captain McMahon and joined his exertions. In fact he took the whole burthen of my distresses on his own shoulders and employed his own lawyer to examine and investigate my affairs."

After about two months' correspondence with George at Calais, Tarleton kindly came over to visit him at Tattersall's desire, "as he could in a few hours make me more fully master of my affairs than by writing fifty letters by the post." Tarleton stayed four or five days, nor would George ever forget the letter he brought from Tattersall, which "ought to be written in letters of gold:"

My dear Major

I do insist on it that you will come home directly to England to my house, where you shall be made happy. You have been robbed and plundered. I will bail you from every body who may arrest you, and if you cannot pay, I will.

I am, dear Major, etc

RICHARD TATTERSALL

George adds that before he quit England he had lived when in affluence in the strictest terms of intimacy and friendship with

---

[44] Richard Tattersall (1724-1795), the founder of "Tattersall's", had set up a stud-farm at Dawley in Middlesex, which, together with his reputation for integrity, was the cornerstone of his large fortune. In 1766 he had purchased from the Earl of Grosvenor a 99 years' lease of a property at Hyde Park Corner, where he fitted up two rooms for the use of members of the Jockey Club. It was his and George's mutual interest in the turf that had led to their friendship. Politically a Whig, Tattersall was acquainted with the Prince of Wales and Charles James Fox.

"this worthy old man" and had constantly kept up a correspondence with him during the whole of the American War. "He
proved himself one of those few men in this world who do not
desert an old friend in distress."

Before Tarleton returned to England, it was agreed that
George should not repair there until he had heard further from
him and Tattersall. In about ten days he received letters, and
taking passage in the next packet for Dover, he arrived at
Tattersall's house at Hyde Park Corner, where he was received
with the truest friendship and remained under its hospitable
roof for near twelve months. "I here held a consultation with my
lawyers, when they were of opinion, from the securities I had
given before my departure from England for every farthing
I owed, that I could not be cast in any action by which I might be
arrested. However, to make things more secure my lawyers
were prepared to plead the Statute of Limitations."

From Tattersall's house George sailed into the world and in
a short time was arrested for between seven and eight hundred
pounds — "that was all that was against me." Tattersall and his
son Edmund, another of George's friends, were his constant bail.
"I brought the actions into court," states George, "and the first
cause I tried, the jury never left the box, nor even consulted
together for more than a couple of minutes, and gave a verdict
for me, after which all the rest withdrew their actions, of which
I believe there were nine or ten."

In the meantime George had been introduced by his friends
Rawdon and Tarleton to George Augustus Frederick, the Prince
of Wales and heir to the throne. Charmed by George's engaging
personality, the Prince at once admitted him, like Rawdon and
Tarleton, to his coterie of convivial companions, appointing him
in due course his equerry at a salary of £300 per year.[45]

---

[45] Approximately £42,000 in today's money.

The Prince by now had just attained his majority and resided with his own establishment at Carlton House in Pall Mall. By inclination as well as position he had become the leader of fashion and gaiety in high society. Superficially charming, graceful and chivalrous, he was tall and finely formed with a handsome and manly appearance heightened by the richness and variety of his dress. Among his accomplishments was a fluency in French, Italian and German; he was well read in the classics; he cultivated an interest in music, excelling both as a vocal and as an instrumental performer; and he was a connoisseur of the fine arts. Nor did he lack physical pursuits. He loved outdoor exercise and showed to great advantage on horseback; he was a good shot and an accomplished fencer; and he was skilful in the noble art. using on occasion his fists to good effect. Yet beneath the glossy surface lay a character rooted in depravity. Led on by his dissolute uncle, the Duke of Cumberland and Strathearn, he had descended into debauchery and licentiousness. Less a sensualist than a voluptuary, he like George had come to display an extravagant, boundless appetite for women of all backgrounds, whether they be common prostitutes, courtesans, demi-reps or members of the aristocracy. It was, in the words of honest Sancho[46], the beginning of a career attended with "a larger and more continuous share of the tarts and cheesecakes of life" than has fallen to the lot of any prince of olden or modern times in any part of Europe. Otherwise, profligacy, gaming — at which he was a great loser, bacchanalian orgies, and a keen interest in the turf typified much of his existence.

It was not, however, to the unsavoury conduct of the Prince that George would later pay tribute: "For above sixteen years I have had the honour of [the Prince's] protection and acquaintance. It is hard indeed if I did not know him in so long a period of time, when I have viewed him in every stage: in health, on the bed of sickness, in convivial, and in serious hours.

---

[46] Sancho Panza in Cervantes' *Don Quixote*.

This Prince is but little known to the world at large, who judge him from report only. What is common report but a common prostitute? To make her the standard of truth is as erroneous as to make the chameleon the standard of colour. A day shall come, vipers, when ye shall be compelled to swallow the poison you here spit forth. By my honour and the sacred love and reverence I bear to truth, I am not induced to speak of him from his dignified station in life. I speak not of him as being Prince of Wales. Were he an ensign on half pay with no other support than that scanty pittance, or a clergyman serving three churches for forty pounds a year — two situations most deplorable and the least to be envied in life — I would select him above all mankind for a companion and friend, and by his judgement I would be guided in the most weighty and intricate concerns. His enemies even acknowledge that he is the most accomplished and best bred gentleman of the age, a master of languages, and an elegant classical scholar — three distinguished qualities rarely to be met in one man."

Of all the brilliant, pleasure-loving crowd who at this time surrounded the Prince, undoubtedly the two persons who exercised the most influence over him were Charles James Fox[47] and Georgiana, the Duchess of Devonshire[48], both of whom were also close friends of George from his entry into the *beau monde* over ten years before. By now Fox was about 34 years of age, a man of great abilities and at the zenith of his fame. The *de facto* leader of the Whig Party, of which George was a staunch supporter, he had lately served as Secretary of State for Foreign Affairs, but hated by the King for his politics and opposition to the American War, he with his

---

[47] Fox (1749-1806) was the third son of Henry Fox, later Lord Holland, and Lady Caroline Georgiana Lennox, daughter of Charles Lennox, the second Duke of Richmond and grandson of Charles II.
[48] The eldest daughter of the first Earl Spencer, Georgiana was born in 1757 and married the fifth Duke of Devonshire in 1774. She died in 1806.

coalition partner, Lord North, had been dismissed from office in December 1783 — only two months earlier — and replaced with William Pitt and the Tories.

Fox had inherited from his ancestor, Charles II, not only his swarthy, saturnine appearance but also his love of vicious pursuits, especially of gaming and women, no matter what their background or class. He was stout, heavily built and unwieldy, negligent in his dress, and slovenly in his personal appearance, but when he smiled or spoke, his whole being seemed transformed and he won to his side almost all he might. He was a good friend — eager, warm-hearted and unselfish; his personal creed was frankly hedonistic; in religious matters he had no fixed belief; yet in his political life he was a man of lofty ideals and high principles. Such was this remarkable man, the "My dear Charles" of so many of the young Prince's letters. The King strove in vain to break the friendship between them — and of course the Prince's support for the Whigs, and desperately implored his Lord Chancellor, Thurlow, to tell him what to do. "Sir," replied Thurlow, "you will never have peace until you clap 'em both into the Tower."

The Duchess of Devonshire, who was devoted heart and soul to Fox, exercised an influence over the Prince socially as well as politically. Socially, her influence lay in the fact that she was a leader of fashion whose life was a constant round of receptions, balls, masquerades, parties of pleasure, and visits to the opera and theatre. Politically, she hosted at Devonshire House, her mansion in Piccadilly, an active and high-ranking circle of Whigs whose influence over the fortunes of the Whig Party was profound. It was a select circle of which George had now become a member. A vivacious and inspiring personality, the Duchess was not classically beautiful but her charms were described by almost all contemporary writers as beyond compare. As Wraxall put it, who knew her well, "... her beauty [did not] consist of features and faultless formation of limbs and shape; it lay in the amenity and graces of her deportment, in her irresistible manners and the seduction of her society ... In addition to the external advantages which she had received from nature and fortune, she possessed an ardent temper, susceptible of deep as well as strong impressions; a cultivated understanding, illuminated by a taste for poetry and the fine arts; much sensibility, not exempt perhaps from vanity and coquetry." Yet the Duchess was an intriguing paradox. On one side she was extremely charming, graceful and witty, kind-hearted and philanthropic, full of generous impulses and high ideals. On the other she was incredibly reckless and foolish, willing to risk everything at the gaming table on the turn of a card and losing in one winter alone over £100,000.[49] With a restless energy ever seeking something new, she was eager for fame, living always for the hour, but despite her faults, inescapably endearing.

As George became a close confidant of Fox and February advanced into March, it became increasingly clear from a Whig perspective that something had gone badly wrong in constitutional practice. Despite the numerous limitations placed upon royal power since 1660, the King remained the dominant figure in political life. Of all the prerogatives with which he was endowed the vital one was his constitutional right to choose his own ministers, through which he controlled national policy and distributed patronage. It was nevertheless accepted — at least till now — that the will of the House of Commons must ultimately override all other authority in the state and that if the King's ministers could not command a majority there and enable "the King's business" to be done, they must resign. Yet, to the Whigs' dismay, the King had changed the rules of the game without notice and appointed a minority administration under Pitt which, though opposed by the Commons, refused to fall on its sword. To resolve the impasse, only a dissolution of Parliament remained.

---

[49] Approximately £13,850,000 in today's money.

As Fox became too well aware that a general election was imminent, he appointed George as a principal lieutenant to run his campaign for a seat in Westminster and began to take part in a series of pre-electoral public meetings. Of one of these held in February Charles Jenkinson, one of the King's "secret advisers", wrote, "I am assured that Mr Fox was defeated today in Westminster Hall by 5 to 1. Others make the parties more even. It is clear, however, that Mr Fox was forced to leave the hall and to leave the other party in possession of it and that he harangued the mob from one of the windows of the King's Tavern. He was then drawn in his chariot by a low mob of about a hundred to Devonshire House; but what will astonish you is that Colonel Stanhope [and] Mr Hanger were on the coachbox and that Mr George North, Mr Adam and a third person stood as footmen behind. How disgraceful!"

Meanwhile the Commons' support for Fox's coalition with North was steadily draining away as Northites and members with unsafe seats either gravitated out of self-interest towards the party in power or otherwise began supporting Pitt for fear that the coalition was a potential threat to the smooth running of government. By 1 March the coalition's majority had shrunk to one. Materially influencing many was the knowledge that Pit was widely and assiduously using Treasury money to bribe borough-mongers and men of influence to secure a majority in the new House, it being well-nigh impossible for the Whigs to outbid him. All in all, as both Whigs and Tories knew, the popular will would have little to do with the outcome of the election. On 25 March the King dissolved Parliament.

The Westminster seat, to which Fox now stood for re-election, occupied a unique place among parliamentary constituencies, since every male "inhabitant householder" had a right to vote for Members of Parliament. *Ipso facto* there was a better opportunity to secure a genuine expression of the popular will in an election there than in any other constituency in the kingdom. Aware that the outcome was of peculiar significance, the King and Pitt would make strenuous efforts to secure Fox's defeat.

Besides Fox the candidates were Lord Hood from the navy, whom the Whigs did not oppose, and Sir Cecil Wray, a former Whig who had defected to the Tories. Only two could be elected. The platform on which Fox — "the Man of the People" — stood was an abridgement of the King's prerogative to appoint a ministry of his own choice. Fox's recent experience had convinced him that confidence between a Whig ministry and the Crown was impossible and that where he could not trust, he had to control. The King had to be tied down with the strength of party and the authority of the House of Commons — "the true, simple question of the present dispute" being, as Fox declared to a meeting of his supporters, "whether the House of Lords and Court influence shall predominate over the House of Commons and annihilate its existence or whether the House of Commons, whom you elected, shall have power to maintain the privileges of the people, to support its liberties, and check the unconstitutional proceedings of a House of Lords, whom you never elected, and regulate the prerogatives of the Crown." For his part Wray, like Pitt, stood for maintaining the status quo.

The poll opened on 1 April and would close six weeks later. Fox and his election committee were centred in Devonshire House, supported enthusiastically by the Prince, who would constantly invite them to Carlton House for entertainments of every description. It was, however, George, working out of the Shakespeare Tavern, who was largely responsible for managing the campaign on the streets, and a prodigious task it was, for in no other electoral contest in the eighteenth century was there such a prevalence of drunkenness, tumult, disorder, loss of life, and corrupt practices. Throughout the campaign the entire western quarter of London, and especially Covent Garden, the site of the hustings, presented a scene of uproar which it is difficult to describe. In fact, the latter locality might better be termed a bear garden, so flagrant were the outrages against decency and so riotous was the violence of which it was the scene.

As the hustings were erected in Covent Garden, the bailiff and his deputies repaired there to record the votes for the respective candidates. There was no registration, and the right of each elector to poll was determined on the spot as and when he appeared. The immediate and continuing problem faced by George was that Wray began by employing gangs of thugs, disguised as sailors, ostensibly to keep a way clear to the hustings but in reality to intimidate those who offered to vote for Fox. George's answer was to hire the sedan chairmen of St James's Street to frustrate them. There ensued numerous brawls and riots in which George with his trademark shillelagh, which he carried all his life, took a leading part.

The King himself did not scruple to influence the poll. Two hundred and eighty of his guardsmen were marched to the hustings and ordered *en masse* to vote for Wray, whilst a groom of the bedchamber publicly announced that he had been directed to do so by the Lord Chamberlain. Fox for his part brought his personal magnetism to bear. Writing to her sister during the campaign, Hannah Moore maintained her loyalty to Pitt, but added: "Unluckily for my principles I met Fox canvassing the other day and he looks so sensible and agreeable that if I had not turned my eyes another way, I believe it would have been all over with me."

It is not easy to determine the exact amount of money at the disposal of either party but it was immense. Bribery was widespread, as when an agent of Fox sportingly approached a prospective elector. "I'll lay you five guineas, and stake the money in your hands, that you will not vote for Fox," he cried. "Done!" replied the householder, who went into the polling booth, winning the bet and the bribe.

Of course not all the money was used for bribery. Rife was treating and related expenses, for which George was partly responsible. Illegal nowadays, treating involved the procurement of food, alcoholic liquor and other refreshments in order to influence voters, the upshot being a marked increase in riotous behaviour as those partaking of the largesse became rapidly drunk, proceeded to quarrel, and took to brawling in the taverns or streets. Then there were to be paid the innkeepers for keeping open house, the sedan chairmen at five shillings per day with their food and drink, the publishers of newspapers for their support, the printers of handbills or posters, and others too numerous to name.

And so the election went on its merry way, but as voting steadily progressed Fox found that he was trailing Wray and began to despair. It was then that the Duchess of Devonshire came into her own. As Wraxall recalled, "the month of April verging to its close and almost all the inhabitants of the metropolis who possessed votes for Westminster having been already polled, there remained no resource equal to the emergency except by bringing up the voters residing in the outskirts of the town or in the circumjacent villages. This task, however irksome it might be to a female of so elevated a class, and little consonant as it seemed even to female delicacy under certain points of view, the Duchess of Devonshire cheerfully undertook in such a cause. Having associated to the execution her sister, Viscountess Duncannon, who participated the Duchess's political enthusiasm, these ladies, being previously furnished with lists of outlying voters, drove to their respective dwellings. Neither entreaties nor promises were spared. In some instances even personal caresses were said to have been permitted in order to prevail on the surly or inflexible, and there can be no doubt of common mechanics having been conveyed to the hustings on more than one occasion by the Duchess in her own coach." Almost immediately two prints appeared of the Duchess canvassing for votes: "Female Influence, or the Devonshire Canvas" and "The Devonshire, or Most Approved Method of Securing Votes".

FEMALE INFLUENCE; or. the DEVONS^{hir}—E CANVAS.

THE DEVONSHIRE, or Most Approved Method of Securing Votes

Kisses indeed were the order of the day, as a voter related many years later: "Lord, sir, it was a fine sight to see a grand lady come right smack to us hardworking mortals, with a hand held out and a 'Master, how d'ye do?' and a laugh so loud and talk so kind, and shake us by the hand and say, 'Give us your vote, worthy sir, a plumper for the people's friend, our friend, everybody's friend.' And then, sir, we hummed and hawed, they would ask after our wives and families, and if that didn't do they'd think nothing of a kiss, aye, a dozen of them. Lord, sir, kissing was nothing to them, and it came all natural!"

"The effect," says Wraxall, "of so powerful an intervention soon manifested itself. During the first days of May Fox, who a month earlier had fallen above a hundred votes behind Sir Cecil, passed him by at least that number. Conscious never-theless that the least relaxation in their efforts might probably enable the adversary to resume his superiority, and aware of the exertions which Government would make to ensure the success of their candidate, the Duchess, sacrificing her time wholly to the object, never intermitted for a single day her laborious toils."

Of this stage in Fox's campaign *Fraser's Magazine* provides an interesting vignette:

We recollect a procession, one among many of the same kind about this period, which, setting out from the St Alban's Tavern, mustered in Pall Mall opposite Carlton House at ten in the forenoon, composed of fifty of the finest women of the land with the Duchess of Devonshire and other ladies of the *haut ton* at their head, forming together such a galaxy of beauty as most certainly will never be seen again on such an occasion. These fascinating ladies were termed the blue and buff squadron, being dressed in blue riding habits with York tan gloves[50] and each wearing in her hat or bonnet a large fox's brush. And so great was the influence of these political gaieties that half the beautiful women in Westminster perambulated the public places wearing similar symbols.

---

[50] Blue and buff were Fox's party colours, having been those of Washington's troops during the American Revolutionary War.

Immediately at their gay heels followed standard bearers, bands of music etc, and then Mr Fox, arm in arm with Sam House[51], with certain noblemen and gentlemen of the election committees, amongst whom was conspicuously prominent Colonel George Hanger with his preposterous cudgel and white frill plaited down to his waistband; after him four and twenty fresh-looking butchers, all clad in white jackets, nankeen breeches, and blue aprons tucked round their waists, sounding a merry peal with marrowbones and cleavers, followed by numerous Whig lords and gentlemen, all well mounted, and a motley group of tag-rag and bobtail in their wake. Thus equipped, they marched off to the hustings in Covent Garden market, erected in front of St Paul's Church. The ladies, halting at the Royal Hotel, corner of King Street, were received with boisterous huzzas.

What transpired next is recorded by Karl Philipp Moritz, a visitor from Berlin. In the area before the hustings an immense multitude was assembled "of whom the greatest part seemed to be of the lowest order." They were addressed from the hustings by Wray and then by Fox, both of whom bowed very low and invariably referred to them as "gentlemen". The moment Wray began to speak, "this rude rabble" became as quiet as the raging sea after a storm, only now and then rending the air with cries of "Hear him! Hear him!" Even little boys clambered up on rails or lampposts as if Wray's, and later Fox's, speech was addressed to them, and they too testified their approbation by joining lustily in three cheers and waving their hats. At length, when Wray was almost finished, the crowd pressed Fox to speak, calling out "Fox! Fox!", and he came forward. "When the whole

---

[51] A devoted friend of Fox, to whose election expenses and general upkeep he contributed greatly, Sam House was landlord of the Coach and Horses Tavern in Wardour Street, Soho. He was about five feet ten in height and "as cleanly cut in nature's mint as a newly coined Tower guinea". He had but little hair upon his head and rarely wore a coat, being usually attired in a jacket and breeches of nankeen, diamond knee buckles when in dress, and fine silk hose. His waistcoat was white damask and his entire clothing was without speck or blemish, his linen vying in whiteness "with the down under the wing of a swan". He died at an early age.

was over, the rampant spirit of liberty and the wild impatience of a genuine English mob were exhibited to perfection." In a very few minutes the entire scaffolding, benches, chairs and everything else were completely destroyed and the mat with which the whole was covered torn into ten thousand long strips or pieces and used to encircle crowds of people of all ranks. Hurrying away, the mob seized whatever lay in its path "and thus, in the midst of exaltation and triumph, they paraded through many of the most populous streets of London." A print of such a riot was promptly published: "The Humours of Covent Garden or Freedom of Election".

The poll closed on 17 May. Topping it was Hood and in second place Fox, having defeated Wray by 236 votes. Great was the rejoicing of the Whigs, who, accompanied by a huge crowd, proceeded in procession from the hustings. Acting as Fox's coachman was George, dressed in a coachman's coat, hat and wig, and preceded by a lofty white silk banner inscribed "Sacred to Female Patriotism". Immediately following was the Duchess of Devonshire in a laurel-festooned coach drawn by six horses.

Having circled Covent Garden three times, the procession wended its way down King Street and Bedford Street into the Strand, finding at the corner of Cockspur Street and Pall Mall barrels of refreshment set out by Sam House. Carrying on from there, it reached the courtyard of Carlton House, where the Prince cheered Fox from the windows. Then down Pall Mall, up St James's Street to Devonshire House, in the courtyard of which a platform had been erected against the wall in Piccadilly for the Prince to receive Fox, who addressed the crowd.

The same night, arrayed in blue and buff, the Prince attended a supper party given by the fair and fascinating Mrs Crewe[52] in honour of the event. Fox, the Duchess and George were there, all arrayed in the same colours. The Prince gave the toast, "True blue and Mrs Crewe!" to which she wittily replied, "True blue and all of you!" A day later the Prince gave a magnificent *fête* at Carlton House. He showed to great advantage — no host ever did the honours more gracefully — and on this occasion the gentlemen, including the Prince, waited on the ladies at table before being seated themselves. The King regarded his son's behaviour as the last straw of insubordination and revenged himself by taking no notice of the Prince's next birthday.

The rejoicings, nevertheless, could not disguise the fact that the Whigs had lost heavily in the rest of the country, where "Fox's martyrs" fell prey in droves to the electoral chicanery of Pitt. He had, however, failed to command the support of a majority of the electors in the democratic constituency of Westminster, and this being so, it seems fair to question whether he remained in power as the choice of a majority of the British people in 1784.

---

[52] Frances Anne Crewe (née Greville) of Crewe Hall, Cheshire, was one of the most interesting and brilliant hostesses in London society. Keenly interested in politics, she maintained a salon at her house in Grosvenor Street, Mayfair, that was a resort of the principal Whig politicians. "In her character," says Stokes, "there was a spice of devilry, a bohemian charm of unconventionality, which, added to a quick wit and unparalleled beauty, rendered her presence a joy to all beholders." She died in 1818.

Many years later George had a few concluding words to offer about the contest for Fox's seat: "The year I came to England the contested election for Westminster took place. The walking travellers, Spillard and Stewart, the Abyssinian Bruce, who has feasted on steaks cut from the rump of a living ox, and various others who in their extensive travels have encountered wild beasts, serpents and crocodiles, breakfasted and toasted muffins at the mouth of a volcano — whom hunger has with joy compelled to banquet on the leavings of a lion or a tiger or the carcase of a dead alligator — who can boast of smoking the pipe of peace with the Little Carpenter and the Mad Dog — and lived on terms of the strictest intimacy with the Cherokees, the Chickesaws and Chuctaws, and with all the *aws* and *ees* of that immense continent — who, from the more temperate shore of the Mississippi, have extended their course to the burning soil of India and to the banks of the Ganges — from the frozen north European seas to the banks of the temperate and more genial Po — may boast their worldly experience and knowledge of human life, but no one, in my humble opinion, has seen *real life*, or can know it, unless he has taken an active part in a contested election for Westminster. In no school can a man be taught a better lesson of human life. There can he view human nature in her basest attire. Riot, murder and drunkenness are the order of the day, and bribery and perjury walk hand in hand, for men who had no pretensions to vote were as plenty to be found in the Garden[53] as turnips, who at a very moderate rate were induced to poll. A gentleman, to make himself of any considerable use to either party, must possess a number of engaging, familiar, and condescending qualities. He must help a porter up with his load, shake hands with a fishwoman, pull his hat off to an oyster wench, kiss a ballad singer, and be familiar with a beggar. If, in addition to these amiable good qualities, he is a tolerable good boxer, can play a good stick, and in the evening drink a pail-full of all sorts of liquors in going the

---

[53] Covent Garden.

rounds to solicit voters at their various clubs, then, indeed, he is a most highly finished and useful agent. In all the above accomplishments and sciences, except drinking, which I never was fond of, I have the vanity to believe that I arrived nearer perfection than any of my rivals.

"I should," continues George, "be ungrateful indeed if I did not testify my thanks to those gallant troops of high rank and distinguished fame, the knights of the strap and the black diamond knights[54], who displayed so much bravery and attachment to our cause. By my soul, they are higher in my estimation than all the knights in Christendom together, not excepting even the Knights of Malta with Quixote Paul at their head. At that time I formed a great intimacy with them which has continued to this day, for I never forget my old acquaintances whenever I meet them nor look upon my *old* friends with a *new face*, which is too much in general the custom of the world. We have shaken hands and drank together frequently since the time of our active services and I trust I shall live to taste many a good pot more of brown stout with them. I will ever acknowledge their gallantry and honest attachment.

"I beg it may be well understood," George goes on, "that it is very far from my intent to sing a recantation of my own actions, but after years of cool reflection I reflect with horror that the capital should have been so convulsed for four or five weeks by the faction of two parties contending for power. I trust I shall live to see the time that all elections will finish in one day and the votes taken parochially, which would effectually prevent riot and perjury and many other inferior crimes which at present are committed at all elections. Fine speeches every day were delivered from the hustings, endeavouring to impress the minds of the people with the freedom of elections and how disinterestedly both parties acted for the public good, for the liberty of the

---

[54] The sedan chairmen and coal heavers.

people, and freedom of the nation. I am bound in honour to render justice to each party for the *striking proofs* they gave of the sincerity of their professions, as it must be admitted that they manifested it to an eminent degree by the freedom they displayed in breaking each other's heads. Of that species of liberty each were abundantly lavish."

On 21 May, only four days after the close of the Westminster election, there began a series of amusing events involving George of which Huish provides a most interesting account. They will, he claims, "be read as a rich treat to the lovers of fun and mischief," showing "the extraordinary gaiety of the disposition of the Prince of Wales and the familiar manner in which he lived with his companions:"

It was at the celebration of Her Majesty's birthday that Major Hanger made his first appearance at court, and it may be said to have been a debut which proved a source of infinite amusement to all who were present, and to no one more so than the Prince of Wales, who was no stranger to the singularity of his character and the general eccentricity of his actions. Being a major in the Hessian service, he wore his uniform at the ball, which was a short blue coat with gold frogs with a belt unusually broad across his shoulders, from which his sword depended. This dress — being a little particular when compared with the full-trimmed suits of velvet and satin about him, though, as professional, strictly conformable to the etiquette of the court — attracted the notice of His Majesty and his attendants, and the buzz, "Who is he?" "Whence does he come?" etc etc, was heard in all parts of the room. Thus he became the focus of attraction, and especially when the contrast presented itself of his selecting the beautiful Miss Gunning as his partner. He led her out to dance a minuet but when, on the first crossing of his lovely partner, he put on his hat, which was of the largest Kevenhüller kind ornamented with two large black and white feathers, the figure which he cut was so truly ridiculous and preposterous that even the gravity of His Majesty could not be restrained. The grave faces of his Ministers relaxed into a smile and the Prince of Wales was actually thrown into a convulsive fit of laughter. There was such an irresistible provocation to risibility in the *tout ensemble* of his appearance and style of movement that his fair partner was reluctantly obliged to lose sight of good manners and could scarcely finish the minuet, but Hanger himself joined in the laugh which was raised at his expense and thereby extricated his partner from her embarrassment. This is perhaps the first time that the *pas grave* of a minuet has been considered as a mighty good jest, but there are moments when even the most serious circumstances serve only to produce a comic effect.

The Major now stood up to dance a country dance, but here his motions were so completely antic and so much resembling those of a mountebank that he totally discomfited his partner, put the whole set into confusion, and excited a degree of laughter throughout the room, such as had never before been witnessed in a royal drawing room.

Shortly afterwards George's ludicrous debut at court became the subject of conversation at Carlton House, when the Prince proposed that a letter should be written to him thanking him, in the name of the company which had assembled in the drawing room, for the pleasure and gratification which he had afforded them. The joke was considered a good one. Writing materials were ordered and the Prince himself dictated the following letter for copying and dispatch by Richard Brinsley Sheridan, a convivial companion, whose handwriting George was not acquainted with:

St James's Street
Sunday morning

The company who attended the ball on Friday last at St James's present their compliments to Major Hanger and return him their unfeigned thanks for the variety with which he enlivened the insipidity of that evening's entertainment. The gentlemen want words to describe their admiration of the truly grotesque and humorous figure which he exhibited, and the ladies beg leave to express their acknowledgements for the lively and animated emotions that his stately, erect and perpendicular form could not fail to excite in their delicate and susceptible bosoms. His gesticulations and martial deportment were truly admirable and have raised an impression that will not soon be effaced at St James's.

According to Huish, the letter produced a highly ludicrous scene, which often excited a laugh when the Prince related it to guests as one of the most humorous that had occurred to him during his life.

The day after George received the letter the Prince purposely invited him to dine at Carlton House, and it formed part of the Prince's plot that Sheridan should not be there. After dinner the conversation turned designedly on the leading circumstances of the recent ball. When the Prince ironically complimented George on the serious effect that his appearance must have had on the hearts of the ladies, he in a very indignant manner drew from his pocket the letter, declaring that it was a complete affront to him and that the sole motive of the writer was to insult him and turn him into ridicule. The Prince requested to see the letter, and having perused it, he fully concurred with George that no other motive could have actuated the writer than to offer him the greatest affront.

George's anger rose. "Blitz and Hölle!" he exclaimed, " If I could discover the writer, he should give me immediate satisfaction."

"I admire your spirit," replied the Prince. "How insulting to talk of your grotesque figure!"

"And then to turn your stately, erect and perpendicular form into ridicule," added Fox.

"And to talk of your gesticulations," said Captain Charles Morris, another of the Prince's jovial friends.

"Sapperment!"[55] exclaimed George, "but the writer shall be discovered."

"Have you not the slightest knowledge of the handwriting?" asked the Prince. "The characters are, I think, somewhat familiar to me. Allow me to peruse the letter again." It was handed to the Prince. "I am certain I am not mistaken," he said. "This is the handwriting of that mischievous fellow Sheridan."

"Sheridan!" exclaimed George. "Impossible, it cannot be!"

"Hand the letter to Fox," replied the Prince. "He knows Sheridan's handwriting well."

"This is undoubtedly the handwriting of Sheridan," said Fox, looking at the letter.

"Then he shall give me immediate satisfaction," declared George, and rising from the table, he requested Captain Morris to be the bearer of his message to Sheridan. In it he demanded either a full and public apology or the appointment of a place for their *rencontre*. In the meantime, as Morris went on his way, George prepared to retire to his lodgings to await the answer. The Prince now pretended to interfere, expressing his readiness to mediate between the parties, but at the same time he contrived every now and then to increase the flame of George's resentment by some artful insinuations as to the grossness of the affront, besides complimenting him on the spirited manner in which he had behaved. George was determined not to be appeased and left the room muttering, "Damn the impudent fellow! Grotesque figure! — perpendicular form! — gesticulations!"

George had no sooner retired than the whole party burst into loud laughter. The Prince had brought him to the very

---

[55] A German oath.

point he wished and in about an hour Morris returned with Sheridan, who immediately entered into the spirit of the adventure. It was then agreed that Sheridan should accept the challenge, appointing the next morning at daybreak in Battersea Fields, and that Fox should be the bearer of his answer to George. Sheridan for his part undertook to provide medical assistance.

As dawn arose, the parties were punctually at the spot, George accompanied by Morris, Sheridan by Fox, and the Prince disguised as a surgeon and seated in a carriage. After the customary preliminaries had taken place, the parties took their places. The signal to fire was given — no effect took place. The seconds reloaded the pistols — the parties fired again — still no effect.

"Damn the fellow!" exclaimed George to his second, "I can't hit him."

"The third fire generally takes effect," remarked Morris, who with the utmost difficulty could hardly keep his amused faculties in order, while the Prince in his carriage was almost convulsed with laughter.

The signal to fire was given the third time, the effect was decisive, and Sheridan fell, as if dead, on his back.

"Killed, by God!" exclaimed Morris, "Let us fly immediately." And without giving George time to collect himself, he hurried him to his carriage and drove away at once towards town. Alighting from his, the Prince, almost faint with laughter, joined Sheridan and Fox, the former of whom, as soon as George's carriage was out of sight, had risen from his prostrate position, unscathed as when he entered the field, for, to complete the farce, it had been arranged that no ball should be put into the pistols and that Sheridan was to fall on the third fire. The Prince and his two companions soon drove off to town, and a message was sent to George desiring his immediate attendance at Carlton House. George obeyed and entered the Prince's apartment with a most dolorous countenance. "Bad business this," said the Prince, "a very bad business, Hanger, but I have the satisfaction to tell you that Sheridan is not materially hurt and if you will dine with me today, I will invite a gentleman who will give you an exact account of the state in which your late antagonist lies. Remain here till dinner time and all may yet be well."

George looked forward with some anxiety to learning the fate of one of his and the Prince's most convivial companions. The hour arrived and the party was assembled in the drawing room. "Now, Hanger," said the Prince, "I'll introduce to you a gentleman who will give you all the information you can wish." The door opened and Sheridan came in. George started back in wonder. "How! how! how is this?" he stammered, "I thought I had killed you!" "Not quite, my good fellow," replied Sheridan, offering George his hand. "I am not yet quite good enough to go to the world above, and as to that below, I am not yet fully qualified for it. I therefore considered it better to defer my departure from this to a future period. And now I doubt not that His Royal Highness will give you an explicit explanation of the whole business — but I died well, did I not, Hanger?"

The Prince now declared that the whole plot was concocted by himself and hoped that when George next fought such a duel, he might be in a coach to view it. Conviviality reigned throughout the rest of the evening, the song and glass went round, and the Prince sang the parody on "There's a difference between a beggar and a queen".[56]

It was only two weeks later that the Prince dispatched George to Germany with secret information for his beloved

---

[56] Composed by Morris, the parody appears in his *Songs Political and Convivial* (24th edition, London, 1802).

brother Frederick, who had been exiled there by the King to remove his elder brother's corrupting influence. What was the nature of the information we do not know. By July George was back in England, ready to attend the Prince on his second sojourn in Brighton.

CHAPTER 11

BRIGHTON — THE EARLY YEARS

Accompanied by George, the Prince set off for Brighton on 22 July 1784. As George later recalled, "The summer after I came to England His Royal Highness the Prince of Wales did me the honour to take me down with him to Brighton. I never shall forget the two or three first seasons I had the honour of being with him there. In all my days before and since, I never passed my time more agreeably or with greater happiness. They were indeed the pleasantest days of my life."

A fishing village of some 3,500 souls on the south coast of England, Brighton was rapidly becoming the favoured health resort of the aristocratic and fashionable world. Formed of six principal streets, many lanes and some squares, it contained mostly flint-stoned buildings, the most prominent of which were the theatre and two coaching inns, The Castle and The Old Ship. To the east, beyond the village proper, lay a few houses fronting The Steine,[57] an open grassy area bordered by wooden railings and a track. It was in 1752 that the village had come into prominence, when Dr Richard Russell, a resident there, published a dissertation on the healing effects of seawater.

Brighton offered a range of fashionable amusements from the innocent to those less so. Whether, for example, it was bathing in the sea or boating, strolling or sunning oneself on the beach, walking on the adjacent plain or nearby Downs, riding out, going for country drives or picnics, or attending tea parties at the assembly rooms of the two coaching inns, the opportunities

---

[57] Pronounced "Steen".

for what were mostly innocent pastimes were varied. Among them a particular pleasure was promenading on The Steine, especially on Sunday evenings when a band played. Otherwise, there were, for instance, card parties, a favourite pastime of the age, held privately or at the assembly rooms, where stakes were often high; "libraries", mostly near The Steine, where games of chance for small stakes were played and every conceivable kind of merchandise sold; the theatre or public concerts; and balls of every description, from the dress to the masked or cotillion, of which several took place each week in the summer season. Finally, there were sporting amusements ranging from cock-fights, bull-baiting or race days at Brighton and Lewes to deer or fox hunting. Inevitably, as Brighton's reputation for amusements grew, and as the nobility and gentry increasingly patronised it, so did it attract an ever larger number of disreputable or lawless characters, whether they were prostitutes, blacklegs, cardsharpers, pickpockets or the like.

Waiting to welcome the Prince was a large concourse of people on The Steine. Delighted that he was again to sojourn with them, numbers waited till every light was extinguished, but all in vain, for the Prince and his party did not arrive till three to four o'clock in the morning of the 23rd, taking up residence in a house beside The Steine that Louis Weltje, the Prince's clerk of the kitchen, had rented from Thomas Kemp — a house which Samuel Rogers, who had dined there as a boy, described contemptuously as "a respectable farmhouse". The Prince would in due course acquire it and in the meantime undertook extensive alterations and additions that were completed in 1787. It became known as the Marine Pavilion. Throughout the rest of the century the Prince would visit Brighton every summer for the "season", the period of more or less three months when he was resident there.

On the 26th, only three days after his arrival, the Prince performed a remarkable feat of endurance. Leaving Brighton at five o'clock in the morning, he rode on horseback to London in only four and a half hours, returning likewise, but one hour longer — a round trip of 114 miles in one day! It was a record that stood for many years. Of course he would not have travelled alone, it being unthinkable for the foremost prince of the realm to embark on such a venture unaccompanied — and who better than George, his equerry and a skilled horseman, to have been at his side?

The press added the not altogether surprising news that the Prince "immediately on his return very prudently retired to his rest," although by doing so he disappointed company at The Castle ballroom, who had assembled in expectation of seeing him.

Among the Prince's companions, besides George, were those "three bottles a day" men, Fox and Sheridan, the Lades, and the Dukes of Norfolk and Orléans, all of whom had a licentious reputation. Also present were Captain Morris and the Hon Thomas Onslow, the eldest son of Lord Onslow.

Sheridan was the foremost dramatist of the day, the author of *The Rivals* and *The School for Scandal*, but had forsaken the theatre for politics when he entered the Commons as the Member for Stafford in 1780. A gamester and a rake, he had already attained the height of celebrity as a politician and gifted orator. Besides his political acumen, it was his social qualities, his brilliant and ready wit, his serenity of temper, which nothing ruffled, that had made him a great favourite with the Prince, whose pleasures and sensual enjoyments he promoted. He was a young man, still in his thirties, and his handsome features had not yet been marred by his excessive drinking, which, together with his gaming, would ultimately lead to his downfall. Like the Prince, he was, as we have seen, a keen practical joker.

A country squire, Sir John Lade Bt of Haremere in Sussex had attained his majority in 1780, inheriting a fair fortune which

148

he soon dissipated. It was an event anticipated by Dr Samuel Johnson who, on Sir John's coming of age, had written the following prophetic lines:

Long-expected one-and-twenty,
Ling'ring year, at length is flown;
Pride and pleasure, pomp and plenty,
Great Sir John, are now your own.

Loosen'd from the minor's tether,
Free to mortgage or to sell;
Wild as wind, and light as feather,
Bid the sons of thrift farewell.

Call the Betsies, Kates, and Jennies
All the names that banish care;
Lavish of your grandsire's guineas,
Show the spirit of an heir.

All that prey on vice and folly,
Joy to see their quarry fly;
There the gamester, light and jolly,
There the lender, grave and sly.

Wealth, my lad, was made to wander,
Let it wander at its will;
Call the jockey, call the pander,
Bid them come and take their fill.

When the bonny blade carouses,
Pockets full and spirits high —
What are acres? what are houses?
Only dirt, or wet and dry.

Should the guardian, friend or mother
Tell the woes of wilful waste,
Scorn their counsels, scorn their pother,
You can hang, or drown, at last.

A gamester with a string of race horses, Sir John had taught the Prince the art of driving and, together with George, would manage his racing stable. He also taught the Prince much else besides, mostly of a disreputable nature. After a run of ill luck at gaming and racing he eventually fell upon evil days and was imprisoned in 1814 for debt. Penniless when released, he was granted a pension by the Prince, which was continued by William IV and Queen Victoria. He died in the second year of her reign, one of the last survivors of the Prince's dissolute coterie.

Sir John's wife, Lady Letitia Lade, was a foulmouthed Cockney who had reputedly belonged to a brothel in Broad Street, St Giles's, before becoming the mistress of John "Sixteen String Jack" Rann, a notorious highwayman hanged in 1774. So deplorable was her language that whenever the Prince wanted an object of comparison in the vulgar art of swearing, he was wont to say, "He swears like Letty Lade." A skilled horsewoman, even better than her husband, she was unrivalled in the technical arts of driving, particularly a phaeton and four:

> More than one steed Letitia's empire feels,
> Who sits triumphant o'er the flying wheels;
> And, as she guides them through th' admiring throng,
> With what an air she smacks the silken thong.
>
> Graceful as John, she moderates the reins,
> And whistles sweet her diuretic strains;
> Sosostris-like[58], such charioteers as these
> May drive six harness'd princes, if they please.

Yet it was not so much her horsemanship that appealed to the Prince as her role as a procuress in pandering to the Prince's sexual desires, a role that George also played. She died in 1825.

---

[58] A reference to Madame Sosostris, a noted clairvoyante.

"The Jockey of Norfolk", the eleventh Duke, was a frequent guest at the Pavilion, driving over from Arundel Castle. Now in his late thirties and a coarse voluptuary, gross in his tastes and addicted to low pleasures, he has been described as "a vulgar, heavy, dirty mass of matter that could swill wine like a Silenus[59] and gorge beefsteaks like a buckhorse," an opinion broadly shared by Wraxall, who knew him well. "In his youth," he says, "he led a most licentious life, having frequently passed the whole night in excesses of every kind and even laid down when intoxicated, occasionally, to sleep in the streets or on a block of wood. At the Beefsteak Club, where I have dined with him, he seemed to be in his proper element. But few individuals of that society could sustain a contest with such an antagonist when the cloth was removed. In cleanliness he was negligent to so great a degree that he rarely made use of water for purposes of bodily refreshment and comfort. He even carried the neglect of his person so far that his servants were accustomed to avail themselves of his fits of intoxification for the purpose of washing him. On those occasions, being wholly insensible of all that passed about him, they stripped him as they would have done a corpse and performed on his body the necessary ablutions. Nor did he change his linen more frequently than he washed himself." One day he complained to Dudley North that he was a martyr to rheumatism and had ineffectually tried every remedy. "Pray, My Lord," said he, "did you ever try a clean shirt?". He died aged 69.

Another frequent visitor to the Pavilion was the Duc d'Orléans, a young nobleman whose private life was steeped in debauchery. Professing enlightened principles so at variance with his private character, he would in due course serve as a deputy to the Paris Convention, vote for the execution of Louis XVI, and renounce his title — but all to no avail. He was guillotined in 1793.

---

[59] A companion and tutor of the wine god Dionysus, Silenus was a notorious consumer of wine.

By comparison the Prince's other companions, Charles Morris and "Tommy" Onslow, were of relatively unblemished character. Of Morris the only fault, if fault it be, was his conviviality. For many years — till 1831 — he was bard and punchmaker to the Beefsteak Club, of which the Prince became a member in 1785. There, at evening gatherings, he was wont to sing songs of his own composition, sometimes tender, sometimes jovial, at all times clever.[60] Born of a well respected family, he was a feature of high society, remaining throughout the Prince's life one of his favourite companions. He died in 1838, aged 92, at his home in Brockham, Surrey.

Now the MP for Guildford, Onslow was a young man respected by the Prince for his skill in driving, particularly a phaeton and four. Of him many epigrams were published, for example:

> What can little Tommy do?
> Why, drive a phaeton and two!
> Can little Tommy do no more?
> Yes, drive a phaeton and four!

Soon he would play a part in the Prince's courtship of, and secret marriage to, Mrs Maria Fitzherbert. For some unknown reason he later fell out of favour with the Prince, dying aged 72 in 1827. By then he had succeeded to the Earldom.

Almost always attended by George, the Prince would begin his day innocently enough, bathing in the sea, as his physicians had recommended, in order to relieve the swollen glands in his neck. Then, as often as not, off to the assembly rooms at The Castle, where, dispensing with the parade of royalty, he would drink tea "just as other people did." Occasionally he attended or took part in sporting events. When not otherwise engaged, he dined at the Pavilion about six o'clock, sometimes going on to

---

[60] See his *Lyra Urbanica*, 2 vols (London, 1840).

the theatre or a ball, at other times — or afterwards — carousing with his cronies and, together with them, dallying with female adventurers procured for the night. Unsurprisingly, the Pavilion soon acquired a scandalous reputation.

It was only a few days after his round trip to London that the Prince was involved with George in another amusing event related by Huish. The Prince, he claims, was attracted to Brighton, not so much by its salubrity, as by the angelic figure of "a sea-nymph" whom he had encountered reclining on one of the groynes on the beach. "In this amour, however, His Royal Highness was completely the dupe. As far as personal charms extended, Charlotte Fortescue was of 'the first order of fine forms,' but as far as mental qualifications were to be considered, she was one of the most illiterate and ignorant of human beings. In artifice and intrigue she was unparalleled, and withal she knew how to throw such an air of simplicity and innocence over her actions as would have deceived even a greater adept than His Royal Highness in the real nature of her character." She soon discovered the exalted station of the person she had captivated by her charms, and on the principle that a thing is of little value if cheaply or easily obtained, she for a time frustrated every attempt of the Prince to obtain a private interview with her. She kept her residence a complete secret and for some days was neither seen nor heard of. On a sudden she would make her appearance and then, suffused in tears, speak of her approaching marriage and consequent departure from the country. Could that idea be borne by the Prince? "Heaven and earth were to be moved to avert such a direful calamity!" A regular elopement was proposed, and in order to give the affair a highly romantic air it was arranged that the dress of a footman was to be found for the angelic Charlotte and that the Prince was to have a postchaise in waiting a few miles on the London road to bear her away. "There is, however, an old adage which says that much falls between the cup and the lip, and in this instance the truth of it was fully confirmed." The hour was anxiously awaited that would bring the two together, but as the Prince was dressing for dinner, the arrival of George was announced. The Prince invited him to dine, excusing himself at the same time for the early hour in which he would be obliged to leave him as he had most important business to transact that night in London. Why, the Prince asked, was George so out of sorts?

"A hunt, a hunt, Your Royal Highness," replied George, "I am in chase of a damned fine girl, who I met with at Mrs Simpson's in Duke's Place,[61] and although I have taken private apartments for her in St Anne's East,[62] yet the hussy takes it in her head every now and then to absent herself for a few days. And I have now been given to understand that she is carrying on some intrigue with a fellow at this place. Let me but catch him and I will souse him over the head and ears in the ocean."

The Prince now enquired what kind of girl he was in pursuit of. By George's description he did not doubt that the one with whom he was to elope that very evening was the same as had cut and run from George's protection. Accordingly he began to consider how to extricate himself with the best possible grace from the dilemma in which he found himself. That he was a dupe to the artifices of a cunning, designing woman was now apparent to him, so that it would be his greatest pride and joy to outwit her. He therefore disclosed to George the whole of his intrigue. It was then decided that George should put on one of the coats in which she had been accustomed to see the Prince and take his place in the chaise. The whole affair was well managed. The Prince remained at Brighton, and George bore off the girl to London, not a little chagrined, as she was, at such an unexpected termination of her romantic adventure.

Crowded while the Prince was there, Brighton became deserted when he departed at the close of the season, as a report in February concisely described: "This is a dead time with

---

[61] A brothel in the parish of Aldgate, London.
[62] A precinct of Brighton.

us — nothing going on — not a soul in the place except a few invalids, who crawl out in the sunshine along the cliffs. The Steine looks quite forlorn ... The libraries, instead of exhibiting all the charms of fashion, are deserted except by a few sentimental maid servants and gossiping town's people who sometimes subscribe for a toasting fork or tea caddy by way of *keeping it up*. A club of three meets now and then at Ragget's[63] and plays dummy for a supper ... Those tradesmen who favour us with their company ... are mostly gone."

Fortunately, it was not long after that the Prince came back, again attended by George. Leaving town on 22 June 1785, they first called at Tunbridge Wells, from where Lord Sheffield wrote to William Eden: "The Prince of Wales passed this way and dined with Lady Betty Delmé,[64] but shocked this place by his want of curiosity. He neither saw the Well nor the Pantiles[65] ... Charles Fox also passed this way another day and dined at the same place. The Prince's comrade was George Hanger."

As a year ago, the Prince reached Brighton in the early hours of the morning, once again disappointing a crowd that had waited in vain to greet him. A few days later the press reported: "The visit of a certain gay, illustrious character at Brighton has frightened away a number of old maids who used constantly to frequent that place. The history of the gallantries of the last season, which is in constant circulation, has something in it so voluminous and tremendous to boot that the old tabbies shake in their shoes whenever His Royal Highness is mentioned." Those few individuals apart, the inhabitants in general were prepared to forgive the outrageous rowdyism and joking of the Pavilion set, given the many advantages they derived from the Prince's sojourn with them. The Prince was indeed the hero

---

[63] Raggett, the proprietor of White's Club in St James's Street, London, had opened a clubhouse on The Steine.
[64] A sister of Lord Carlisle.
[65] The fashionable promenade at Tunbridge Wells.

of Brighton and it seemed that nothing he could do would alienate its affection.

As before, the Prince would at times entertain members of high society at the Pavilion whilst there was a ready supply of prostitutes and other loose women for his and his companions' delectation there. According to a press report of 10 September, "Half the fashionable persons and about one fourth of the whores of London have visited Brighton in the course of the summer."

For George, whether he was attending the Prince or not, life was a giddy round of pleasure. Particularly in the mornings, when he was left to his own devices, he would race chariots through the village at considerable risk to himself and others or engage in many other amusements, as when, for a wager of a hundred guineas, he raced a bullock across The Steine while carrying on his back a jockey booted and spurred. "A great concourse of people were assembled to see this uncommon race," a contemporary journal noted, and to the surprise of all, George won. Another time, again on The Steine, he arranged a footrace between his servant and a Horsham carrier named Scutt, who, declining at the last moment to race, paid the forfeit of half a guinea. Determined not to disappoint the many onlookers, George induced five girls to race for a new smock, "which afforded most excellent diversion, as did another female race for a hat." The Steine was indeed the venue for a variety of events in which George was involved: donkey races, pony races, jumping in sacks, jingling matches[66], races against octogenarians run by officers ridden by officers, fencing matches, "pugilistic encounters", and so on.

In the afternoons, when the Prince's other engagements allowed, George would play cricket with him and members of the aristocracy on the Level, an open space just above The Steine.

---

[66] A game in which blindfolded players try to catch one not blindfolded who keeps jingling a bell.

George and Lord Darnley were excellent bats, Bob the postillion a first-rate wicketkeeper, whereas the Prince, an indifferent player, displayed "great condescension and affability."

It was an age of practical jokes, of which the Prince and his companions were arch practitioners. According to Thomas Creevey, the Prince, whom he never saw drunk but once, had the playful habit at dinner "of making any newcomer drunk by drinking wine with him very frequently, always recommending his strongest wines, and at last some remarkably strong old brandy which he called Diabolino." On another occasion the Prince, attended by George and another companion, accompanied to the beach the Marquis de Conflans, an old friend, who was about to embark for France. Waiting for him was a boat to convey him to a packet lying close offshore. At this point the Prince decided to make sport of his friend, who was not in the best of physical condition. He threw down a challenge to swim out to the packet with him and his companions, which the Marquis, "for the honour of France", could not refuse. "All rushed into the water breast-high until they reached the packet, which received the drenched and shivering Frenchman in a bad plight for the voyage, whilst his English friends regained the beach and saluted him with a joyous 'Bon voyage!'" On another day it happened that the Prince entered his kitchen just as Old Martha Gunn, his bathing attendant, was given a pound of butter by one of his servants, a present that the old lady hastily put in her pocket. Chancing to see this, and never averse to a practical joke, the Prince entered into conversation with her, getting the "butter-side" of her nearer and nearer to the great kitchen fire. It was a sad dilemma: the Prince kept talking and talking and the butter kept melting and melting, but the venerable lady was afraid to move! When the butter began to stream through her clothes on to the floor, the Prince, laughing heartily, took his leave.

Numberless were the escapades of this nature in which the Prince and his cronies indulged, as when Sheridan, dressed as a policeman, entered the Dowager Lady Sefton's abode and arrested her for illegally playing faro. Sir John Lade, for his part, was not averse to a humorous wager. Small in stature, he bet Lord Cholmondeley, a portly giant of a man, that he would carry him twice round The Steine on his back. A great crowd including many ladies assembled "to be spectators," as a contemporary journal put it, "of this extraordinary feat of the dwarf carrying the giant." All was ready, when Lord Cholmondeley asked Sir John why he was waiting. "Till you strip, My Lord," he replied with a twinkle in his eye. "I engaged to carry you, but not an ounce of clothing. So hurry, My Lord, make ready lest we disappoint the ladies." "Sharp practice," retorted his lordship as the crowd began to laugh, but rather than comply, he paid up.

And so life at Brighton continued on its merry way till September when the Prince, accompanied by George, departed. All was set to change, at least during the next few seasons there, for the Prince had fallen deeply and lastingly in love with Mrs Maria Fitzherbert, a wealthy widow of the Roman Catholic persuasion.

CHAPTER 12

LONDON AND
ELSEWHERE — 1785 TO 1786

Carlton House, the Prince of Wales's residence in St James's, London, had been purchased from Lord Burlington in 1725 for Frederick, the Prince's grandfather, whose widow had occupied it till her death in 1772. Demolished in 1828, it occupied a site now forming part of Waterloo Place, the Duke of York's Memorial, Carlton House Terrace, and the Athenæum and old United Service Clubs. On finding the mansion in a wretchedly dilapidated condition when he set up his establishment there in 1783, the Prince called in Henry Holland, the architect, to renovate and improve it — works which, though initially completed one year later, would continue long after. Despite the Prince's limited income of £62,000 per year[67], money was no object, and his profligacy both here and elsewhere had now caused him to fall head over ears into debt. Screened from Pall Mall by a row of columns, the mansion boasted an imposing entrance hall from where a great staircase with gilded railings led to magnificent and well lit state apartments such as the cupola room, the rose satin drawing room, and the armoury, said to be one of the finest in Europe. The Prince's private apartments were located on the ground floor and looked over gardens extending westward to Marlborough House.

By now, the autumn of 1785, George had become so insepara- ble from the Prince that he soon gained the nickname, not "the Constant Hanger", but "the Constant Hanger-on". It is well- known, says Huish, that he was the Prince's "particular

---

[67] Approximately £8,475,000 in today's money.

companion", and that many of the Prince's youthful improprieties "were ascribed by the King to the company which he kept, and particularly to the society of Sheridan and Major Hanger." Indeed, the King went so far as to exclaim, "Damn Sherry, and I must hang — hang — Hanger, for they will break my heart and ruin the hopes of my country!" Unsurprisingly, George was later to remark that "from the very moment I came into the Guards as an ensign to the day I went to the American War, and to this hour, after having served my King and country faithfully for seven long years, I never have been honoured with one word from His Majesty's lips."

It was not the public face of Carlton House — the banquets, balls, and other entertainments to which high society was invited — that infuriated the King so much as the seedy side of private life there, which the Prince was careful to keep apart. As to the latter, a magazine later observed, "Nothing could exceed the immoral, the licentious conduct of [the Prince's] table at this period, which was most gorgeously supplied and most wantonly abused. The orgies of the night in such company as there assembled should never be recorded, for the entire annals of the house for several years would be a never-ceasing history of ribald conversation, drunkenness, and debauchery." Whether it was dissolute ladies of the nobility, demi-reps, courtesans, or common prostitutes, for whom the brothels of London were ransacked, all were grist to the mill. According to Huish, "The bacchanalian orgies of Carlton House were at this time of a most extraordinary description and might be said to resemble more the interior of a Turkish seraglio than the abode of a British prince, in which it might be supposed that some respect ought to have been paid to the customary forms of decency and morality." Nor did the Prince's philandering remain in-house, for he was wont to visit, not always incognito, some of the more noted houses of ill repute, over whose portals a madam or two affixed the Prince's coat of arms as a sign that her establishment was "patronised" by him. Throughout, George took an active part.

They were not the only occasions where a like event occurred. The Prince, who was fond of seeing society in all its guises, frequently visited places where his presence was least expected, again at times incognito. One evening, accompanied by Lord Southampton, the Groom of the Stole, he entered a tavern in Gray's Inn Lane to taste its celebrated Burton Ale. After sampling it for a short while, he was discovered and the two abruptly departed in a hackney carriage for Carlton House. A few days later the publican surprised his neighbours by placing the Prince's crest over his door with the inscription "Purveyor of Burton Ale to HRH the Prince of Wales"!

George too was not averse to venturing out. Besides President of the dissolute Adam and Eve Club in Marylebone, he was, for example, President of the celebrated Beggars Club, an Augean night cellar located in St Giles's, a parish notorious for its iniquity, beggars, and vice. Here, as portrayed in the cartoon "Courtiers Carousing in a Cadgers Ken[68]". he made merry with cronies such as Sheridan and Fox, surrounded by low life who had been invited to take part. On other occasions things did go awry, as when George, Sheridan and Fox paid a visit to a well-known hostelry, the Staffordshire Arms. After sending for some sportive prostitutes and carousing with them, they discovered that their combined resources could not defray the expenses of the evening. Sheridan, who was so worse for wear that he was put to bed, found himself hostage in the morning till the debts were paid.

Courtiers Carousing in a Cadgers Ken

[68] Slang for a den of scroungers.

George's finances at this time were indeed precarious, dependent as he was on the uncertain payment of his salary. One day at Carlton House, after the bottle had been circulated for some time, his good-humoured patter came suddenly to a halt and he seemed to be wholly lost in thought. As he continued to ruminate, the Prince noted his unusual quiescence and interrupted it by enquiring the subject of his meditation. "I have been reflecting, Sir," replied George, "on the lofty independence of my present situation. I have compromised with my creditors, paid my washerwoman, and have three shillings and sixpence left for the pleasures and necessities of life." At this point he exhibited his coin of the realm on the splendid table at which he sat.

Against this background it is not altogether surprising that George should have turned to inventive ways in which to restore his shattered finances. Accordingly it transpired that during one of the convivial parties at Carlton House George designedly introduced the subject of the travelling qualities of the turkey and the goose, and he pronounced it as his opinion — though directly contrary to his real one — that the turkey would outstrip the goose. The Prince, who placed great reliance on George's judgement in such matters, backed his opinion. As there were some of the party who favoured the goose, the dispute ended in the Prince's making a match of twenty turkeys against twenty geese for a distance of ten miles, the competitors to start at four o' clock in the afternoon. The race was to be run for £500, and as George and the turkey party did not hesitate to lay two to one in favour of their birds, the Prince did the same to a considerable amount, not in the least suspecting that the whole was a deep-laid plot to extract money from his purse, for, given the natural propensity of the turkey, a win was, he believed, a certainty. The Prince took great interest in this extraordinary wager and deputed George to select twenty of the most wholesome and fine-feathered birds that could be procured. On the appointed day the Prince and his party of turkeys, and the Hon George Berkeley[69] and his party of geese, set off to decide the match. For the first three hours everything seemed to indicate that the turkeys would be the winners, being then two miles ahead of the geese, but as night came on, the turkeys began to stretch out their necks towards the branches of the trees lining the road. In vain the Prince attempted to urge them on with his pole, to which a red cloth was attached. In vain George dislodged one from its roosting place, only to see it and three or four others perch comfortably elsewhere among the branches. In vain was barley strewn upon the road, but no art, no stratagem, no compulsion could prevent them from taking to their roosting places. Meanwhile the geese came waddling on and in a short time passed the turkey party, who were all busy in the trees trying to dislodge their obstinate birds. It was found impossible to make the turkeys progress farther. The geese were declared the winners and the Prince, ever a dupe to titled gamers and sharpers, lost his wager to the tune of several thousand pounds.

And so the merriment displayed convivially at Carlton House continued, as when the Prince at table filled his glass with wine and wantonly threw it in George's face. Without being in the least disconcerted, George immediately filled his own with wine and, throwing it in the face of the companion seated next to him, bid him pass it around — an admirable instance of his presence of mind.

Despite being equerry to the Prince, George like Fox did not hold the rest of the royal family in high regard. At this time it was common in parliamentary debates to refer to "the majesty of the people", and this phrase came into George's mind as he and a friend, a Whig MP, were walking along a London street on May Day 1785. There they met a company of chimneysweeps who according to ancient custom were dancing around in robes

---

[69] He was the younger son of the 4th Earl of Berkeley.

of gilt paper while crowned with artificial flowers. Leaning on his friend, George quipped, "Ah! I have often heard speak of the majesty of the people, but I have never had the pleasure before of seeing the majesty of the young princes."

Another day, when rain was bucketing down, George was again walking along a London street with a male companion. Encountering two ladies with whom he was acquainted, he doffed, not his own hat, but that of his companion!

The carousing at Carlton House came to an abrupt end — at least for the time being — on 15 December 1785 when the Prince entered into a secret morganatic marriage with Mrs Maria Fitzherbert and began to taste the pleasures of tranquil wedded domesticity. In his early devotion to her, states Wilkins, "he showed a constancy, a firmness, and a persistency worthy of all praise, and not at all in keeping with the fickle character generally attributed to him. There is no doubt that his love for her was deep and genuine, and that it was the great passion of his life. She was in truth the only woman whom he ever really loved."

That Mrs Fitzherbert was a Roman Catholic constituted an almost insuperable obstacle to the avowal of the marriage. Apart from the Royal Marriage Act 1772, which required that the King's consent be obtained, there was more importantly the Bill of Rights 1689, which declared that "all and every person and persons that is, are, or shall be reconciled to, or shall hold communion with, the See or Church of Rome, or shall profess the Popish religion, *or shall marry a Papist*, shall be excluded and be for ever incapable to inherit, possess, or enjoy the Crown and Government of this realm, and Ireland, and the dominions thereunto belonging, or any part of the same, or to have, use, or exercise any regal power, authority, or jurisdiction within the same."

So secrecy was essential, but almost inevitably rumours began to circulate and eventually gain ground that a marriage had indeed taken place. At last there appeared a series of caricatures proclaiming the wedding, in most of which, as set out below, George is mistakenly included, although he played no part in the arrangements and was not present at the ceremony:

13 March 1786: "The Follies of a Day, or the Marriage of Figaro", in which the Prince is putting a ring on Mrs Fitzherbert's finger, a sham parson — Weltje — is officiating, and George is a witness.

21 March 1786: "Wedding Night, or the Fashionable Frolic", in which the Prince and Mrs Fitzherbert are dancing, George is playing the "Black Joke" on a fiddle, and a torn up marriage certificate lies on the floor.

21 March 1786: "The Lovers' Leap", in which the Prince and Mrs Fitzherbert are preparing to jump over a broom lying on the floor between them — a supposed feature of gypsies' marriage ceremonies, George is pushing the Prince on, and a cat is jumping out of a bag.

27 March 1786: "Wife or no Wife, or A Trip to the Continent", in which the Prince is about to put a ring on Mrs Fitzherbert's finger, Fox is giving her away, George and Sheridan are witnesses, Edmund Burke — another of the Prince's companions — is officiating as a Jesuit priest, and Lord North, dressed as a coachman, is fast asleep.

1 May 1786: "The April Fool, or the Follies of a Night, as performed at the Theatre Royal, C[arlto]n House, for the Benefit of the Widow Wadman", in which the Prince, Mrs Fitzherbert, and George are dancing; Fox, drumming with a pistol on a warming-pan, exclaims, "Damme, but 'tis sublime;" and Burke, playing on a gridiron with a pair of tongs, says, "Burn the pan, is it not beautiful?" On the walls are two scenes from *Hamlet,* one where Polonius says to the King, "I will be brief, your noble son is mad," and on the ground lie two plays, Susanna Centlivre's *A Bold Stroke for a Wife* and George Colman and David Garrick's *The Clandestine Marriage.*

3 May 1786: "The Introduction of F[itzherbert] to St James's", in which there is a view of St James's Palace; the Prince is carrying

Mrs Fitzherbert on his shoulders; he is preceded by George beating a drum, and by Fox and Captain Morris playing a trumpet and a horn; and Burke brings up the rear playing on a flageolet.

Like George, none of the other persons portrayed, apart of course from the bride and groom, attended the marriage ceremony or were involved in the arrangements for it.

The FOLLIES of a DAY or the MARRIAGE of FIGARO.

WEDDING NIGHT or the FASHONABLE FROLIC.

THE 'LOVER's LEAP.

WIFE & no WIFE ____ or ____ A trip to the Continent.

THE APRIL FOOL or the FOLLIES of a NIGHT.
As performed at the Theatre Royal, C——n House, for the Benefit of the Widow Wadman.
Published 1st April 1786, by S. W. Fores at the Caricature Warehouse, No 3, Piccadilly.

THE INTRODUCTION OF F____ TO Sᵗ. JAMES'S.

As a result of the marriage George became freer to attend to his own affairs, gaining employment as the East India Company's recruiting officer for its army in India. "There was," George explains, "no salary attached to the employment. The more active my services were in behalf of the Hon Company, the

168

greater were my profits. I brought this business to such perfection that I never, any year after the first, made less than £600 profit. During the first year I intrinsically lost £500, which was expended to set this great machine going. After having once wound up this recruiting dial, it wanted but little regulating, which my subsequent successes and regularity proved." His communications were extended so wide and general that "there was not a town in England of consequence in which I had not established a regular rendezvous." On the odd occasion George was accompanied by the Prince, who mischievously, for the sake of seeing a scramble, threw money in great quantities to the assembled mobs.

A sportsman in the wider sense, George embraced his new-found freedom by becoming a patron of the noble art, at times in association with Tarleton, and was not averse to taking part in prize-fights himself, having been trained by Sam Martin of Bath, a first-rate pugilist. One of many spectators, Henry Angelo attended a contest at Banbury, where "Colonel Tarleton was conspicuous there on stage, as was Colonel Hanger," whilst William Windham watched another at Croydon that "was in consequence of a purse collected by subscription under the direction of Hervey Aston, George Hanger, etc." Among all classes of society, be they commoners, gentry or nobility, prize-fighting was then the rage.

With a reputation as a "bruiser" George was not one to be crossed, but once at Newmarket he did come a cropper. In the coffee-room there, which he was wont to frequent, as ever with his shillelagh, he came to blows with Tom Bullock, whose father James had once been a Whig MP. George was worsted, but his opponent had the modesty to arrogate no merit to himself, claiming to have been educated in the noble art at a better school under a more scientific master[70].

---

[70] Thomas Johnson.

Like George, the Prince, who was adept with his fists, took a keen interest in prize-fighting. All changed on 6 August 1786 when he witnessed the death of a prize-fighter in a contest at Brighton racecourse. The Prince then declared that he would never again attend another and settled an annuity on the widow and her family.

George had now a wider opportunity to enjoy the sports of the field and took himself yearly to The Hoo, the estate of his old friend Thomas Brand, a former Whig MP, near Kimpton, Hertfordshire, "where I generally used to shoot the first week in September and thence proceed to Suffolk and Norfolk." There, as often as not, he would lodge at a hostelry in Thetford, where welcoming farmers would invite him "to come and sport on their grounds, saying, 'Go you and shoot on my farm, and on my neighbour's farm, who dines with us today, and if anyone asks what right you have to shoot there, tell them you have [our] leave.'" At other times George would be invited to stay and shoot with other nearby friends, for example Thomas Coke of Holkham Hall, a 30,000-acre estate in north Norfolk. A former Whig MP who had become one of "Fox's martyrs" in 1784, Coke would be raised to the Earldom of Leicester in later life.

At the close of the season George would return to London to enjoy the myriad pleasures there, among which was his consorting as ever with prostitutes, whether, for example, he picked them up on the street or in the theatre — events portrayed in two contemporary prints, "Street Walkers" and "Box Office Loungers". Otherwise he now had few royal duties to perform, the most important of which was to manage the Prince's racing stable at Newmarket in conjunction with Sir John Lade. They were remarkably successful. Between 1784 and 1792 the Prince's horses won 185 races, including the Derby in 1788, and his total winnings came to 32,688 guineas.[71]

---

[71] Approximately £4,750,000 in today's money.

STREET WALKERS

Publish'd April 28 1786 by B Smith N°10 Pleasant Row Battle Bridge

28 ap. 1786

171

BOX LOBBY LOUNGERS

Meanwhile, under the influence of Mrs Fitzherbert, the Prince drank less, gambled not at all, gave up brothels and clubs, moderated his language, was less wild in his conduct, and seemed in every way determined to lead a new life. At Carlton House Mrs Fitzherbert was the presiding divinity and played hostess at all parties to which ladies were invited. She accompanied the Prince to every entertainment or assembly that he attended and was received, if not with the formal homage accorded to a Princess of Wales, then with a delicate deference due to her unique position. All in all, the Prince had become quite a reformed character.

Yet despite his reformation the Prince remained in dire financial straits, having amassed debits of some £300,000 in total.[72] Harassed by his creditors and unable to obtain relief from the King and Parliament, he decided on 9 July 1786 to

---

[72] Approximately £43,250,000 in today's money.

adopt a programme of severe retrenchment, curtailing his household, halting all renovation work at Carlton House, selling off his race and carriage horses, and economising in other ways. Two days later, accompanied by George, he came down to Brighton.

CHAPTER 13

BRIGHTON — THE LATER YEARS

Having put his carriage horses up for sale, the Prince was reduced to travelling to Brighton by less commodious means. On 13 July the *Morning Post* gleefully reported, "A morning paper of yesterday says that the Prince of Wales set off for Brighton in a *hired chaise and hack horses*, but we are informed by authority, which we trust will meet with equal credit, that His Royal Highness was an *outdoor passenger* by the *Brighton Dilly*[73]." Quickly the satirists followed, not failing to include George in their prints:

15 July 1786: "A Trip to Brighton, or the P[rince] and his reduced Household returning for the summer season", in which the Prince and Mrs Fitzherbert are leaving London in a hired carriage; she is studying "The Principles of Economy"; the carriage is piled high with furniture, vegetables, meat, small beer, and raisin wine; Weltje is driving; and one of the footmen is Fox, the other George, who is reading "For Sale at Tattersall's, the Prince's Stud". In fact Mrs Fitzherbert did not accompany the Prince but followed a fortnight later.

Undated but contemporaneous: "The Brighton Stud", in which a groom leads three donkeys — George, Fox, and Sheridan; the Prince rides another — Mrs Fitzherbert; and Lord Derby — as another — looks on. Evidently the print had in view the projected sale of the Prince's racing stable.

Undated but contemporaneous: "A Scene in the School for Scandal", in which the break-up of the Prince's establishment is

---

[73] Slang for a stagecoach, from the French *carrosse de diligence*.

marked by parodying a scene from Sheridan's play where Charles Surface helps to knock down the portraits of his ancestors. George as Careless is the auctioneer, and while offering Lot 1 — a portrait of the King and Queen ("Farmer George and His Wife"), he cries out, "Going for no more than one Crown!" to whom the Prince as Charles Surface encouragingly remarks, "Careless, knock down the Farmer." One of the audience bids five shillings for the lot. A portrait of Mrs Fitzherbert is Lot 2, and Lot 3 is one of Mary "Perdita" Robinson, an old flame of the Prince's. Through the open door may be seen Tattersall's, where the Prince's racing stable was sold. To the extravagance of maintaining it a carriage numbered Lot 1,000 alludes.

Later in the season an equally amusing print appeared. Dated 23 August 1786, it is entitled "The Jovial Crew, or Merry Beggars. A Comic Opera, as performed at Brighton by the Carleton Company". The Prince and Mrs Fitzherbert form the centre. He has a hat full of money: "£7,586. By sale of the Stud", whereas she carries a child on her back. On either side of them, mostly on crutches, are the rest of the beggars, including George. A set of verses is appended:

First Beggar, Mr S[heridan]
    I was once a poet at London,
    I kept my heart still full of glee;
    There's no man can say I'm undone,
    For begging's no new trade to me.

Second Beggar, [The Prince of Wales]
    In London I once shone with *éclat,*
    A stud and brave household could boast;
    Give me a brisk wench in clean straw,
    And I value not who rules the roast.

Third Beggar, Mrs F[itzherbert]
    A widow I was, buxom and bold,
    So closed with a royal attack;
    Though 'tis said the marriage won't hold,
    But, ecod, I'll stick to his back.

Fourth Beggar, Mr F[ox]
    Here comes a patriot polite, sir,
    Who flattered the K[ing] to his face;
    Now railing is all his delight, sir,
    Because he's turned out of his place.

Fifth Beggar, Mr B[urke]
    I was a jesuitical preacher,
    I turned up my eyes when I pray'd;
    But my hearers half starved their teacher,
    For they believed not a word that I said.

Sixth Beggar, Captain M[orris]
    I still am a merry song-maker,
    My heart never yet felt a qualm;
    Though poor, I can fiddle and caper,
    And sing any tune but a psalm.

Seventh Beggar, Colonel H[anger]
    Make room for a soldier in buff,
    Who valiantly strutted about;
    And if the peace should be broken off,
    Why then he'll most wisely sell out.

Eighth Beggar, Mr W[eltje]
    De beggar vos I in Germany,
    But alms vos here better agree;
    For by begging in goot company,
    Begging vos de making of me.

Ninth Beggar, Lord N[orth]
    Since, beggars then, we are happy and free,
    Pray talk no more of state axes;
    For by the war you'll surely agree,
    That all I have beggared with taxes.

A TRIP TO BRIGHTON,
OR THE P— AND HIS REDUCED HOUSEHOLD RETIRING FOR THE SUMMER SEASON.

THE BRIGHTON STUD

A SCENE in the SCHOOL for SCANDAL

THE JOVIAL CREW OR MERRY BEGGARS.
A COMIC OPERA AS PERFORMED AT BRIGHTON BY THE CARLETON COMPANY.

The Prince and Mrs Fitzherbert spent the season of 1786 very quietly, as they did those of 1787 and 1788, but to avoid scandal she rented a separate house on the west side of Castle Square.

Apart from bathing each morning in the sea, the Prince usually stayed in his private apartments at the Pavilion till three o'clock, transacting such business as he personally had to attend to, and then would ride for an hour before dismounting at Mrs Fitzherbert's. Every evening he held a small dinner party at the Pavilion, the covers averaging sixteen. Served as usual at six o'clock, dinner was always accompanied by a band playing horns and other noisy instruments, which to the majority of the illustrious guests seemed a maddening imposition, though the host delighted in it and often joined in, beating time on the dinner-gong. Unless the Prince took his party to the theatre or to a ball at The Castle or The Old Ship, other guests were invited for the evening. Mrs Fitzherbert, a great card-player, who was always present, immediately after dinner made up her table and remained there until the company departed. The Prince, who had forsaken gaming, never touched a card. He talked to his guests and listened to the music till twelve o'clock, when, as a rule, the band stopped, wine and other refreshments were handed round, and shortly after, the guests were dismissed.

Occasionally the Prince and Mrs Fitzherbert would spend their afternoons driving out in a phaeton and four. At other times they would promenade on The Steine. Now and then the Prince went shooting.

Among the highlights of the season were Brighton Races in the first week of August and the race balls at the two coaching inns — events which the Prince and Mrs Fitzherbert, splendidly attired as ever, did not fail to attend. Later the same month the races at Lewes were graced with their presence. Always conspicuously celebrated — and by the whole village — was the Prince's birthday on 12 August. Church bells were rung; festive sports were held; sailing matches took place; an ox was roasted on The Steine and distributed to the populace, together with a plentiful supply of ale; there were fireworks and illuminations; and the Prince and Mrs Fitzherbert would attend a ball and supper at The Castle, where they were cheered to the echo.

As a consequence of the Prince's reformed lifestyle George was no longer needed to pander to his master's roistering and licentiousness, which were for now quiescent, though he did continue to fulfil the mundane duties of an aide. In doing so, he did, for example, cross the path of Mrs Phillippina Burton Hill, an actress of some repute who had come down from London hopefully to perform for the Prince and Mrs Fitzherbert, with whom she had corresponded. One evening, she recalls, she went to the playhouse, "where the Hon George Hanger joined me, paid me many compliments — a repetition of what he had said some years ago, [but] they never produced the desired effect ... He entreated permission to call on me after the play. I positively refused it," with no doubt George's reputation in mind. Soon after, on Monday evening, 27 September 1786, "I heard a double knock at my door. I was indisposed in bed with lowness of spirits. My servant looked from the window and asked who was there, when a gentleman answered in these ominous terms, 'It is neither a thief or robber but Mr Hanger come with a message to Mrs Hill from His Royal Highness the Prince of Wales or from Mrs Fitzherbert.' I desired her to say I could not see him, concluding within myself that it was only to get admittance and not wanting to see him. She ran downstairs, said 'twas from the Prince or Mrs Fitzherbert, and he was in the apartment in a minute — behaved with such politeness, courtesy, and respect that I forgot his former solicitation and beheld him not as a foe. He expressed great concern for my indisposition, hoped I should soon recover, etc, etc, then thus began with suppliant mien and flatteries, 'I come, Mrs Hill, with Mrs Fitzherbert's compliments. She desired me to say in answer to your letter, which indeed I saw, that all her interest, in whatever you undertake, should be exerted to promote it, but that she could not point out what was proper for you to do.

180

This is her message. Next, His Royal Highness, with whom I have been shooting this morning, and we were talking about you. He sent his compliments and said that he should be glad to assist you and that whatever you undertake, his patronage should sanction it.' What could be more pleasing to a drooping mind than this high honour? I was transported with sudden joy [and] begged him to say that my gratitude was too great for expression."

At this point George, joker that he was, could not help himself and suggested an answer to the part that she might play, one that could not fail, as she well knew, to cast her in a ridiculous light. "Mr Hanger," she goes on, " after making an apology for what he was going to propose," put forward "the mighty part" of Scrub, a breeches part[74] in George Farquhar's *The Beaux' Stratagem*. "Had a poisoned arrow shot through my heart, I could not have felt a pang more dreadful!" Nevertheless, she consented. "He caught me at my word [and] said he would let the Prince know that I would do it. He was going from me to Mrs Fitzherbert."

Five days later she performed the part at the theatre. "There was a most brilliant audience and such applause that 'twas said no person ever received in that character, the immortal Garrick only excepted, not that I think it any feather of adornment to have shown in so ridiculous a point of view. Still, I should be ungrateful in the extreme if I did not acknowledge myself sensible of the high honour conferred on me by the great and condescending applause which His Royal Highness gave, and all the nobility and gentry — but there was a little hissing from two persons, which a gentleman took pains to find out, one of whom proved to be an intimate of the Hon Major [Hanger]."

---

[74] A part that is regularly or frequently played by an actress in male costume.

Sadly, the event left Mrs Hill out of pocket. Besieged by her creditors, she repeatedly wrote to the Prince for aid till he threatened to prosecute her. She then left Brighton but, returning in 1787, attempted to perform a work of hers at The Castle's assembly rooms, only to be hooted off stage by her *bête noir*, George, and his "female troop".

When the Prince and Mrs Fitzherbert came down to Brighton in early July 1787, as ever accompanied by George, the works to the Pavilion had just been completed under the superintendence of Henry Holland. The front to The Steine now extended about 160 feet and was surmounted by a cupola atop a circular room. On either side a wing had been added, forming with the centre a square court in which there was a handsome dial supported by a finely sculptured figure. Between the court and The Steine a lawn had been laid out. The ground floor of one wing comprised a drawing room, and that of the other a dining room. The second floor of each contained bedchambers. From almost every window the sea was visible. Fitted up in the French style was a library, and there was an extensive billiard room that comprised not only billiard but also hazard and money tables. The entrance from the anteroom to the staircase was spacious and grand, a striking feature being four pillars in Scagliola marble by Richter. To the rear, facing East Street, were the offices, kitchen and stables, together with Weltje's house.

Yet, despite the care lavished on the renovation, all was not well. According to Anthony Pasquin, the dining room "may be compared to a sort of oven. When the fire is lighted, the inmates are nearly baked and encrusted." So, while dining there one day, Sheridan asked of George, "How do you feel yourself, Hanger?"

"Hot, hot, hot as hell," replied George.

"It is quite right," quipped Sheridan, "that we should be prepared in this world for that which we know will be our lot in another."

182

Again, the Prince's sojourn passed very quietly, the highlight of which was his reunion with Frederick, the Duke of York, who, returning from exile in Germany, came down to stay. On the new lawn they would often play cricket, in which George and at times Tarleton, an occasional visitor, took part.

Although the following season was passed no differently, it saw the first appearance of Richard Barry, the 7th Earl of Barrymore, who was destined to become another of the Prince's convivial companions. A shooting star whose life would soon be extinguished, he was aged but eighteen.

By the season of 1789 a further sea change had occurred in the Prince's behaviour. So disappointed was he at the King's recovery from madness, which had dashed his expectation of a Regency, that he had regressed into a life of carousing and licentiousness, relying on George and others to pander again to his pleasures. In vain did Mrs Fitzherbert plead for moderation as the Prince's amours with titled ladies ensued, but at length she came to adopt a course of philosophic toleration, ever mindful that, as Sheridan put it, "The Prince is too much every lady's man to be the man of any lady."

As the Prince strove at Brighton to forget his disappointment, he let himself go, thinking of nothing but pleasure from morning till night — and pleasure of the most reckless kind. Surrounding him were the wildest of his companions, none of whom surpassed Lord Barrymore, who had now joined the Prince's coterie. According to Henry Angelo, who knew him well, "His Lordship alternated between a gentleman and a blackguard. The refined wit and the most vulgar bully, he was equally well-known in St Giles's's or St James's. He could fence, dance, drive, or drink, box or bet, with any man in the kingdom. He could discourse slang as trippingly as French, relish porter after port, and compliment her ladyship at a ball with as much ease and brilliance as he could bespatter blood in a cider cellar." A keen practical joker whose escapades were legendary, he did, for example, place a shrouded dummy in a coffin one dark Brighton night and, aided by his brother Henry, stood it on end before the door of a house. Ringing the bell, the pair retired to a safe distance to watch the fun. A maid came to the door, saw in the dim light what she took to be a ghost, shrieked, and fainted. Her cry summoned the other occupants, who began to shout for help. In the confusion the brothers seized the coffin and ran off, leaving the victims to the derision of their neighbours, who had hastened by. On a second occasion the joke misfired. A live shrouded footman took the place of the dummy but was fired on by the master of the house. The discharge from a blunderbuss missed his head by no more than one inch. Wisely, he fled for dear life. Another escapade is perhaps best related by Lord Lennox:

Not only respect but a sort of homage was paid the Prince and Mrs Fitzherbert whenever they appeared together in public. At Brighton they were the lions of the place and the common theme of conversation in public circles. Their privacy, however, was held sacred by even the most privileged of their circle of intimates. Nevertheless, it did once or twice happen that one of those daring spirits who hang loose upon society chose to invade it. A story went the round of the clubs of an incident of this nature that we have not seen in print:-

One evening the Prince of Wales was enjoying his *otium cum dignitate* with his temporary *cara sposa*, when his ears were suddenly startled by the sounds of a guitar under the window.

"Who the deuce can that be?" he enquired sharply.

"Only some poor *émigré*," replied the lady.

The music continued and presently a male voice commenced a French *chanson* of an amorous nature, pretty well-known on both sides the Channel.

"Confound his impudence!" cried His Royal Highness.

The lady laughed with her habitual good nature. Twang! twang! continued the instrument, and the refrain was repeated over and over again.

"Chère amie! chère amie!"

The Prince looked annoyed, though his fair companion did not and said all she could to make him regard the thing as a joke. He was curious to know the audacious serenader but did not like to present himself at the window.

Twang! twang! continued the guitar.

"Chère amie! chère amie!" repeated the voice with increased fervour.

The singer was a young man apparently but his features were concealed by a large wide-brimmed hat, and his figure by the folds of an ample roquelaire[75]. As he kept his eyes directed towards the window above him, there could be no mistake as to the object of his gallantry.

Twang! twang! went the accompaniment for the twentieth time. *"Chère amie! chère amie!"* added the voice.

The window above cautiously opened and a head enveloped in an unquestionably feminine cap, with the upper part of the body to which it belonged wrapped in a white dressing gown, appeared holding a letter in the left hand. The back being to the light, the figure could be but imperfectly seen from the dark street, but the *billet-doux* was clearly discernible, and immediately it was shown, the serenader sprang eagerly forward and placed himself close under the window to receive it.

"Chère amie!" murmured a soft voice from above.

"Here, adorable creature!" replied the serenader passionately, stretching out his arms to receive the *billet*.

---

[75] A knee-length cloak.

"Share that!" added more masculine tones, and on the head of the serenader descended the contents of a large water-jug. The sudden movement disarranged the headdress, and a formidable pair of whiskers became visible. A burst of loud laughter, as the window descended, added to the discomfiture of the too daring gallant. But worse than all were the congratulations of certain of his intimate friends who from a distance had been watching the experiment.

Next day the story was known all over Brighton. The cavalier who had met with so cool a reception proved to be Lord Barrymore, who, for once in his life at least, received a fitting reward for his indiscretion.

As a result of his rakehelly behaviour Barrymore gained the nickname "Hellgate"; the Hon Henry Barry "Cripplegate" on account of his club foot; the Hon Augustus Barry, who was a clergyman, "Newgate" because, it was said, he had been imprisoned in every jail except there; and Lady Caroline Barry "Billingsgate" due to her foul language. All were regular visitors to the Pavilion, the brothers being satirised in Gillray's *Les Trois Magots* ("The Three Scamps").

Not to be outdone, Henry too was a practical joker. He rode, for example, a horse up the stairs of Mrs Fitzherbert's house to the topmost room but, unable to get it down, had at last to call in two blacksmiths to do the job, rewarding them with a bowl of punch at The Castle.

George became involved with Barrymore in events on The Steine. Ill mounted, they would, for instance, take part in pony races, which were, says Wallace, "more entertaining as a display of whim and drollery than of horsemanship and speed." A still more whimsical sport they organised, not simply for amusement but for large bets — the racing of country girls for smocks. As these "Sussex Atlantas" were not trained for the course and fell down frequently, each patron was allowed to assist his favourite to her legs. George, the Prince and Barrymore were seen running to help their fallen racers, "greatly to the amusement of the multitude."

Having married a niece of Letty Lade, Barrymore met his end in 1793 when, as an officer in the militia, he was in charge of escorting French prisoners to Dover. While he was seated in his coach, a gun accidentally went off and shot him in the head.

As in earlier days, the Lades were frequent guests at the Pavilion, as was the Jockey of Norfolk, now satirised in a print by Gillray, "*Le Cochon et ses deux petites*".

Le Cochon et ses deux petits __ or __ Rich pickings for a Noble appetite. vide. Smith...Topps Bar. No. No. 99.

Joining them was that old roué the Duke of Queensberry, of whom it was written:

And there, insatiate yet with folly's sport,
That polished, sin-worn fragment of the Court,
The shade of Queensb'ry should with Clermont meet
Ogling and hobbling down St James's Street.

Absent from 1794 was Mrs Fitzherbert, with whom the Prince had broken in a dastardly way. The same year George's sojourns in Brighton ended.

CHAPTER 14

LONDON AND ELSEWHERE —
1787 TO SPRING 1795

George left Brighton for London in September 1786. Little did he know that he would remain in the Prince's service for less than nine more years, as ever a convivial companion fulfilling whatever duties came his way. Aside from those of an unsavoury nature, he would, for example, attend the Prince on royal visits and be with him when he chose to stay at a country estate.

It was on a royal visit that George again came something of a cropper. As *The Times* reported on 24 January 1788, "Major Hanger, on his late tour to Plymouth with the Prince of Wales, met with an accident which might have produced very disagreeable consequences. In walking before His Royal Highness, a portly fishwife, whom he had pushed aside rather disrespectfully, gave the Major a fisticuff which, unluckily for his situation, knocked him into a kennel to the no small entertainment of the Prince and his party, who laughed most heartily at the dismal distress of the Major." A cartoon of the rencounter — "The Battle Royal between the Prig Major and Big Bess" — was published.

The Battle Royal between the Prig Major and Big Bess

On a royal visit to Yorkshire in late autumn 1789, where George was again present, another accident took place, this time involving the Prince. Having attended York races and received the Freedom of the City, he was lavishly entertained at Wentworth House, the seat of Earl Fitzwilliam, a prominent Whig who was one of the richest men in England. While returning to London, the Prince had reached some two miles north of Newark when the axle of his coach was struck by a cart crossing the road. The coach overturned and fell a considerable way down an adjoining slope, being shivered to pieces. Fortunately, he escaped with only a sprained wrist and a slight contusion to the shoulder.

When not at Brighton, the Prince was often out of town at places in the country, where, always accompanied by George, he lived the life of a country gentleman, giving himself up completely to sporting pursuits. Of the estates most frequented by him, the most pleasurable one was Kempshott Park near Basingstoke, Hampshire. There he would shoot, but his chief occupation was hunting, for which, it was said, he possessed the finest set of foxhounds and the most splendid stable of hunters in the county. Hampshire was indeed his favourite choice for hunting, though he did not always resort to Kempshott, staying, for example, at The Grange near Alton, the seat of Lord Ashburton. Among other estates to which he was invited were the Duke of Gloucester's at Bagshot Park near Windsor and Lord North's at Bushey Park, Middlesex. Christmases too he would spend out of town, for instance at Hinchinbroke, the seat of that *bon vivant* the Earl of Sandwich.

By 1788 the King and Parliament had relieved the Prince of his debts, augmented his income by £10,000 per year,[76] and set aside £20,000 for works to Carlton House — a settlement ending his nine long months of relative poverty and severe retrenchment, during which the satirists had had a field day. Typical are the following two prints, one of which includes George, who as ever is distinguishable by his large nose, supplemented at other times by his conspicuous shillelagh:

18 January 1787: "The Prodigal Son", in which the Prince is seated on bare earth feeding swine; his coat is out at the elbows and his breeches unfastened; his garter is gone; and on the ground lie three feathers, the symbol of his princedom.

26 February 1787: "Love's Last Shift", in which the Prince and Mrs Fitzherbert are portrayed in the last stage of poverty; he sits before a fire, turning a sheep's head, and rocks a cradle in which a sleeping child lies; he wears no breeches as Mrs Fitzherbert is mending them; Weltje has just brought in some potatoes; and George has in hand a small measure of beer.

---

[76] Approximately £1,385,000 in today's money.

The PRODIGAL SON. P.of. Wales
Kingsbury
18 Jan. 1787

LOVE'S Last SHIFT.

It was during the 1780s that George began to go into print. Described over the years as semi-literate by writers who should have known better, he was tolerably well read and would in later life become something of a bookworm. His first offering was "An Ode to Bacchus", published in *The Times* on 27 July 1787, the opening lines of which dedicate to the Prince the recently completed Pavilion in Brighton:

> Illustrious son of Jove and Semele,
> Who once lay snug on high,
> Within the muscles of your father's thigh,
> To thee we dedicate this pile,
> Built for the royal tenant of your isle,
> Who must one day,
> When Death shall call his powers into play,
> Embrace his subjects as a monstrous family:
> Oh! guard this consecrated haunt
> From prostitution vile, and bailiff dire;
> The means to celebrate thy glory grant;
> Oh! give us fuel to support the fire.
> Thus prim'd and loaded, boldly we'll advance,
> And follow Pleasure in the mazy dance,
> With jocund step we'll nimbly trip,
> As the high-mettled tribe,
> The grape's celestial joys imbibe,
> And press the goblet to the parched lip.

Of two later lines below Anthony Pasquin suggests an explanation:

> Guard us, blithe deity, whene'er we sleep,
> Oh, lead us from the dangers of the deep.

"The Major," he says, "is supposed to allude to his providential escape in the summer of 1787 from the fangs of a shark on the coast of Brighton, which seized him by the glutei while he was bathing with the Prince."

About the same time as the Ode George is reputed to have written the lyrics for the ballad "Kitty of Coleraine":

As beautiful Kitty one morning was tripping,
With a pitcher of milk from the fair of Coleraine,
When she saw him she stumbled, the pitcher it tumbled,
And all the sweet buttermilk watered the plain.
Oh! What shall I do now, 'twas looking at you now,
Sure, sure, such a pitcher I'll ne'er meet again.
'Twas the pride of my dairy, Oh, Barney McCleary,
You're sent as a plague on the girls of Coleraine.

He sat down beside her and gently did chide her,
That such a misfortune should give her such pain.
A kiss then he gave her, and before he did leave her,
She vowed for such pleasure she'd break it again.
'Twas haymaking season, I can't tell the reason,
Misfortune will never come single 'tis plain,
For very soon after poor Kitty's disaster,
The divil a pitcher was whole in Coleraine.

Two years later George published his *Address to the Army*, a work which rebuts criticism of Tarleton's *A History of the Campaigns of 1780 and 1781 in the Southern Provinces of North America*. One of the relatively few works by a British participant, George's provides a wealth of first-hand information interspersed with a critique of British strategy and tactics that has stood the test of time. Historians — including myself[77] — rely on it to this day.

It was about this time that George had a well publicised encounter with a highwayman west of London, an event to which he returns in his memoirs. Bemoaning the fact that in general civil highwaymen were no longer to be met, he goes on,

---

[77] See, for example, Ian Saberton, "Was the American Revolutionary War in the south winnable by the British?" in his *The American Revolutionary War in the south: A Re-evaluation from a British perspective in the light of The Cornwallis Papers* (Grosvenor House Publishing, 2018).

"Especially in these days I am sorry to say that they seem to be bent as much on murder as to relieve their wants. I myself did not experience a few years past any marks of civilities from one of these gentlemen who stopped my chaise near Gunesbury Lane, for he fired directly in my face and his pistol was not three feet from my head. But I do not complain, for I confess I was not over ceremonious with him, as luckily I fired first and hit him, which I have reason to suppose rather deranged him and prevented his taking any effectual aim at me."

Politically, the 1780s gave rise to two events in particular that affected George: one, in which he was directly involved, was a relatively minor affair — the Westminster by-election of 1788; the other, which affected not only him but the entire country, was the cataclysm of the French Revolution one year later, which in its aftermath would lead to war with France and the disintegration of the Whig Party.

The Westminster by-election was brought on by Lord Hood resigning his seat when appointed by Pitt to the Admiralty Board. Standing now as the Tory candidate for re-election, he was opposed by Lord John Townshend, the Whig candidate, who was a personal friend of Fox. The poll was held in July and, as on earlier occasions, was characterised by drunkenness, tumult, widespread disorder, loss of life, and corrupt practices. Working again out of the Shakespeare Tavern, George reverted to his role of largely managing the Whig campaign on the streets, but this time more proactively.

Canvassing, for example, was conducted with greater vigour and sometimes led to violence, as when Charles Simpson's home was entered — a visit that ended with words and then blows being exchanged. A few days later a print based on the event appeared: "Canvassing Macaroni and True British Elector", in which an elector is threatened by Townshend's bludgeon-bearing canvassers, among whom George, Fox, and Burke are clearly identifiable. Part of the print comprises the following threatening lines:

> Your Vote and Interest for my Friend I earnestly solicit.
> By me his Compliments he sends, and begs I be explicit.
> If you to vote for him agree, no Harm to you shall come, Sir;
> But if you don't. take care! Gad's me! Our men will make you run, Sir!

Aping the Tories in the 1784 election, George began employing ruffians at the hustings to intimidate those minded to vote for Hood. Sir George Young, who was there, records vividly what went on: "On the hustings were posted a set of young men neatly dressed in buff and blue for the occasion:[78] blacklegs from all the race courses and all the faro and E-O tables in town.[79] Their business was to affront every gentleman who came on the hustings without their livery. 'You lie!' 'Who are you? Damn you!' and a variety of such terms echoed in every quarter. Something of the sort soon tingled in my ears."

As to the Tories, they adopted at the hustings the ploy of challenging prospective voters of the Whig persuasion no matter what their station or celebrity, as Burke found out to his cost. George recalled the event some years later: "When the numbers for Lord John Townshend began to increase rapidly on the poll, the adverse party, to delay our polling so many in the day, substituted a device to delay our exertions and to lessen the numbers on the poll book, and insisted that every man who came to vote should take the test oath[80]. The celebrated Edmund Burke of pensioned memory came before the hustings to give his vote, accompanied with Peter Delmé Esquire, when the poll clerk for the opposite party informed Mr Burke that he had

---

[78] The party colours of the Whigs.

[79] Even-Odd was a game with a wheel and a ball just like roulette but instead of numbers there were just 20 sections marked E for Even and 20 marked O for Odd. Instead of zero, a portion of the sections was allocated for the house.

[80] Administered under the Test Act 1678, the oath in effect affirmed that the subscriber was not of the Roman Catholic persuasion.

positive orders not to permit any person's name whatever to be entered on the books unless they had taken the test oath. Mr Burke began to expatiate with him on the subject, presuming that, as he was a Member of Parliament, he would not insist on his taking the test oath. But the clerk was positive and Mr Delmé, though he also was in Parliament, took the test oath and accordingly gave his vote. But when the clerk offered Mr Burke the Testament, Mr Burke, with an indignant look and a rage not to be described, snatched the book out of the clerk's hands and threw it at his head, then walked indignantly away, muttering his resentment but without giving his vote."

Aided again by the sedan chairmen of St James's Street, George attempted more rigorously to control the streets and even carried the fight to the doors of the opposing party's dens. Absolute mayhem ensued — a field day for the cartoonists:

16 July 1788: "The Butchers of Freedom", in which George, Fox, Sheridan and Townshend, armed with cleavers and marrowbones, assail a bastion of the Tories.

July 1788: "Opposition Music, Or Freedom of Election", in which George, Fox and Sheridan, likewise armed, are about to strike a woman and her child.

The BUTCHERS of FREEDOM.

OPPOSITION MUSIC. *Or* FREEDOM *of* ELECTION.

It was not only the Tories' bastions that were threatened. So too was the Shakespeare Tavern, the centre of George's operations. Sir Sampson Wright, a Bow Street magistrate, therefore arranged for guardsmen to be posted outside, two of whom were later arrested for thrusting at Fox with their bayonets on one of his visits. Accompanied by Sheridan, he proceeded to remonstrate with Wright in a fit of "violent passion". Within days Gillray followed with a cartoon, "The Battle of Bow-Street", in which Fox is being jabbed with a bayonet and Sheridan is threatening a kneeling Wright.

The BATTLE of BOW-STREET.

One year later Charles Macklin was asked if he remembered the elections for Westminster. Aged 89, he replied, "I remember them, but most of them as chaos."

There was no lack of money. The Whigs were reputed to have a war chest of £15,000 and the Tories £5,000 more,[81] both of which, besides covering incidental expenses, were devoted to bribery and treating on a vast scale. And so proceedings continued on their merry way — much as four years earlier — until the result was announced. Townshend had won with a majority of 823 votes. Appalled at the expense, both parties now agreed a truce by which they would share the two seats unopposed. It was the last contested election in Westminster for several years.

The onset of the French Revolution in June 1789 was enthusiastically welcomed by George, as it was by Fox, given their instinctive compassion for freedom and hatred of despotism. "How much the greatest event it is that ever happened in the

---

[81] Respectively some £2,075,000 and £2,770,000 in today's money.

world, and how much the best," declared Fox, adding later, "Considered together, [it was] the most stupendous and glorious edifice of liberty which had been erected on the foundations of human integrity in any time or country," sentiments with which George agreed. Yet as the revolution gravitated from constitutional reform to an egalitarian republic tainted by the horrors that accompanied it, many influential Whigs became increasingly uneasy that the spread of republican principles constituted a threat not only to the very foundations of British society but also to the very stability of Europe. So when on 1 February 1793 Pitt declared war on France with the object of reinstating a monarchy there, he was, though vehemently opposed by Fox, supported by a large section of the Whig Party in both Houses of Parliament. One year later the Party split into Foxites and those under Portland, who soon entered into a coalition with Pitt.

That George was at one with Fox throughout is confirmed by an opinion expressed in his *Anticipation of the Freedom of Brabant*, a work that he published only two months before the declaration of war. In it he says, "I am astonished that there is to be found one single person in the whole British nation, from the first nobleman to the poorest peasant that loves his native country, *who does not rejoice as much as I do*[82] in the French Revolution. Were they not actuated by the same principles as I am (the pleasure and satisfaction of seeing not only the most despotick, most cruel, oppressive, and profuse government overturned but liberty given to above 20 millions of souls who for ages have groaned under the lash of the most oppressive tyranny), they ought at least, if true lovers of their country, to reflect on that dagger which that despotick government attempted to plunge in the vitals of their country and which would have been accomplished had not the French Revolution taken place." Here George has in mind Louis XVI's intention to subvert British rule in India, a course that would have led inescapably to war.

---

[82] George's italics.

What then was George to do when Pitt almost immediately declared war on revolutionary France? Well, patriot that he was, he repeatedly applied to be transferred from the half-pay to the active list, but was unsuccessful due to his notoriety. He therefore took it upon himself to contribute to the nation's defence by publishing in 1795 his *Military Reflections on the Attack and Defence of London*. Much to his satisfaction he saw some of his recommendations promptly enacted by Parliament. A few months earlier he had been promoted to lt colonel, though still on the half-pay list.

As the war clouds began to gather, George and Sir John Lade's management of the Prince's racing stable came to an end. On 20 October 1791 the Prince's horse Escape, though well fancied, was beaten by two horses of very inferior reputation. The odds, which had greatly favoured Escape, were adjusted and large bets were laid against him when he ran again the next day. He won. Sam Chifney, the Prince's jockey, was much suspected of pulling him in the first race and was warned off by the presiding steward, Sir Charles Bunbury. The Prince rightly took the view that the decision reflected badly on his integrity and withdrew from the turf, ordering his racing stable to be sold. Always free with his language, George's reaction may well be imagined. According to *The Times*, "George Hanger swears in common conversation more in an hour than a Chancery Lane buffer in Court does in a term."

It was in 1791 that George was caricatured in a famous print by Holland: "Don Hangerando a Lilliputian Champion". In it he stands full face with a frown, his hands on his hips. Sporting a large moustache, he wears spatterdashes, gauntlet gloves, and his customary large Kevenhüller hat. Completing his attire are a sabre and huge epaulettes. Beneath the title is etched:

Don't raise my courage — if you do,
By Jove I'll cleave your scull in two!

Don Hangerando a Lilliputian Champion

Don't raise my courage — if you do,
By Jove I'll clave your scull in two!

About this time William, George's elder brother, now Lord Coleraine, sought his urgent advice on what to do to get out of a scrape. He was, notes Raikes, "a beau of the first water, always beautifully powdered, in a light-green coat with a rose in his buttonhole. He had not much wit or talent but affected the *vieille cour* and the manners of the French court. He had lived a good deal in Paris before the revolution and used always to say, 'The English are a very good nation but they positively know not how to make anything but a kitchen poker.' I remember many years ago the Duchess of York made a party to go by water to Richmond in which Coleraine was included. We all met at a given hour at Whitehall Stairs and found the Admiralty barge with the Royal Standard ready to receive us; but by some miscalculation of the tide it was not possible to embark for near half an hour and one of the watermen said to the Duchess, 'Your Royal Highness must wait for the tide.' Upon which Coleraine with a profound bow remarked, 'If I had been the tide, I should have waited for Your Royal Highness.' Nothing could have been more stupid, but there was something in the manner in which it was said that made everyone burst out a-laughing."

So what was the scrape that William had got into? It transpired that one evening at Drury Lane a stranger wearing top-boots sat next to him in the dress-circle. Such legwear would have been a gross breach of etiquette in France, so much so, that William was driven to treat it as a like affront in London.

"I beg, sir, you will make an apology," he remarked with an innocent and reassuring air.

His neighbour stared in blank amazement. "Apology, sir! Apology for what?" he demanded angrily.

"Why," replied William, pointing to the offending boots, "that you did not bring your horse with you into the box."

"Perhaps it is lucky for you I did not bring my horse-whip," retorted the other in a fine frenzy, "but I have a remedy at hand — I will pull your nose for your impertinence!" Thereupon he threw himself on William, only to be dragged away by those sitting on the other side of him.

Cards were exchanged and a duel seemed imminent. William went at once to George to beg his assistance. "I acknowledge I was the first aggressor," he confessed, though not in a humble frame of mind, "but it was too bad to threaten to pull my nose. What had I better do?" George unfeelingly replied, "*Soap it well*, and then it will slip easily through the fingers!"

It was advice George was never weary of repeating to any gentleman wishing to calumniate another. Indeed he returns to it in his memoirs: "Since I have taken upon myself the charge of my own sacred person, I never have been pulled by the nose or been compelled to soap it. Many gentlemen of distinguished rank in this country are indebted to the protecting qualities of soap for the present enjoyment of their noses, it being as difficult to hold a soaped nose between the fingers as it is for a countryman at a country wake to catch a pig turned out with his tail soaped and shaved for the amusement of the spectators."

Meanwhile the Prince had again spiralled massively into debt and by mid 1793 owed £375,000,[83] a sum that he had no immediate prospect of paying. Desperately he applied to the King for relief, but found him obdurate. Unless the Prince married a German princess of the Protestant persuasion, his father would move no step to help him and instruct His Government to oppose any application to Parliament. Breaking with Mrs Fitzherbert in June 1794, the Prince soon after accepted the King's terms and on 8 April 1795 married Princess Caroline of Brunswick. Securing only partial relief of his debts, he began promptly to economise by reducing almost the whole of his household.

George was dismissed.

---

[83] Approximately £41,400,000 in today's money.

CHAPTER 15

DESCENT INTO DEBT AND
THE KING'S BENCH PRISON

No longer in the Prince's service, George found his income reduced by £300 per year, but worse was to come. Shortly after, the East India Company terminated his employment as a recruiting officer with the loss of his remaining income of over £600 annually.[84]

"One misfortune seldom comes alone," maintains George, "Indeed I am convinced of it." So how did he become a victim for the second time? Basically, he explains, because of a dispute between the Board of Control and the Directors of the East India Company over the Board's plan to build barracks in England to receive the Company's recruits before their dispatch to India. "This system the Directors opposed to a man excepting the Chairman and Deputy Chairman. A long debate took place on this subject (at which I was present) in the public court-room, and a very great majority by vote threw out the plan. The Board of Control, after that question was carried by a very great majority of Proprietors against them, thought fit to change the whole system of recruiting for the Hon Company's army in India and gave them recruits from Chatham barracks. This put it out of the power of the Hon Company to employ me any longer.

"I have reason," adds George, "to complain bitterly of my misfortunes at this period of my life, for I am of opinion there is no other instance of any person losing an income of £900 a year

---

[84] His lost income from both posts amounted together to over £100,000 a year in today's money.

without having been guilty of some misconduct or malpractices; but it was my misfortune that my pecuniary resources should be subjected to events which could not be foreseen or avoided.

"Once again I had risen to a state of ease and happiness after the various misfortunes I had suffered, when I was again most suddenly reduced to the greatest distress. I had fondly brought my mind to think that I had weathered all the storms in life and brought my vessel into a quiet snug harbour; but how was I deceived! for the hurricane of misfortune, without giving me notice, drove me from my comfortable moorings into the troubled ocean, once more to seek the necessaries of life. I now began gradually to measure my steps towards the King's Bench Prison."

Practically destitute as George was, recourse to money-lenders was his only option, but with no means of repaying them he has provided an interesting vignette of his evasion: "When hunted by bailiffs, the bloodhounds of unrelenting usurers and their more rapacious attorneys, how often have I secreted myself in the house of some fair one or with her fled the town to some distant scene of freedom and security! When I have experienced that balm to a distracted mind which female converse only can impart, although oppressed by anxious care and sinful poverty (that worst of crimes), give me but health and the affections of some kind sympathising fair one and I will oppose a sea of troubles."

Yet George could not always evade his creditors, as evinced by the recovery of a debt of £48 which he describes: "When the bailiffs came for my coat and cloak to my house, they also had my stockings, shoes, shirts and breeches, to which I submitted with all humility, although it would have been very distressing to me and a wonderful loss, for those very clothes would have been sold at public auction for a trifle when compared with their real value to me (as it would have cost me at least £150 to replace them for a debt of £48) had they not perchance been given by the sheriff's officer to my friend Mr Graham, the auctioneer, who generously paid the money for me and preserved my clothes, for pay the debt I absolutely could not at that time nor could I liquidate it for many months with my generous friend Graham. Here both the lawyer and Mr Graham verified the Scriptures but the world I trust will give greater credit to the latter, for the lawyer, when I was helpless, *took me in* but Mr Graham, *when I was naked, clothed me.* I cannot help, but with a considerable degree of satisfaction and pleasure, remarking the very moderate costs on this action of £48, they not amounting to much above one half of the original debt, which I think I may say, and I am certain, was for a bill given by me for £26 or £30, not exceeding that sum."

Even in adversity, there was never a better subject for the caricaturist than George, and Gillray was not one to miss an opportunity. In 1796, when George's debts had not become acute, he was at the height of his notoriety and might be seen every day in St James's, riding on his little pony on the way to The Mount Tavern in Lower Grosvenor Street, his hat cocked on one side in the fashion of the day, an Indian silk handkerchief round his neck, and his shillelagh in his hand. "Georgey a' Cock-Horse" he was called, and as "Georgey a' Cock-Horse" Gillray immortalised him. Punch, the pony, was George's delight and he would tell his cronies how Punch was a great weight carrier and how in Scotland he had seen as many as thirteen dead calves carried on a similar horse. The boast reached Gillray, who in another cartoon — "Staggering Bobs, a Tale for Scotchmen, or Munchausen driving his Calves to Market" — drew Punch staggering beneath the weight of George and thirteen calves. Etched on the cartoon is the following conversation:

"Here they are, my Lord [Galloway]. Here's the stuck calves, by G[od]. No allusion, d[a]mme! Almost forgot you was a north-countryman! Runt carries weight well! No less than thirteen, d[a]mme! Come, push about the bottle and I'll tell you the story. In Scotland they eat no veal — no veal, by G[od]! Nothing but staggering bobs, by G[od]! On my honour and soul I mean no insult! but Tattersall, he swore — d[am]n me if he didn't, that on a small Scotch runt he saw, G[od] d[am]n my blood — how many d'ye think he saw?"

"Saw what, Georgey?"

"Why, calves. Staggering bobs, to be sure! Why, d'ye think he saw seventeen? No! but d[a]mme, by G[od], he saw thirteen!!! and all just upon such another little cock-horse as my own."

GEORGEY a' Cock-horse.

George Hanger, Lord Coleraine.

"Here they are my Lord, here's the slunk Calves, by Gᵪx
— no allusion, dᵪmme! — almost forget you was a North-Country-
Man! — Runt carries weight well! no less than Thirteen
dᵪmme! — come push about the Bottle, & I'll tell you
the Story; —— In Scotland they eat no Veal, —
no Veal, by Gᵪs! nothing but Staggering Bobs. — by Gᵪs! —
on my Honor & Soul I mean no insult? — but Tattersal he
swore, d — n me, if he didn't, that on a small Scotch Runt,
he saw, Gᵪx dᵪn my blood, how many d'ye think he saw ?
(" Saw what, George?) — why Calves! — Staggering Bobs
to-be-sure! — why d'ye think he saw Seventeen? — no!
but dᵪxme, by Gᵪx he saw Thirteen !!! — & all just
upon such another little Cock-Horse as my own !!!

STAGGERING-BOBS, a Tale for Scotchmen.___or.__MUNCHAUSEN driving his Calves to Market
This Poem is dedicated to Lord Eᵪᵪl, his Party, & the Frequenters of Stevens's in general.

Meanwhile, as George's descent continued, he began a lawsuit against his brother William, about which, and his penury, he wrote to the Prince, seeking a loan of £100 to tide him over till the case was decided:

London, 10 August 1797

Most honored and dearest Prince, Sir

Your Royal Highness must of course long before now have been acquainted with the dispute in litigation between me and my brother. As there is nothing on earth, Sir, that I value more than your good opinion (which as hitherto I have the vanity to believe that I have fully possessed), I most humbly sollicit Your Royal Highness to suspend all judgment and opinion until the case is decided, when I shall take the earliest opportunity of laying before you, Sir, and some few more friends several letters that have passed between me and my brother before I was reduced to the necessity of appealing to the laws of my country. By these letters I wish to be judged. Your Royal Highness, I trust, will believe me when I assure you *every means* have been employed by my brother's lawyers to delay this business and to protract it so that I might not be able to gain any favourable decision till the first term in November, thinking that my distresses may oblige me to compromise the affair, for I would not willingly lay so heavy a charge against a brother. Unfortunately for me in some degree they have effected it, though it will avail my brother nothing in the end but will only protract it to the middle of November, by which time Lord Kenyon[85] has decreed that the report shall be made. On the day that the tryal was to have come on, both partys (in Court) agreed that the case in dispute should be refered to the arbitration of a Master of the Court of King's Bench (a Mr Bailey) on condition that Mr Bailey should appoint an immediate meeting and, upon finding a sum above £300 to be due to me, that he should immediately order the prompt payment of a sum not exceeding £300 to me. That sum by agreement was specifyed to be wanted to supply my immediate demands; the remainder and further and final sums to be litigated were then to stand over till the end of October when all partys were to meet for the final decision.

---

[85] The Chief Justice of the King's Bench.

Mr Bailey, the arbitrator appointed, was so kind as to fix on *this day* for the partys to meet. My council, solicitor and witnesses and self were all present. No soul appeared on the part of my brother, not even his attorney, but when sent for said he was not prepared, that my brother was out of town, that his agent, Timothy Brent Esq, was also out of town, and that the witnesses he should call were not ready. The arbitrator, Mr Bailey, then said that he would give us a meeting next Saturday evening. The attorney said my brother could not come to town so soon nor could he find others that were wanting to appear by that time; but what is more unfortunate for me is that all the judges of the King's Bench after this week will not be in town all the summer, they being some gone on the circuit and others retire to their country houses, and as it is necessary for the principal evidences to be sworn before one of them, the whole must now be putt off till the very *latter end of October.* Thus, Sir, do not only my relations but fortune combine to keep me for near three months longer in suspense and misery. I cannot help mentioning to Your Royal Highness that my brother in one of his letters had the audacity to offer me £300 provided I would give him an acknowledgment under my hand that I had no further demand on him whatever. I rejected it with contempt, for in giving such an acknowledgment I must have owned myself to have been a villain and to have made a false demand on him. Shortly afterwards I sent my worthy friend, Colonel McMahon (who Your Royal Highness well knows) to my brother to inform him of my present wants and requesting him to lett me have the £300 which he said he had ready for me, but not on the terms he had required of me, but to lett me have it on account and that it should go to the general account on the final settlement. My brother refused Colonel McMahon and had the affrontery again to tell him that he could not lett me have that sum unless I acknowledged under my hand that I had no further demands on him whatever, although he was at the same time told of my distressed situation and that by the middle of July I must pay some debts to the amount of about 200 or be fixed in judgment attended with great expence. All this he was informed of but would do nothing. To mention to Your Royal Highness the particulars of my situation for these six weeks past would be only grieving a heart that I know to be so sensible of and so truly feeling for all affliction. It is sufficient to say that I have been shutt up in

211

the house of a friend in London for three weeks, not being able to retire into the country at a distance, not having had the command of a guinea. I have not a second decent coat to my back, not any linen but what I took with me, as all my cloaths, linen, etc have been siezed and will soon be sold. It is absolutely necessary that I should retire for a time at a distance into the country, but I have not the means even to supply the necessarys of life (upon my sacred word and honor it is true) nor have I any means of acquiring it. In my absence my creditors will take a security assignment on the arbitration and all will go well. My India recruiting business will begin again,[86] also in November, but till then I solemnly declare I have no means of existing. I must pay some few things before I can leave the town and must have a small sum to retire on. I throw myself on Your Royal Highness's bounty and on that protection which I hope I have not yett done anything to induce you to withdraw your kindness from me , and if you, Sir, will be gratiously pleased to afford me the loan of £100 till the decision takes place in November, I will most honorably and most humbly lay both myself and the money before Your Royal Highness and with every submission, attatchment and respect return you my gratefull thanks for so signal a relief in so distressed a situation. That sum will pay some few things that are absolutely necessary and will support me to the time of decision.

Etc

GEORGE HANGER

PS: If Your Royal Highness gratiously should condescend me a reply, be pleased, Sir, to lett my letter be enclosed under cover to Captain Tuck, No 3 Stangate, Lambeth, Surry.

As 1798 came to pass, George had received no financial assistance from the Prince, his lawsuit against his brother was still undecided, and he could forestall his creditors no longer. Arrested by a bailiff and locked up in a sponging house,[87] he was committed to the King's Bench Prison on 2 June.

---

[86] No, it would not.

[87] A bailiff's house in which debtors were put before being taken to jail.

CHAPTER 16

INCARCERATION

Burnt down by the Gordon rioters in 1780, but promptly rebuilt, the King's Bench Prison was located south of the Thames in Southwark, immediately north of Borough Road as it now enters Newington Causeway.

The prison consisted of one larger building, one smaller, and St George's Fields, an extensive open space. Comprising some 200 rooms, "occupied by persons of the lowest order," the larger building included a chapel, coffee-house, two public houses, and shops or stalls for meat, vegetables, and other necessaries. A small paved court led to the smaller building, where some ten well-furnished state rooms were provided "for the reception of the better sort of Crown prisoners." Surrounding the buildings was a thirty-foot wall surmounted by *chevaux de frise.* To St George's Fields the "Rules" applied, whereby residence, or access for the day, might be purchased.

THE KING'S BENCH. SOUTHWARK. IN 1830.

"The discipline of the prison," writes Richardson, "was tyrannical, yet lax, capricious and undefined. The regulations were either enforced with violence or suffered to become a dead letter. Nobody cared much about them." At any one time the prison housed between 800 and 1,000 inmates.

If George is to believed, the real and true state of the prison, and the misery and distress that prisoners suffered in it, was very little known to the world in general. It was the public's perception that no persons surrendered to the King's Bench but such as had money in their possession which their creditors could not lay their hands on, so enabling them to live there in some degree of comfort; that it was a place of mirth, festivity and joy; that no prisoner was in want; and that in general those who surrendered there did so only till a proper arrangement of their affairs could be accomplished. Yet nothing was further from the truth.

In George's opinion the prison rivalled the purlieus of Wapping, St Giles's's and St James's in vice, drunkenness and debauchery. "Setting aside the indulgence of unnatural propensities, it may be said to out-Herod Sodom and Gomorrah." Unless a man was of a certain age, of a bold and firm mind, and of undaunted resolution to bear with fortitude and manly dignity the oppression and heartbraking agonies he suffered from his persecutors, he would soon sink into drunkenness and dissipation, and what is worse, lose every sense of honour and dignity of sentiment, every moral principle and virtuous disposition, from the immoral contagion that was to be found within the walls. Unless, therefore, he lived alone or contrived to live only with such as brought honour and gentlemanly manners with them, he was lost. As to the women to whose lot it fell to be doomed to this miserable and corrupting abode, those who were good became bad, and those who were bad became worse.

By nine o'clock on Monday mornings a creditor or his attorney was required by law to deposit three shillings and six pence in the hands of the doorkeeper for the use of their prisoner,

214

and if the sum was unpaid or deficient, the action against the prisoner was superseded and he was released. As to the liberality of the payment, George enquires, "Will any man venture to assert that a man can live on such a stipend? Let those who make this law try, only for one day, what they can purchase for such a sum and they will find that they will go to bed both hungry and thirsty unless they drink water, for a sufficient quantity of bread and small beer cannot be purchased for that money to satisfy their appetite and their thirst."

In fact the payment was often not made, as George makes clear: A prisoner can "be deprived of the sixpence a day,[88] at best a miserable pittance, by the pettifogging reptile, yclept an attorney, who, by some quirk or quibble or litigious oath or process, can for twelve months prevent the prisoner from receiving the allowance which the law of the land intended should be paid him instantly on his committal to keep him from starving."

An example he gives: "If a prisoner be arrested and surrenders to the King's Bench in the month of June after the term is over, there being no term till the next November, during a period of near five months he may starve, for until the Court is sitting he cannot apply for his groats; but when November arrives and he applies for them, then the attorney may by a litigious process prevent him from recovering the miserable boon until the following May. Many prisoners during the five months of this long vacation have suffered cruelly, and some would have absolutely starved if it had not been for the generosity of some gentlemen who themselves are prisoners and have it in their power to contribute to the wants of the wretched sufferer. Many gentlemen as well as others of superior stations in life, for several weeks, have to my knowledge, for successive days, never known what it was to enjoy one good meal. Nor is

---

[88] Approximately £3 in today's money.

this all. From the scanty fare and irregularity of their diet they frequently contract diseases which they have carried with them to their graves and [have] made them miserable objects during their lives."

Of the rogueries perpetrated by attorneys, the principal one followed on from their practice of purchasing bills of exchange. "When," says George, "money is scarce and a gentleman wants a little cash but cannot get his bill discounted at his banker's, having overdrawn his account considerably, ... he goes to some advertising money-broker and gives him a bill, we will say for £100, to get discounted." The money-broker would then go to some tradesman in the habit of discounting bills and the gentleman would be given part in cash and part in goods. Usually the bill began to circulate among other tradesmen, each endorsing it, until eventually the last approached an attorney whose constant habit was to purchase them. "The attorney never examines the face of the bill but looks directly on the back of it to see how many names are there endorsed. If there are three names, it is a matter worthy of his attention. If four, it is excellent, that making five names with the drawer's." Should this be so, the attorney would purchase the bill in the hope that the gentleman who drew it would not be punctual at the day it was due, so that he might bring an action against the drawer and make him pay costs, not only for his name appearing on the face of the bill, but also for each separate name endorsed on the back. "If," adds George, "you defend the action by various ingenious methods such as sham plea, writ of error, and some other very clever inventions, you may postpone the payment of the bill for many months; but at the final arrangement, when neither sham nor fudge can avail any longer, then you must be contented to pay," otherwise you are committed to prison. Costs might be exceedingly high, as when an attorney compelled a lady of George's acquaintance to pay as many as eight or nine sets, but, as George ironically remarks: compared to the rest of his fraternity, "he was *a jewel* of an attorney and as transcendent in real honour as a brilliant is to a rose diamond."

No matter how small were debts, attorneys were devoted as ever to loading their recovery with most extravagant costs, of which George gives three examples affecting him. In the first he says:

I built a one-horse chair some years past. The price was, to the best of my recollection, between £50 and £60. The first day I drove it for two hours, merely to try it and to have it properly hung. I then left it a few days with the maker to regulate it and, before I took it away, I paid one half of the price in money and gave a bill for the other half at a short date, which was paid. However, I happened to send the chaise back to be screwed up and to have some trifling alteration made etc, the expence of which amounted to £5-6s-0d or £6-5s-0d,[89] I forget which. After owing this trifle for a considerable space of time, I was served with a copy of a writ. I had been out of town for above two months and totally forgot that I had been served with [it]. In December following, a sheriff's officer met me, who had oftentimes arrested me, and told me he had a warrant against me. I asked him why he did not call at my house in the morning early that I might have gone out with him and settled it, as it was then near my time of dinner. He gave me a very satisfactory reason why he did not. I asked him the sum it amounted to. "A small sum, somewhat above twenty," he replied. As it was rather late in the day and near dinnertime, I desired him to call on me the next morning and I would settle it. "I would with pleasure, Colonel," said he, "but it is an execution." "That is impossible," I replied, "for I have not signed any bond or warrant of attorney to any person existing." "I assure you, Colonel," continued he, "it is an execution. You ought to know the law and what lawyers can do, for you have paid enough to know it in your lifetime." "I now understand you," I replied, "I suppose it is some small debt under £10 brought to judgment by the attorney." "Exactly so." To cut this matter very short, I went to my friend Mr Wright in Carey Street and surrendered to him. My agent very kindly brought me the money to discharge the debt and costs,

---

[89] Respectively some £645 and £720 in today's money.

which amounted to above £24.[90] Now, if I had not been able to pay it, I must have surrendered to the King's Bench or Fleet and there I might have lain until I had rotted, unless I had paid the £24, for I have no reason to believe that the attorney employed against me would have deviated from the line adopted by his brethren and have shewn me any very distinguished favour.

In the second example George writes:

Many years ago I kept horses at the livery stables of my old friend Mr Fozard. I had for some time given over keeping horses and had settled all accounts with him for many months, when a man called on me and told me that I owed him £4 and some shillings for the keeping of a horse at grass some distance from London. I told him that I knew nothing of the matter, that I never had put any horse to grass with him, and that I did not even know the place where he lived, which I literally believed was the fact. In about three days after, I was served with a copy of a writ. I then began to reflect, and did recollect, that Fozard had put a horse one winter into a straw yard for me, but having settled my account with him, I of course concluded that I had paid that expence with the rest. I accordingly went to his stables and examined the books, when I found that he had not made such a charge and of course that I owed it. I was served with the copy of a writ on a Friday evening, and on Monday morning quitted town for the neighbourhood of Ascot Heath preparatory to the races. I was so incautious as not to look at the date of the writ to see when it was returnable, nor did I send it to my lawyer, thinking that a week would make but little difference as I should be in town the following Saturday. The writ, however, was made returnable in three days and a fresh term commenced in four days. Thus the lawyer had the start of me by two terms in one week, which enabled him to make such rapid progress in his expences. On the Saturday afternoon, only eight days from the time I was served with the copy of a writ, I went to his house to pay the debt and, judging that I should not have above twenty shillings to pay for

---

[90] Approximately £2,775 in today's money, of which over £2,000 comprised the costs.

the expences at first incurred, was surprised, when his clerk made the amount out, that the £4 were in eight days accumulated by the attorney's costs to £11 or £13,[91] I really forget which, but either of them is sufficient for my purpose. On my expostulations relative to the exorbitant charges produced in so short a time, the clerk informed me that another term had commenced since the issuing of the writ and consoled me by the assurance that it was very fortunate I happened to call that day, as, from my having neglected to plead through my attorney to the writ, judgment would have been entered up against me on the Monday morning following, which would have been £3 more, and that then I should have been taken in execution. I now began to understand the affair. ... Nought was left for me but to pay the whole sum ... and content myself with having had the good fortune to call that day, the moment I came to town, by which I saved the additional charge of £3. This all took place in eight days. I had indeed seen, during my absence at Ascot Heath, some tolerable good racing, but this attorney, it must be allowed by all sportsmen, beat everything for speed.

In the third example George is briefer:

Before I surrendered as a prisoner to the King's Bench, I gave a bill to a tradesman, not for any debt contracted by me but for a lady of my acquaintance. This bill was kept back by a lawyer into whose hands it fell, and not being a debt of my own, it escaped my notice. After I was liberated, it was demanded of me but, as I could not pay it, I was arrested and compelled from actual necessity to bail it and defend it for some time till I was able to pay it, when I gave my attorney a sum of money to discharge that bill and some other matters I had to settle; but not having sufficient money given him, he left £6 unpaid and informed me of his so doing. The lawyer was perfectly satisfied and assured him that he would put me to no trouble for the remaining trifle, and that I might pay it when convenient. My lawyer, however, went out of town for two

---

[91] If we assume that George is talking of the mid 1770s, the figures in this sentence amount to some £600, £1,650 and £1,950 respectively in today's money, making the costs over £1,000.

months on business, in which time this gentleman carried on the process against me and, having brought it to an execution, fixed me in judgment for £16-16s-0d. In addition to this the customary expences attending on a judgment, such as sheriffs poundage, caption fee, one guinea, searching the office, and some small perquisite to the house of the officer I went to, amounted to above £2 more.[92]

This is law, aye, and very sound — legal and excellent law too, and what is practised *every day in the year* to the emolument of the attorney and ruin of the debtor, who, when it is a distressing circumstance to him to pay £6, is compelled to pay £16 or be sent to jail and there to lay until he rots or can pay the costs to the attorney as well as the principal debt.

Ipso facto, it may be seen how great an object it was for an attorney, who bought a bill from a tradesman, to have four or five names endorsed on the back of it, otherwise it was not worth having, nor did he think it worth negotiating if there was a probability that the drawer would pay it at the day when it was due. Occasionally, however, an attorney would come unstuck, as George goes on amusingly to relate:

A friend of mine, who was not always, as well as myself and many others, rigidly punctual in taking up his bills at the hour when due, discounted a bill in the [usual] manner. There were four or five names on the back of the bill, which made it very eligible. An attorney readily purchased this bill. The morning when due it was presented at his house with the customary notice left in writing: "Your bill for £100 lies due at Messrs ————, bankers. Please to call this day between the hours of three and five." My friend that day, a happy day for him but a day of disappointment to the attorney, was per chance more in cash than usual and sent his servant with the money between three and five o'clock to take up the bill, which he did and brought it to his master cancelled. A few weeks after, the same tradesman, who sold this bill drawn on my

---

[92] In today's money the figures in this paragraph amount respectively to some £630, £1,760, and £210.

friend to the attorney, called again on him with another bill drawn on the same gentleman, asking him to discount it. The moment he saw on whom the bill was drawn he threw it with indignation on the floor, saying, "I am astonished, sir, at your offering me such a bill. I will have nothing to do with that gentleman's bills, for the last which I gave you money for to oblige you *was paid the day it was presented.*" The tradesman, much to his mortification, was obliged to depart without getting cash for his bill and had the trouble to seek for some other attorney who dealt in bills, to whom the unusual punctuality of my friend was not yet known.

George continues by questioning both the policy and the morality of imprisonment for debt. "We," he says, "who live in a land of liberty, who boast of the justice and lenity of our laws, who profess Christianity, can we without remorse of conscience reflect on the miseries the oppressed debtor suffers? Can we pretend to possess any feeling, and any religion or humanity, and with indifference view one part of our fellow creatures persecuted and half-starved by unfeeling, remorseless creditors?" He himself was of opinion that in a free country there should be no confinement of a person for debt, though he would have made it a felony for anyone to secrete one shilling of his property. It was fallacious to assert that had there been no law to confine a debtor's person, England's trade and commerce would have suffered. There was no law in Scotland to confine a debtor who gave up his property, and had the trade of Edinburgh and Glasgow decreased? Look also to Holland, a country where the true interests of trade and commerce were as well understood as in England. "There is no law there to imprison a debtor, yet Holland had arrived at its wealth and grandeur by trade alone."

Reverting to the King's Bench, George firmly believed that had it not been for attorneys and their pursuit of exorbitant costs, above half of the inmates would have been freed immediately, many of whom owed less than £6 to their creditor but costs exceeding £20 or £30 to the attorney. In fact, many a creditor was most willing to take the original debt and release the debtor from the prison, but was inhibited from doing so, for, if he did, the attorney would fix him with the debtor's costs. As respects George's own confinement there, he fared better than most.

Although housed in the larger building, he had a room to himself, in which he proceeded to write his memoirs. How this arrangement came about he explains: "When anyone surrenders to the King's Bench and has a command of money, he can procure a room by paying his chum or chamber companion out, as it is called — that is, by giving some poor man a weekly sum to let him have the room to himself to the mutual convenience of both, as the latter, for the sake of getting a stipend to purchase food, will be content to get a lodging where he can find it at a cheap rate, [whether] by sleeping ten or twelve in a small room or, without any expence at all, by preferring a soft plank in the taproom or a smooth stone on a staircase."

George also gained access to St George's Fields. "By the kind assistance of my worthy and best friend, Jacob Wilkinson, who was my bondsman to the marshal [*the governor of the prison*], I had procured the blessing of a liberty to walk and enjoy the open air within the boundaries of the King's Bench, called the 'Rules'."

"On average," George adds, "I never spent above three shillings any one day during my residence in those blessed regions. I had two reasons for living so cheap: first, being of opinion a prisoner for debt should not be squandering money, nor should he live sumptuously, yet he should not deny himself the necessaries of life; secondly, I was determined to ascertain how cheap a gentleman could live and want for nothing necessary to his maintenance, namely a hearty breakfast and dinner every day. Bread and beer were cheaper at that period, but meat was much the same. I drank nothing but porter."

What ended George's incarceration followed on from the successful outcome of his action against his brother, at which stage, while still confined, he wrote to the Prince, not to thank him for financial assistance, which he did not receive, but for the Prince's support in other ways:

30 November 1798

Most honored and dearest Prince

Lett me entreat Your Royal Highness to accept the sincere thanks of a heart truly impressed with the sincerest and unshaken gratitude for manyfold favours, but most particularly, dear Sir, for Your Royal Highnesses recent conduct in taking the part of an injured man very early in the dispute between Lord Coleraine and me. Had it not been for that goodness of heart which I so fully know Your Royal Highness to possess, untill the law had cleared my character I should have appeared both in the eyes of His Royal Highness the Duke of York and of the world a *perjured villain*. Permitt me also to express, dear Sir, the heartfelt gratitude I feel from Your Royal Highness's expressions in my favour communicated to me by the honest Tyndale, sentiments which, while they shew that I am still so happy as to retain your good opinion and friendship, [are] a source of consolation to my mind superior to all calumny and malignity, lett it come from every other quarter of the sensorious world as well as from a base calumniating brother. Proud and happy in that protection which I have uninterruptedly enjoyed for the space of twelve years (during which period not one single undertaking or transaction in life that might have had a tendency to induce the censorious world to lament Your Royal Highness's having countenanced a man capable of disgracing your patronage has passed without being previously submitted to Your Royal Highness's approbation), it is scarcely to be imagined that at my present period of life, and with my *dear-bought experience*, that I should be guilty of any act which would forfeit *that* which constitutes *its* chief happyness. No, dear Sir, disgusted and sickened with the false glare and base deciept of the world, and with a mind wholly abstracted from former follies and foibles, I am secure from any danger of ever forfeiting that place in your esteem which I reflect on with such heartfelt satisfaction and [which] consoles me under all misfortunes. Enclosed I send for Your Royal Highness's perusal a coppy of a letter to the Duke of York which I have thought it my duty as a much injured man to adress to His Royal Highness in my own vindication.

Most ardently wishing Your Royal Highness every happyness and blessing in life, I remain, most honored and dearest Prince, your Royal Highness's most gratefull, faithfull, and devoted humble servant

GEORGE HANGER

Although the lawsuit was decided in George's favour, it took several months before he negotiated a settlement with his creditors, a period during which he remained confined. "I was," he says, "engaged in a family lawsuit which was decided by arbitration before a Master of the Court of King's Bench. By this I gained a considerable sum of money, when I compounded for my debts and was discharged. My affairs on this occasion were settled in the following manner: my creditors were paid seven shillings and sixpence in the pound in cash and I signed a bond to them to pay them the remainder in future from every property I might have to receive by will, reversion or entail. After allotting to them the various sums assigned them, there were forty odd pounds remaining, which I took for my own use, and that was all I reserved to myself. I therefore started again to run the course of life with £40[93] capital stock."

He was released from the King's Bench Prison on 6 April 1799.

_____

[93] Approximately £4,200 in today's money.

CHAPTER 17

THE FINAL YEARS

Welcoming George on his release was an old friend, Edmund Tattersall, who like his deceased father invited George to lodge with him till he had regained his feet.

Finding his solicitations for employment blocked at every channel, George resolved to apply himself to trade and in May 1800 became a coal merchant. At once his detractors began to portray him in a menial light, but George was quick to respond: "It has been circulated and reported in order to injure me in my new profession that I receive a certain sum per chaldron[94] commission. On my honour the report is absolutely false! I am allowed an annual salary, which with prudence will keep me from want, by a generous friend, who has undertaken this business to serve me and to set the trade a-going."

George was confident of his prospects: "By the distin-guished favours I have already been honoured with, by a further protection from the public in favouring me with their commands to supply their families with coals, and by the orders which are weekly increasing, I shall, I trust, be able to relieve my friend from his anxious exertions and to establish the trade myself in a few months on a solid and permanent commercial basis. *Sunt mihi deliciæ, sint mihi divitiæ, carbones*[95] is my motto. May the black-diamond trade flourish with me! which, if it receives,

---

[94] An obsolete spelling of "cauldron", a chaldron was an English measure of dry volume, mostly used for coal.
[95] A Latin expression meaning: "Coals are my delight. Let them be my riches."

as I trust it will, a generous support from the public, cannot fail of success."

As ever Gillray was quick to pounce. Only two months after George started up he published a cartoon entitled "Georgey in the Coal-Hole". The location is the interior of a small brick shed heaped with coal. In profile to the left is George carrying a sack towards the doorway, through which a coal-cart may be seen. He is thin and wears tattered but fashionable clothes.

GEORGEY in the COAL-HOLE.

One day the Prince on horseback happened to pass by. "Well, George, how go coals now," he enquired in a friendly way, to which George replied with a twinkle in his eye, "Black as ever, please Your Royal Highness."

Yet despite George's initial optimism he did not fare well and by the spring of 1804 was again in dire straits. On 1 May his close friend Rawdon, now Lord Moira, the GOC in Scotland, wrote from Edinburgh to John McMahon, the Prince's private secretary, "If it be practicable to save poor Hanger, it can only be done by immediate intervention. Surely there are enough of us who, under the Prince's countenance, would form a sufficient subscription to secure him from a jail, which would now be utter ruin."

It was indeed Moira who saved him. When the Ministry of All the Talents was formed in February 1806, Moira became Master General of the Ordnance and promptly appointed George a Captain-commissary of Royal Artillery Drivers, a sinecure from which he was allowed to retire on full pay two years later. Involving such a notorious personality, the affair was bound to attract adverse public notice, which it did. Unsurprisingly, the Commissioners of Military Inquiry were led to investigate and in their 17th Report came up with trenchant criticism, to which George published a reply.

A few years earlier George had again gone into print. Percipient and farsighted politically, he gave vent to his enlightened views in *The Life, Adventures, and Opinions of Col. George Hanger*, the work by which he is remembered today, though almost entirely amid the groves of academe.[96] A roller coaster of a ride in which he plays to the gallery, it in many respects has stood the test of time, often dealing with subjects

---

[96] The work was assembled by William Combe, a hack author, from George's writings in prison, but the words are unmistakably George's.

tacitly avoided by later writers. Containing common-sense views on social subjects — views far in advance of the general opinions of his day, it reveals a deep compassion for the poor and downtrodden, particularly women, and advocates measures to relieve their condition. Among other things too numerous to mention, he calls for a moderate, partial reform of Parliament and, in words laced with irony, addresses the failings of the established church. Whatever his frailties, of which we have provided ample evidence, George — a committed Christian — convincingly demonstrates that he was blessed with an innate goodness of heart.

George retained the Prince's friendship and, though no longer in his service, was to be found occasionally in his company. Only a few months after his dismissal he had been invited to dine at Carlton House, where a well publicised incident took place in which he was involved. At dinner the Prince's wife Caroline was of course seated next to the Prince, but much to her dismay, so too was his mistress, Lady Jersey. When her ladyship with great deliberation drank from the Prince's glass, Caroline reacted by swiftly turning to George beside her, seizing his pipe, and puffing a cloud of smoke ostentatiously into her husband's face.

In 1805 the press reported that George was attending the Prince in Brighton, but it was left till 2 November 1812 for the most savage caricature of them roistering together to be published. By Cruikshank, it is entitled "The Prince Regent, the Duke of York, George Hanger, and other distinguished *Beaux*" and portrays George as tall and full-faced, wearing a long drab-coloured coat with a cape. On his right breast is a star. Each of his arms encircles a gin-drinking old woman while at his feet, one of which is cloven, sprawls a young woman applying a bottle to her lips. Standing nearby, a dandy inspects the scene through a quizzing glass and exclaims: "Hang her! She's quite drunk!" Appended to the print is a reference to George: "A tall, strapping-looking person, shabbily but buckishly attired, with a peculiar cast of countenance, now stepped forward and cried out, 'My *name* is sufficient. Whoever has heard of [Hanger] must know that I am without rival in the annals of debauchery. I claim no higher honour than to be my *Prince's friend!*'" The print was in fact based on George's lingering reputation rather than his life as it then was, for he had long since forsaken his bacchanalian, dissolute ways.

On at least two occasions George invited the Prince to his abode, though the first turned out none too well. Hearing George, then a captain-commissary, expatiate on the advantages of his office, the Prince remarked that now he was rich, he would so far impose upon his hospitality as to dine with him. "I shall give Your Royal Highness a leg of mutton and nothing more, by God!" George replied warmly, yet as the day arrived, his pocket could boast little more than a half-crown and a shilling. Etiquette demanded that an aide to the Prince should examine and report back on the proposed meal. Well that he did, for he found George with a dirty scullion zealously preparing for his illustrious guest. His sleeves rolled up, he was vigorously basting a solitary leg of mutton on a spit, and in the pan beneath were potatoes to catch the exudations. "Although the colonel's culinary skill left no doubt that the leg of mutton would have sustained a critical discussion on its intrinsic merits, and although the dinner might have been endured by royalty, yet His Royal Highness's poodles would assuredly have perspired at the very mention of what a certain nobleman used to term a 'jig-hot', so the feast was dispensed with and due acknowledgement made for the evident proofs of hospitality which had been displayed."

The second occasion was a success. According to the relater, he heard the account from someone accompanied by George, who freely admitted it to be founded on fact:

It was on one of those festive occasions, when whim, wit and sparkling wine combined to render the festive scene "the Feast of reason and the flow of soul", that the Prince of Wales invited himself and his brother, the Duke of York, to dine with George Hanger. An honour so unlooked for and one for which George was so little prepared (as he then resided in obscure lodgings near Soho Square) quite overpowered the Colonel, who, however, quickly recovering his surprise, assured His Royal Highness of the very high sense he entertained of the honour intended him, but lamented it was not in his power to receive him and his illustrious brother in a manner suitable to their royal dignity. "You only wish to save your viands, George," replied the Prince. "We shall certainly dine with you on the day appointed, and whether you reside on the first floor or the third, never mind. The feast will not be less agreeable from the altitude of the apartment or the plainness of the repast." Thus encouraged, George was determined to indulge in a joke with his royal visitors. On the appointed day the Prince and Duke arrived and were shown upstairs to George's apartments on the second floor, where a very tasteful banquet was set out, but more distinguished by neatness than splendour. After George had kept his illustrious guests waiting a considerable period beyond the time agreed on by way of sharpening their appetites, the Prince good-humouredly enquired what he meant to give them for dinner. "Only one dish," replied George, "but one that will, I flatter myself, be a novelty to my royal guests and prove highly palatable." "And what may that be?" asked the Prince. "*The wing of a wool-bird,*" George answered facetiously. It was in vain that the Prince and Duke conjectured what this strange title could import, when George appeared before them with a tremendously large red baking dish, smoking hot, in which was supported a fine well-browned shoulder of mutton dripping its rich gravy over some crisp potatoes. The Prince and his brother enjoyed the joke amazingly and they have since been heard to declare that they never ate a heartier meal in their life or one (from its novelty to them in the state in which it was served up) that they have relished more. George had, however, reserved a *bonne bouche* consisting of a superb dessert and most exquisite wines, for which the Prince had heard he was famous, and which was perhaps the principal incitement to the honour conferred."

Gradually, as the century progressed, George retreated ever more into private life, marrying his housekeeper, Mary Anne

Katherine Greenwood, at a ceremony in Wapping. She was born about 1775. The marriage followed on from the birth of their son, whom George acknowledges in a letter of 9 November 1814 to a friend. Written from Thetford, where George had as usual repaired during the shooting season, it includes the following paragraph: "I forgot to tell you something that will make you laugh. When my boy John was appointed to a place in the Custom House, they sent for the register of his birth and christening. It came out that he had never been christened at all. However, I got over it by procuring two persons to make oath of the day of his birth and age. You will fully agree with me that this ceremony having been omitted would be no impediment to his entering the kingdom of heaven, though it appears to be some impediment to his entering the kingdom of the Custom House." When last heard of some 30 years later, John Greenwood Hanger was serving with the Customs in the Channel Islands. Born out of wedlock, he did not inherit the title of Lord Coleraine, which was soon to devolve upon his father.

George did, however, come again to the fore on three occasions. In 1804 and 1808 he published further works on the defence of the realm, and in June 1810, attired in blue and buff and holding his shillelagh, he led on horseback a procession from the Tower of London whose aim had been to escort Sir Francis Burdett MP on his release from imprisonment there for contempt of Parliament. However, much to everyone's dismay, Burdett, who like George was on the radical, reformist wing of the Whig Party (now re-united), was found to have departed by water. Inevitably, a satirical print appeared, in which George is portrayed centrally: "The Burdettes Hoax'd or One Fool makes Many".

The BURDETTITES HOAX'D, or One Fool makes Many. — a Farce perform'd June n'1810 in which the principal character was Double

On 11 December 1814 George's brother William died, leaving George to inherit the title of Lord Coleraine and the estates that went with it. *The Gentleman's Magazine* promptly reported that "the estates of Driffield and Kempsford, county Gloucester, now net £2.000 per annum and, with those in the north of Ireland, make a total rental of £3,000;[97] but should the encumbrances be removed, in four years the rental would be doubled." So George was in clover and would never be faced with monetary worries again.

Yet he refused to assume the title and, when addressed by it, would somewhat peevishly reply, "Plain George Hanger, sir, if you please!" — and for two sound reasons, the first of which he discloses in his memoirs: "As for the reversionary chance that in the wheel of fortune I may have to the title in our family, I am willing to dispose of it at a very cheap rate to any vain man who seeks for empty honours, for, if titles are not bestowed as a

---

[97] Approximately £235,000 per year in today's money.

reward of merit, they are of no value in my estimation." Nevertheless, political animal that he was, George would have been sorely tempted to forgo his reservation and enter public life, had it not been for a second reason, which was the clincher. It is revealed in Westmacott's long-forgotten *roman-à-clef*, *Fitzalleyne of Berkeley*: "Among the few nobility already named, more than one raised modest birth and merit to their own rank; one made a marriage of reparation; nay, even the lord rat-catcher, life-writer (and it was his own), and vendor of the black article of trade, was faithful to his engagements where the law bound him not [*his marriage*], and one of his reasons for forbidding his servants to address him as "My Lord" was that she might bear his name as Mrs Hanger." So there we have it — George simply did not wish to embarrass his wife, who was of lowly estate, by assuming the title.

It was in 1814 that George had published his *Colonel George Hanger to all Sportsmen, and particularly to Farmers and Gamekeepers*, a work containing "the rat-catching secret" and earning him the nickname of "the rat-catcher", to which Westmacott above refers. A few months later George received the pleasing news that he had been promoted to the Hessian rank of major general *à la suite der Armee* and been invested with the Hessian Order *pour la vertu militaire*. They are events that have passed the *Oxford Dictionary of National Biography* by, which accuses him of promoting himself to general.

Two or three years later the sculptor Joseph Nollekens was passing the wall at the end of Portland Road when he overheard George in conversation with an old apple-woman, who was packing up her fruit.

"What are you about, mother?" enquired George.

"Why, Colonel, I am going home to my tea. If, sir, you want any information, I shall come again presently."

"Oh, don't balk trade! Leave your things on the table as they are and I will mind shop till you come back,"

and so saying, George seated himself in the old woman's wooden chair, in which he had often sat while chatting with her. Determined to witness the outcome, Nollekens strolled about till she returned, when George declared his receipts: "Well, mother, I have taken three pence halfpenny for you. Did your daughter Nancy drink tea with you?" It is an anecdote illustrating well the enduring kindness of the man.

George keeping an apple-stall, as sketched in his day

Ever the joker, George was not averse to a humorous bet and about this time wagered a guinea that he would ride on horseback down Bond Street at the most fashionable hour with a chimneysweep behind him. The appointed day arrived, when the course was lined with all that were gay and modish, eager to catch a passing glance at the flying Colonel. Emerging from Piccadilly, he appeared on his old white mare, his shillelagh in his hand and his beaver hat slightly cocked on one side. Proceeding at an ordinary chancery pace, he gravely and politely acknowledged his tittering friends on either side. He completed the course, retraced his steps, and on claiming the guinea, gave it to the chimneysweep.

Bookworm that he was, George spent much time avidly reading as his end approached. Nollekens, for example, recalls seeing him purchase a book, *The American Buccaneers*, from a shop in St Giles's's and sit down close-by to read it in the open street. Cyrus Redding, for his part, recollects that "he might be seen in Pall Mall riding his grey pony without a servant. Dismounting at a bookseller's, he would get a boy to hold his horse while he sat upon the counter for an hour, talking to Burdett, Boswell or Major James, who used to haunt the shop." Then, sometime after the Prince's accession to the throne in 1820, George was permitted to borrow from Carlton House library. Benjamin Jutsham, a longstanding, confidential and much esteemed servant of the King, relates how this came about and sets out his conversations with George, whose singular and extravagant words are so interesting as to quote *in extenso*. Reminded on a visit to the library that he had yet to return a book, George "reiterated a long concatenation of strange curses and unheard of maledictions upon his own head if he had not returned into the hands of Jutsham every book that belonged to the King."

"Don't be positive, My Lord," remarked Jutsham, "When you return home, desire your groom to look for it once more and, trust me, the book will be found. I counted fifteen volumes into your blue broad-cloth wrapper, gave you a correct written list of the same, and you signed it. Here is your own signature."

"Gammon! All Carlton House gammon!" exclaimed George, "I'm too old a soger[98], master thingummybob, to be flummoxed by you or the King, your lord and master, though he is too well-bred to doubt my word!"

"All's one for that," responded Jutsham, "You must, My Lord, find and safely return the missing volume into my hands or I will not allow you to take another — and that is the law"

"Why, you powdered lickspittle! Go to Bath, you demi-reptile! Not take my word! I shall remember you for this, Master Benny Jutsham!"

After this hubbub and within a short week the octavo volume was found and safely returned. With a volley of newly-coined oaths George placed it in the safe custody of Jutsham, saying, "If you doubt my word in future, Benjamin Jutsham, I must whistle Lillibullero and send for the King's old friend and surety, Townshend,[99] the thief-taker, for my character, who will vouch for my being honest as daylight — and, mark ye, as upright mentally as a British grenadier."

After George had departed, a friend of Jutsham's observed, "Why, it has been generally understood that Lord Coleraine's visits to this mansion had ceased many years ago."

"Even so," replied Jutsham, "and the King has never seen him since, nor indeed has anyone belonging to our household. Nevertheless, he is a frequent visitor here at the library. About twelve months ago he sent in his card and asked for me. I met him in the vestibule and he followed me back to the library,

---

[98] Dialect for "soldier".
[99] A reference to Lord John Townshend, whom we have met earlier.

saying, 'How goes it, my old friend Master Benny?' I bowed and returned, 'It is a long time since I had the honour of seeing you, My Lord, and I hope your lordship ———.'

'Gammon!' retorted George, 'I used to be known to you as George Hanger or Georgey, as you prefer, but don't 'My Lord' me. I am ready to entrench myself behind the weed with you at The Sols Arms any night from eight to twelve, and then homewards to tuck into my nest. You may feel surprised to see me, Master Jutsham, but I wish you to do me a favour.'

'With great pleasure, My Lord, if ———.'

'There you go again. Gammon — 'My Lord!' Pshaw, Master Ben!'

'But it is my duty. I must address every nobleman by his title in this house and ———.'

'Gammon!' reiterated George, 'Then I shall keep up the farce and dub you 'My Lord Duke!' I thought you a more cocky fellow, Master Benny. I am only known to myself as GH alias George Hanger. So I mean to live and as such I mean to die! I wish to borrow some of those fine gold-backed books, for I know they are never read in this gingerbread mansion, and I will not keep you long without returning them safe and sound, without speck, spot or blemish outside or inside half as big as the head of a minikin[100] pin.'

'You are requiring me to do that, My Lord, which I never do, never did, and which I never mean to take the liberty of doing. I never took a single book off these shelves but by the order of His Majesty.'

---

[100] Archaic adjective meaning "very small".

'Gammon, Master Ben Jutsham! You know that I am up to snuff! Tell that to the marines, my cock of trumps! I am an old soger and you are an old sailor. Go to! I know that you *do* lend the books whenever you please to whoever you please who wants them, and yet you only refuse them to me. I know why and wherefore, and I am so much the less obliged.'

'Nay, My Lord ———.'

'Oh, bother!' said George.

'Nay, My Lord,' continued Jutsham, 'if you have any request to prefer to His Majesty, I offer to be the bearer of it and I shall feel great pleasure in ———.'

''Thank you, Benny! That's speaking to the mark like a man!'

'What am I to request, My Lord?'

'There you go again,' exclaimed George, — ''My Lord!' Ipecacuanha[101] — you'll make me sick! Well, I leave the negotiation in your own hands. Manage the affair your own way, only procure for me the books. Let me think. Ask for the loan of two folios, four quartos, and about eight to a dozen octavos at the same time, if required, or separate, just as you please, and I promise to be careful in returning them. You may feel surprised,' he added, 'when I tell you that I am become a great reader. I read like hell! — more books by ten to one faster than old Professor Barrett of Trinity in the Emerald Isle. I mean old dirty-faced Barrett — him called the chimneysweep, him who could not tell a living turkey-cock from the painted sign of the Spread Eagle just then standing over his own head.'[102]

---

[101] An emetic or expectorant.
[102] John Barrett (1753-1821) was vice-provost and professor of oriental languages at Trinity College, Dublin. He was as remarkable for his eccentricities as for the extent and profundity of his philological and

'You become a reader, My Lord!' exclaimed Jutsham, 'and a great reader too. For certain, miracles will never cease!'

'It is nevertheless true, so help me Bob! True as the Gospel! You know, Jemmy my boy, I am a miracle! I am a new man at last, snugly tiled in, and have enough of the wherewithal, and summit[103] to spare, to rest my stern quarters on one chair and to squat my trotters on another, to smoke my meerschaum, and to do as I like and care not for the world nor even for your lord and master. No, not even *that,*' which he accompanied with a loud snap of the fingers. 'I have too long been from necessity an idle sort of care-for-nobody-like vagabond, living upon my threadbare wits; and now that I wish to *live* as a gentleman and not skulk out of the world with the blind reputation of a know-nothing ignoramus, I am become a stay-at-home, orderly codger and stick to my reading like a *new one*! Like a pale-faced, moneyless student fagging for a beggarly college prize. Damn it, Benny my trump, if I were to give you a catalogue of the books I have grubbed through, hard and fasting of late, you would stare with wonder. I am no flincher. I take them as they come, as the Irish beggar woman did the bobs. A fig for the damned liar who would call me nice. First, polemics. I found that study staggering mind-rakers. Then I took to controversial writings. These proved moonshine. I then had a go at history — mark me, damned lying history — and by sticking to it night and day, tooth and nail, got through some of the crack works of some of your longwinded, everlasting pagemakers, and am still greasing my heels and pushing onwards to make up for lost time. And you'll not feel a little astonished when I tell you, my cock of trumps, that *I remember all I read*! The Scaligers[104] were noted

---

classical learning. A man of great erudition, he was so ignorant of common life that he literally did not know a duck from a partridge, or mutton as being the flesh of a sheep.

[103] Something.

[104] Julius Scaliger (1484-1558) was an Italian physician and scholar noted for his scientific and philosophical writings. His son Joseph (1540-1609) pioneered the modern study of classical texts.

book-grubbers, as I know. Why, man, I beat them daily by chalks!'"

"My surprise," says Jutsham, "nay, my astonishment at this account which he gave of himself, knowing the man as I did, was great, but when he proceeded to question me on the score of my faith[105], I could hold out no longer and my patience as a listener was relieved by my bursting into a violent fit of laughter that lasted till I felt affected with violent spasms in my breast.

"Nothing daunted, he proceeded, 'Pray, Benny my hearty, let me ask you, are you a believer? I know yours is a damned wicked, profligate house, or are you one of the *forts esprits*[106] or what we now term an infidel?'"

Jutsham endeavoured to assume the appearance of gravity, but in vain. His imagination was so tickled by such unsought questions from such a harum-scarum father confessor that he answered, "My opinions on such awful subjects, My Lord, are preserved in my own private bosom."

"A fig for that!" cried George, "All my eye and blue moon-shine! But I am on the move and will just ask one question ere I cut my stick and brush. Do you really believe the existence of such a vagabond as an atheist in Old England in our enlightened age? You may answer, 'Plenty of such in France,' and quote old death-visaged Voltaire. Why, I've read him clean through, page by page, stops and all, and the writings of old Sam Johnson and all the other bigwigs on the right side of the question, and these have not left him a peg to stand upon. They have reduced them, every mother's son, to whistle,[107]" whereupon George placed his fingers in his mouth and produced a Smithfield drover's shrill whistle. "I'll tell you, all the French priests and laity possess no

---

[105] Jutsham was a Jew.
[106] Freethinkers.
[107] Presumably George means "whistle in the wind".

more real belief in *our* holy religion than mumbo jumbo. Mark my words, my friend Jemmy, all the French, man, woman and child, are shocking infidels."

"Your charity, My Lord, is not much enlarged by your late reading, methinks," replied Jutsham.

The morning after this conversation Jutsham was sitting in the Carlton House armoury when the King came in and seated himself before the fire. After answering a few questions, Jutsham respectfully observed, "Your Majesty, we had a visitor here yesterday who has been many years absent — Lord Coleraine."

"What! George Hanger?" exclaimed the King, "And what brought him hither?"

"He came to endeavour to obtain the loan of some of Your Majesty's books out of the library, sire, and I ventured to promise to prefer to Your Majesty his humble request, for he has lately become a great reader."

"A great reader! George Hanger metamorphosed into a reader! And do you believe it, Jutsham?"

"I have enquired, Your Majesty, and find that he has lately read incessantly, night and day, an immense number of books — indeed, whole series of heavy works such as Gibbon, Tillotson's *Sermons,* the *Philosophical Transactions, Universal History,* and various others — with an avidity that astonishes those who knew him heretofore."

Listening with singular attention, the King appeared to marvel, "This seems to me too preposterous to believe — entirely out of the course of one's moral speculation. Man is certainly a strange compound, an ever-changing sort of miracle: by turns a sinner and then a saint; a reckless spendthrift and then a miser, a rake about the purlieus of Covent Garden and next, by chance, an anchorite. Most men are at best an everlasting anomaly, but to live and to behold George Hanger transformed into a bookworm is a phenomenon indeed. Perfectly unique!" The King laughed long and loud. At last he rose and began to examine some newly imported firearms from India, still laughing at what he had heard about his old companion. At this point Jutsham requested him to signify His royal commands.

"Oh, the books! Ay, certainly! Yes, by all means. Poor man, if they will contribute to his happiness or comfort in any way, as many as he may require, whenever he pleases. Only see that they be safely returned."

And so it transpired that George's groom fetched and returned from time to time all the books that he required, carefully wrapping them in superfine broad cloth purchased expressly for the purpose. No book was ever retained longer than the time prescribed, except the solitary book adverted to earlier.

As mentioned to Jutsham, George would spend his evenings in The Sols Arms, a tavern on Tottenham Court Road not far from George's house in Ridgmount Place.[108] There he would drink a glass or two of porter and smoke his pipe, sitting by the fire in a large chair set aside exclusively for his use.

Sustaining George in his final days, as indeed it had done throughout his life, was his Christian faith. "I am not," he says, "ashamed to own that I am old-fashioned enough to have some religion in me and glory in an ardent, unshaken belief in God. His laws I reverence and adore, and no priestly power sanctioned by custom — human, not divine — will I obey. Yet, at the same time that I view the atheist with abhorrence, I despise bigoted

---

[108] When the writer visited the location in the late 1970s, all the houses had been recently demolished and it appeared that Ridgmount Place had been stopped up.

custom, which is as destructive to true happiness as superstition is to true religion. Society cannot be held together without *religion,* but it may without *priestcraft*," of which he later provides a disapproving example: "I confess my dissatisfaction when I hear a clergyman railing at his congregation and can hardly prevail on myself to keep my seat when I hear them talk of nothing but damnation, hell and the devil, as many of them do, instead of holding up the Christian religion as the purest system of forgiveness, love and chastity, which it really is, and whose spirit is lavish in its promises of pardon and salvation. Man must be led and induced by mild, persuasive and lenient measures to the true sense of religion. He must not be driven or terrified. Religion does not consist in going to church twice a day and carrying a hypocritical, canting, forbidding countenance through the whole week, for, though religious institutions should be observed and public worship should be attended, vital religion does not entirely depend on exterior observances, though they greatly assist it, for a high sense of devotion and piety may be found in nature, in viewing the harmony and connection of all its parts and contemplating the wondrous works of the Divinity, even in the meanest productions of the creation."

George died at home of a convulsive fit on 31 March 1824 and was buried in the graveyard of St Mary's, the family church in Driffield, Gloucestershire. His epitaph reads:

NEAR this place lieth
the Body of GENERAL GEORGE HANGER,
LORD COLERAINE.
He lived and died a firm Believer
in one God and in one God only.
He was also a Practical Christian
as far as his frail nature
did allow him so to be.

Katherine, his wife, died at Ridgmount Place on 26 December 1846 and her body is interred in Kensal Green Cemetery.

Indubitably, as we have revealed, George had seen life, lived it in the fast lane, and done so in his own way. A man of prolific sexual appetite, he exuberantly participated in all the dissipations of high society, yet beneath his rake's veneer lay a bedrock of humanity that he seldom transgressed. A percipient and radical political observer who was a confidant of Fox, he vigorously advocated measures to improve in particular the lot of poor downtrodden women, besides supporting a partial reform of Parliament — an event achieved only eight years after his death. Despite his elevated rank, he counted men and women of all stations in life among his friends, nor did he ever forget them. Indeed, he was capable of serious exertions of friendship, not — till his final years — by pecuniary means, which till then his situation hardly ever admitted, but by persevering zeal when he was likely to achieve a beneficial effect. Well acquainted with military duty, he never lacked courage or the spirit of enterprise. In early life he was generally acknowledged to be a very handsome man, but his person was often disguised by the singularity of his dress. Though free in his manners, he was never inclined to give intentional offence, and none was taken. Despite George IV's comments, he did contrive to devote much of his time to reading, especially in his later years, and was generally well provided with topics for the usual conversations of the table, even in the most convivial circles. Upon the whole, his contemporaries might well have said of him, as Prince Hal said of Falstaff, that they "could have better spared a better man."[109]

---

[109] *Henry IV, Part 1*, Act 5, Scene 4.

BIBLIOGRAPHY

GENERAL

Hanger, George —
The Life, Adventures, and Opinions of Col. George Hanger (London, 1801).
Colonel George Hanger to all Sportsmen, and particularly to Farmers and Gamekeepers (London, 1814).

EARLY LIFE AND ENTRY INTO HIGH SOCIETY

Angier, C J Bruce, "Memoirs of an Eccentric Nobleman", *London Society*, 66 (1894), 137-152.

Bloch, Ivan, *Sexual Life in England Past and Present*, translated from the German by William H Forstern (London: Francis Aldor, 1938).

The Complete Peerage of England, Scotland, Ireland, Great Britain and the United Kingdom extant, extinct or dormant (London, 1910).

Cruikshank, Dan, *The Secret History of Georgian London* (London: Random House Books, 2009).

Greig, Hannah, *The Beau Monde: Fashionable Society in Georgian London* (London: Oxford University Press, 2013).

Highfill Jr, Philip, et al, *A Biographical Dictionary of Actors, Actresses, Musicians, Dancers, Managers & Other Stage Personnel in London, 1660-1800* (Carbondale: Southern Illinois University Press, 1973).

Kelly, Ian, *Beau Brummell: The Ultimate Dandy* (London: Hodder & Stoughton, 2005).

A List of the General and Staff Officers on the Establishment in North America, (New York, 1783), William L Clements Library, University of Michigan.

Lyte, Sir H C Maxwell, *A History of Eton College, 1440-1884* (London, 1889).

Magazine and newspapers:
The Town and Country Magazine, 1772-1777
Morning Chronicle
Morning Post.

Melville, Lewis, *The Beaux of the Regency* (London: Hutchinson & Co, 1908).

Naxton, Michael, *The History of Reading School* (Ringwood: Pardy & Son Printers, 1986).

Oakes, John, and Parsons, Martin, *Reading School: The First 800 Years* (DSM, 2005).

Russell, Gillian, *Women, Sociability and Theatre in Georgian London* (Cambridge: Cambridge University Press, 2007).

Stone Jr, George Washington, *The London Stage 1660-1800, Part 4 (1747-1776)*, (Carbondale: Southern Illinois University Press, 1962).

Thorne, R G, *The History of Parliament: The House of Commons 1790-1820* (Sparkford: Haynes Publishing, 1986).

Valentine, Alan, *The British Establishment 1760-1784: An Eighteenth-Century Biographical Dictionary* (Norman: University of Oklahoma Press, 1970).

THE AMERICAN REVOLUTIONARY WAR

The Central Theatre

Baurmeister, Carl Leopold, *Revolution in America*, translated by Bernhard A Uhlendorf (New Brunswick: Rutgers University Press, 1957).

Ewald, Johann, *Diary of the American War: A Hessian Journal*, translated and edited by Joseph P Tustin (New Haven and London: Yale University Press, 1979).

Fortescue, Sir John, *A History of the British Army*, vol III (London: Macmillan & Co Ltd, 1902).

Hufeland, Otto, *Westchester County during the American Revolution 1775-1783* (New York: Harbor Hill Books, 1974).

Jackson, John W, *With the British Army in Philadelphia 1777-1778* (New York: Presidio Press, 1979).

Journal geführt bey dem Hochlöblich. Hessischen Feld-Jäger Corps während denen Campagnen der Königl. Grossbrittanischen Armee in North-America (Hessisches Staatsarchiv, Marburg).

Krafft, Johann Carl Philip von, "Journal", *Collections of the New-York Historical Society for the Year 1882.*

Martin, David G, *The Philadelphia Campaign June 1777-July 1778* (Boston: Da Capo Press, 2003).

Montresor, John, "Journals", *Collections of the New-York Historical Society for the Year 1881.*

New York Gazette, 1 June 1778.

Pearson, Michael, *Those Damned Rebels: Britain's American Empire in Revolt* (London: Heinemann, 1972).

Reed, John F, *Valley Forge Crucible of Victory* (Monmouth Beach: Philip Freneau Press, 1969).

Stryker, William S, *The Battle of Monmouth* (Princeton: Princeton University Press, 1927).

Syrett, David, and DiNardo, R L, eds, *The Commissioned Sea Officers of the Royal Navy 1660-1815* (London: Navy Records Society, 1994).

Taafe, Stephen R, *The Philadelphia Campaign, 1777-1778* (Lawrence: University Press of Kansas, 2003).

Trevelyan, The Rt Hon Sir George Otto, Bt, *The American Revolution,* 6 vols (London: Longmans, Green & Co, 1915-17).

The Southern Theatre

Alden, John Richard, *The South in the Revolution 1763-1789* (Baton Rouge: Louisiana State University Press, 1976).

Allaire, Anthony, "Diary", Appendix to Lyman C Draper, *King's Mountain and its Heroes* (Cincinnati, 1881).

Bass, Robert D —
The Green Dragoon: The Lives of Banastre Tarleton and Mary Robinson (Columbia: Sandlapper Press Inc, 1973).
Gamecock: The Life and Times of General Thomas Sumter (New York: Holt, Rinehart and Winston, 1961).

Boatner III, Mark Mayo, *Encyclopedia of the American Revolution* (New York: D McKay Co, 1966).

Bridenbaugh, Carl, *Myths & Realities: Societies of the Colonial South* (New York: Atheneum, 1976).

Captain's and Master's Logs of HMS *Pearl* (Kew: UK National Archives).

Caruthers, E W, *Interesting Revolutionary Incidents and Sketches of Character, chiefly in the 'Old North State': Second Series* (Philadelphia, 1856).

Chapman, John Abney, and O'Neall, John Belton, *The Annals of Newberry* (Newberry SC, 1892).

Clinton Papers, William L Clements Library, University of Michigan.

Davie, William Richardson, *The Revolutionary War Sketches of William R Davie*, edited by Blackwell P Robinson (Raleigh: North Carolina Department of Cultural Resources, 1976).

DeMond, Robert O, *The Loyalists in North Carolina during the Revolution* (Durham: Duke University Press, 1940).

Eelking, Max von, *Die Deutschen Hülfstruppen im Nordamericanischen Befreiungskriege* (Charleston: Nabu Press reprint, 2010).

Foote, William Henry, *Sketches of North Carolina, Historical and Biographical, illustrative of the Principles of a Portion of Her Early Settlers* (New York, 1846).

Garden Jr, Alexander —
Anecdotes of the Revolutionary War (Charleston, 1822).
Anecdotes of the American Revolution, Second Series (Charleston, 1828).

Gilchrist, Marianne McLeod, *Patrick Ferguson, "A Man of Some Genius"* (Edinburgh: NMS Publishing, 2003).

Graham, James, *The Life of Daniel Morgan* (New York, 1856).

Graham, Joseph, "Narrative", in William Henry Hoyt ed, *The Papers of Archibald D. Murphey* (Raleigh: Publications of the North Carolina Historical Commission, 1914).

Gray, Robert, "Colonel Robert Gray's Observations on the War in Carolina", *The South Carolina Historical and Genealogical Magazine*, XI (July, 1910), 139-159.

Gregorie, Anne King, *Thomas Sumter* (Columbia: The R L Bryan Co, 1931).

Hanger, George —
An Address to the Army in reply to Strictures of Roderick M'Kenzie (late Lieutenant in the 71st Regiment) on Tarleton's History of the Campaigns of 1780 and 1781 (London, 1789).
Reflections on the Menaced Invasion (London, 1804).
A Letter to the Right Hon. Lord Castlereagh (London, 1808).

Historical Manuscripts Commission, *Report on American Manuscripts in the Royal Institution of Great Britain* (London, 1904 et seq).

Howe, George, *History of the Presbyterian Church in South Carolina* (Columbia, 1870).

Landrum, J B O, *Colonial and Revolutionary History of Upper South Carolina* (Greenville SC, 1897).

Lee, Henry, *Memoirs of the War in the Southern Department of the United States* (Revised edition, New York, 1869).

Logan, John H, *A History of the Upper Country of South Carolina* (Columbia, 1859).

Lowell, Edward J, *The Hessians and other German Auxiliaries of Great Britain in the Revolutionary War* (Whitefish: Kessinger Publishing reprint, 2010).

McCowen Jr, George Smith, *The British Occupation of Charleston, 1780-82* (Columbia: University of South Carolina Press, 1972).

McCrady, Edward, *The History of South Carolina in the Revolution,* 2 vols, (New York: The Macmillan Co, 1901-2).

Moultrie, William, *Memoirs of the American Revolution* (New York, 1802).

Nelson, Paul David, *General Horatio Gates, a Biography* (Baton Rouge: Louisiana State University Press, 1976).

Ramsay, David, *The History of the Revolution of South-Carolina from a British Province to an Independent State,* vol II (Trenton, 1785).

Rankin, Hugh F, *Francis Marion: The Swamp Fox* (New York: Thomas Y Crowell Co, 1973).

Robinson, Blackwell P, *William R. Davie* (Chapel Hill: University of North Carolina Press, 1957).

Saberton, Ian, ed, *The Cornwallis Papers: The Campaigns of 1780 and 1781 in the Southern Theatre of the American Revolutionary War,* 6 vols (Ukfield: The Naval & Military Press Ltd, 2010).

Schenck, David, *North Carolina 1780-1781* (Raleigh, 1889).

Showman, Richard K, et al eds, *The Papers of General Nathanael Greene,* vols VI to VIII (Chapel Hill: University of North Carolina Press, 1991-95).

Simcoe, John Graves, *A Journal of the Operations of the Queen's Rangers* (Exeter, 1787).

Stedman, Charles, *History of the Origin, Progress, and Termination of the American War* (London, 1792).

Tarleton, Banastre, *A History of the Campaigns of 1780 and 1781 in the Southern Provinces of North America* (London, 1787).

Uhlendorf, Bernhard A, trans and ed, *The Siege of Charleston* (Ann Arbor: University of Michigan Press, 1938).

Wallace, David Duncan, *South Carolina: A Short History, 1520-1948* (Columbia: University of South Carolina Press, 1961).

Ward, Christopher, *The War of the Revolution* (New York: The Macmillan Co, 1952).

White, Henry Alexander, *Southern Presbyterian Leaders* (New York, 1911).

Wickwire, Franklin and Mary, *Cornwallis: The American Adventure* (Boston: Houghton Mifflin Co, 1970).

Williams, Otho Holland, "A Narrative of the Campaign of 1780", Appendix B to vol I of William Johnson, *Sketches of the Life and Correspondence of Nathanael Greene* (Charleston, 1822).

Williams, Samuel Cole, *Tennessee during the Revolutionary War* (Knoxville: University of Tennessee Press, 1974).

Woodmason, Charles, *The Carolina Backcountry on the Eve of the Revolution*, edited by Richard J Hooker (Chapel Hill: University of North Carolina Press, 1953).

LATER LIFE

Allen. Thomas, *A History of the County of Surrey* (London, 1831).

Angelo, Henry, *Reminiscences* (London, 1828).

Anon —

Pancratia or a History of Pugilism (London, 1812).

Biographical Sketches of Eccentric Characters (Boston, 1832).

Ashton, John, *Florizel's Folly* (London, 1899).

Aspinall, Arthur, ed, *The Correspondence of George, Prince of Wales 1770-1812* (London: Cassell, 1963-1971).

Baer, Marc, *The Rise and Fall of Radical Westminster, 1780-1890* (London: Palgrave Macmillan, 2012).

Banvard, John, *The Private Life of a King: The Prince of Wales afterwards George IV* (New York, 1875).

Barros, Carolyn A, and Smith, Johanna M, eds, *Life-Writings by British Women 1660-1815* (Boston: Northeastern University Press, 2000).

Bath and Wells, The Bishop of, *The Journal of William, Lord Auckland* (London, 1861).

Bishop, John George, *"A Peep into the Past": Brighton in the Olden Time* (Brighton, 1892).

Blackmantle, Bernard [Charles Molloy Westmacott] —

Fitzalleyne of Berkeley: A Romance of the Present Times (London, 1825).

The English Spy (London, 1826).

Brailsford, Dennis, *Bareknuckles: A Social History of Prize-fighting* (Cambridge: Chadwyk-Healey, 1986).

Broughton, Mrs Vernon Delves, ed, *Court and Private Life in the Time of Queen Charlotte, being the Journals of Mrs Papendick* (London, 1887).

Butler, Frank, *A History of Boxing in Britain* (London: Arthur Barker Ltd, 1972).

Butterfield, H, "Charles James Fox and the Whig Opposition in 1792", *The Cambridge Historical Journal*, IX, 3 (1949).

Christie, Ian R, *Myth and Reality in Late-Eighteenth-Century British Politics* (Berkeley: University of California Press, 1970).

Coleridge, Ernest Hartley, *The Life of Thomas Coutts, Banker* (London: John Lane, 1920).

Curwen, Samuel, *Journal and Letters* (New York, 1842).

Derry, John W, *The Regency Crisis and the Whigs 1788-9* (London: Cambridge University Press, 1967).

The Druid [Henry Hall Dixon], *The Post and the Paddock* (London:, 1862).

Egan, Pierce, *Boxiana or Sketches of Modern Pugilism*, vol I (London, 1818).

Fitzgerald, Percy Hetherington, *The Life of George the Fourth* (London, 1881).

Foord, Archibald S, *His Majesty's Opposition 1714-1830* (Oxford: Clarendon Press, 1964).

George, Mrs Eric, "Fox's Martyrs: The General Election of 1784", *Transactions of the Royal Historical Society*, Fourth series, XXI (1939).

George, M Dorothy, *Catalogue of Political and Personal Satires preserved in the Department of Prints and Drawings in the British Museum*, vols V to VII (London: Trustees of the British Museum, 1935-42).

Greig, James, ed, *The Farrington Diary* (London: Hutchinson & Co, 1923).

Grigson, Geoffrey, "Some Tablets on the Wall", *Country Life*, 17 November 1955.

Hanger, George —
Anticipation of the Freedom of Brabant (London, 1792).
Military Reflections on the Attack and Defence of London (London, 1795).

Hibbert, Christopher, *George IV* (Harmondsworth: Penguin Books, 1976).

Hill, Phillippina Burton, *Mrs Hill's Apology for having been induced ... to appear in the Character of Scrub, Beaux Stratagem, for one night only at Brighthelmstone last Year, 1786* (London, 1787).

Huish, Robert, *Memoirs of George the Fourth* (London, 1830).

Laprade, William Thomas —
"William Pitt and Westminster Elections", *The American Historical Review*, XVIII (London: The Macmillan Co, 1913).
"Public Opinion and the General Election of 1784", *The English Historical Review*, XXXI (London: Longmans, Green, & Co, 1916).

Lennox, Lord William Pitt —
Fifty Years' Biographical Reminiscences (London, 1863).
Celebrities I have known, 2nd series (London, 1877).

Leslie, Doris, *The Great Corinthian: A Portrait of the Prince Regent* (London: Eyre & Spottiswood, 1952).

Leslie, Shane, *George the Fourth* (London: Ernest Benn Ltd, 1926).

Lloyd, Hannibal Evans, *George IV* (London, 1830).

Maxwell, Sir Herbert, Bt, ed, *The Creevey Papers* (London: John Murray, 1904).

Mee, Bob, *Bare Fists: The History of Bare-knuckle Prize-fighting* (Woodstock and New York: The Overlook Press, 2001).

Melville, Lewis —
The First Gentleman of Europe (London: Hutchinson & Co, 1906).
The Beaux of the Regency (London: Hutchinson & Co, 1908).
Brighton: Its History, its Follies, and its Fashions (London: Chapman & Hall Ltd, 1909).
Some Eccentrics & a Woman (London: Martin Secker, 1911).

Mitchell, L G, *Charles James Fox and the Disintegration of the Whig Party 1782-1794* (London: Oxford University Press, 1971).

Moritz, Karl Philipp, *Journeys of a German in England* (London: Eland Books, 2009).

Musgrave, Clifford, *Life in Brighton* (London: Faber & Faber Ltd, 1970).

Newspapers and magazines —
Morning Chronicle
Morning Post
The Times

The Gentleman's Magazine

The Satirist or Monthly Meteor, IV (London, 1808)

The Clydesdale Magazine, vol I, 1 (May, 1818)

The New Monthly Magazine and Literary Journal, Part 2 (London, 1827)

The Mirror of Literature, Amusement, and Instruction, vol X, 276 (London, 1827)

Fraser's Magazine for Town and Country, vol XXIII (London, 1841).

O'Gorman, F, *The Whig Party and the French Revolution* (London: Macmillan & Co Ltd, 1967).

Pasquin, Anthony [John Williams], *The New Brighton Guide* (London:, 1796).

Pigott, Charles, *The Jockey Club or a Sketch of the Manners of the Age* (London, 1792).

Raikes, Thomas *A Portion of the Journal kept by Thomas Raikes Esq from 1831 to 1847* (London, 1858).

Redding, Cyrus, *Fifty Years' Recollections, Literary and Personal, with Observations on Men and Things* (London, 1858).

Richardson, John, *Recollections, practical, literary, dramatic, and miscellaneous of the last half-century* (London, 1855).

Roberts, Michael, *The Whig Party 1807-1812* (London: Frank Cass & Co Ltd, 1965).

Rosebery, The Earl of, ed, *The Windham Papers* (London: Herbert Jenkins Ltd, 1913).

Sichel, Walter, *Sheridan* (Boston and New York: Houghton Mifflin Co, 1909).

Smith, E A, *George IV* (New Haven and London: Yale University Press, 1999).

Smith, John Thomas, *Nollekens and his Times* (London, 1895).

Smollett, Tobias, *The Miscellaneous Works of Tobias Smollett complete in One Volume with a Memoir of the Author by Thomas Roscoe* (London, 1841).

Stokes, Hugh, *The Devonshire House Circle* (London: Herbert Jenkins Ltd, 1917).

Sydney, William Connor, *England and the English in the Eighteenth Century* (Edinburgh: John Grant, 1891).

Thompson, Grace E, *The First Gentleman, being the Story of the Regent, afterwards George IV* (London: Jonathan Cape, 1931).

Timbs, John, *English Eccentrics and Eccentricities* (London, 1898).

Walford, Edward, *Old and New London: A Narrative of its History, its People, and its Places,* vol 6 (London, 1873).

Wallace, William, *The History of the Life and Reign of George the Fourth* (London, 1831).

Wheatley, Henry B, ed, *The Historical and the Posthumous Memoirs of Sir Nathaniel William Wraxall 1772-1784* (London, 1884).

Wilkins, W H, *Mrs Fitzherbert and George IV* (London: Longmans, Green, & Co, 1905).

Worringer'sche Offizierskartei (Hessisches Staatsarchiv, Marburg).

INDEX

Scotia, 119-120; saved from debtors' prison, 121-3; becomes equerry to the Prince of Wales and a member of his fast set, 123; participates in the riotous Westminster election of 1784, 127-139; the butt of the Prince's humour, 139-144; his early sojourns with the Prince in Brighton, 146-158; practical joker, 153-4, 157, 162-3, 181; the pleasures of Brighton, 146-7, 152-3, 155-7; carousing with the Prince and otherwise in London, 159-164; recruiting officer for the East India Company, 168-9; patron of the noble art, 169; shooting game in Hertfordshire and Norfolk, 170; manages the Prince's racing stable, 170; his later sojourns with the Prince in Brighton, 174-188; Brighton's amusements, 187; accompanies the Prince on royal visits and at country houses, 189-191; poet and lyricist, 193-4; participates in the riotous Westminster by-election of 1788, 195-9; a strong supporter of the French Revolution, 199-200; unsuccessfully applies for active service on the declaration of war with France and turns to print, 201; his management of the Prince's racing stable ends,, 201; is dismissed by the Prince, 204; his recruiting for the East India Company ends and he spirals into debt, 205; his incarceration in the King's Bench Prison and release,

213-224; enters trade as a coal merchant but does not succeed, 225-7; obtains a sinecure post, 227; publishes his memoirs,, 227-8; occasionally attends the Prince, 228-230; begets a son and marries his housekeeper, 230-1; inherits the title of Lord Coleraine but refuses to assume it. 232-3; promoted to the Hessian rank of major general, 233; bookworm, 233-242; evenings of his final years spent in a tavern, 242; his ardent, unshaken belief in God and Christianity, 242-3; his death and burial, 243

Hanger, John Greenwood, 231

Hanger, Mary Anne Katherine (née Greenwood), 230-1, 233, 243

Hanger, William, Lord Coleraine, 22, 203-4, 210-12, 232

Hawkes, William, 32-4

Hawkins, James: see Whitshed, Sir James Hawkins

Hayes, Charlotte, 28

Henry Frederick, HRH Prince, Duke of Cumberland and Strathearn, 21

Hessian chasseur companies, 44-8, 52, 66, 68

Hessian Jäger Corps, 39-44, 46-9, 52, 71

Hill, Phillippina Burton, 180-2

Hood, Samuel, Lord, 129, 135, 195

House, Sam, 134, 136

Howard, Charles, Duke of Norfolk, 148, 151, 187

Howe, Sir William, KB, 38

Innes, Alexander, 98

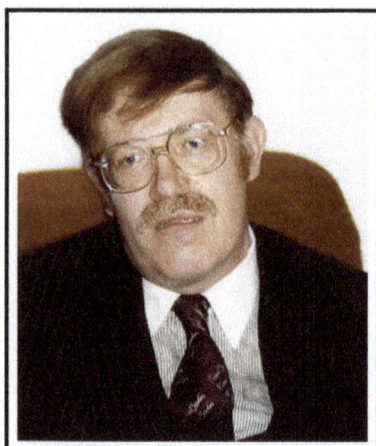

About the author

Ian Saberton was educated at Firth Park Grammar School, Sheffield, and at the Universities of Birmingham and Warwick. He holds a PhD in history from the latter, having previously graduated with a BA (Hons) in Russian from the former. After translating technical Russian for the British Library, he entered the UK Civil Service.

He is editor of *The Cornwallis Papers: The Campaigns of 1780 and 1781 in the Southern Theatre of the American Revolutionary War*, 6 vols (Uckfield: The Naval & Military Press Ltd, 2010) and author of *The American Revolutionary War in the south: A Re-evaluation from a British perspective in the light of The Cornwallis Papers* (Grosvenor House Publishing Ltd, 2018).

It was during the editing of *The Cornwallis Papers* that he came upon George Hanger. Known throughout late Georgian society but unknown to the public today, he has nevertheless been mentioned in passing by various writers over the years, but almost without exception they inaccurately summarise his life and character. It is a purpose of this work to set the record straight.

www.ingramcontent.com/pod-product-compliance
Lightning Source LLC
Chambersburg PA
CBHW040413110426
42812CB00034B/3369/J